Prehistoric

Prehistoric

The Audacious and Improbable
Origin Story of
the Toronto Raptors

Alex Wong

TRIUMPH
B O O K S

First Triumph Books paperback edition 2023

Library of Congress Cataloging-in-Publication Data available upon request.

This book is available in quantity at special discounts for your group or orga-nization. For further information, contact:

Triumph Books LLC
814 North Franklin Street
Chicago, Illinois 60610
(312) 337-0747
www.triumphbooks.com

Printed in U.S.A.

ISBN: 978-1-63727-658-7
Design by Patricia Frey

To Henry and Owen

Contents

Foreword *by Damon Stoudamire*.........ix

Introduction........................xiii

Part One: Beginnings

The Season Ticket Drive 3

The Toronto Raptors 15

Isiah and Brendan.................... 26

The Expansion Draft 37

The Rookie......................... 51

Training Camp 63

The Sharpshooter 75

Part Two: The First Season

Ted Stepien and the Toronto Towers 87

The First Game 97

Fab Five........................... 111

"Practices Were War"................ 117

The Big O 128

John Saunders 135

New Year's Party.................... 148

The Trade Deadline 166

The SkyDome 178

Part Three: Wins and Lessons

"They Should Have Been 73–9" 199

Isiah vs. Brendan 218

Dan and Acie 228

Caribana 238

Part Four: Postscript

Historic 251

Acknowledgments 265

Interviews and Sourcing 267

Foreword

When the Toronto Raptors won the championship in 2019, Kyle Lowry wore my throwback jersey at the championship parade. Seeing him pay homage to both myself and the franchise's history was an honor. My relationship with Kyle dates back to when he joined the NBA as a rookie. I was with the Memphis Grizzlies at the time, coming off major knee surgery and reaching the end of my career, and I took the young point guard under my wing. I took it upon myself to help him be the best player he could be. I shared my experiences with him both on and off the court. The goal was to make him feel like I was always there for him. We both moved on, but from afar, I was proud to watch him end up in Toronto and watch the entire city embrace him.

Seeing my jersey at the parade brought me back to my experience in Toronto. I remember being at the SkyDome at the NBA draft in 1995 and how excited our owner, John Bitove Jr., was when my name was called. He was seated just behind the podium where commissioner David Stern stood, giving a fist pump for the world to see. Coming to a new country to play for an expansion team, I didn't know what to expect, but John and his entire family welcomed me with open arms. I had a wonderful mentor in Isiah Thomas, who shared so much knowledge with me. It brought me back to my teammates. We had a cast of characters. There were a lot of personalities in that locker room. We were a close-knit group. We hung out together all the time. We pushed each other in practice. It didn't matter that we were an expansion team, and no one expected us to win too many games. We played hard and competed every night.

There are so many wonderful memories from the first year. Our first training camp in Hamilton. Our first regular-season game against the New Jersey Nets. That one Sunday afternoon at the SkyDome when we beat Michael Jordan and the Chicago Bulls in front of the largest crowd in Canadian basketball history. I grew so much as a person and a player in my first year with the Raptors. I was the centerpiece of everything that was going on. I was given the ball from Day One and a chance to show and prove. A lot of people don't get that opportunity. We were playing in Canada and didn't have much of a presence over in the United States. I was able to give the fans in Toronto somebody they could see as their own star player. I was this 5'9" point guard, it was easy for fans to identify with me. When I won Rookie of the Year, I like to think it helped give our franchise a bit of recognition and credibility.

Listen, there were some boos on draft night, but the city embraced me from Day One. It didn't matter whether I was going to the grocery store, a walk by my downtown condo, or making an appearance at the mall to sign autographs. The city always showed love. The organization welcomed me with open arms. We were bringing the NBA to Toronto, and all we had was each other. I was spoiled to have such close relationships with people who worked for the team. It wasn't until later in my career that I learned it wasn't like that everywhere. It's hard to convey how appreciative I am of everything Toronto provided me. As I've gotten older, I look back now and realize the first year was about something bigger than what was taking place on the basketball court. We didn't win many games, but we were a success story. We were part of the foundation that's carried on to what the franchise is today. We helped to make the sport more popular in this country. We inspired young kids who identified with us. You can go to Brampton, Mississauga, or Scarborough today and see how we left an impact.

The first year of the Toronto Raptors was the beginning of something special in this city, and a time in my life I will always cherish.

—Damon Stoudamire
Toronto Raptors
(1995–1998)

Introduction

I was 11 years old in 1995 when the Toronto Raptors came into my life.

Three years earlier, my dad walked into the corner room in our tiny apartment in the New Territories region of Hong Kong, where I grew up. It was a school night and I played a Sega Genesis game called *Alex Kidd in Miracle World.* My dad told me we were moving to Canada in a month. He was filling out an application form to enroll me at Central Park Public School in Markham, a town 20 miles northeast of downtown Toronto. I would be starting third grade in September and he needed me to pick an English name. I looked at the video game's main character and decided my new name would be Alex.

When I first moved to Toronto, I was still more into video games, reading *Dragon Ball* manga, and hanging on to every loose thread that connected me to my life back in Hong Kong. I missed my aunts, uncles, cousins, and grandparents. My sister and I were especially close to our grandfather. We used to hang out at the mansion he lived in, a housing unit attached to the factory where he ran his fabric business. I was the youngest intern there, helping out with innocuous tasks during the day at the office and learning how to play Mahjong after hours.

The hardest part about starting life in a new country is the part where you have to let go of the place you used to live in and, at the same time, try to find meaningful connections in the place you are living in now. It wasn't until an NBA team came to Toronto that I started to feel like there was something to tie me to this city. Basketball became a bigger part of my life after my dad installed a basketball hoop on our driveway. At the time, the Orlando Magic were my favorite team. I would pretend to be Dennis Scott and shoot corner threes, and then I would lower the rim and rip down the entire basket with two-handed dunks like Shaquille O'Neal. I would ask my mom to buy me a new basketball almanac every year and study every team's roster and player stats. I never missed the weekend triple-headers on NBC.

But the Raptors coming to Toronto was what changed everything. It's hard to describe what it means to have your own NBA team to root for as a kid. It wasn't just any team too. The Raptors were this weird franchise with a name and logo inspired by *Jurassic Park.* They were one of two teams in Canada. They didn't even have a proper basketball arena and instead played at a baseball stadium downtown. They were led by a rookie point guard who the home fans had booed on draft night. Their general manager was one of the best NBA players of all time who had just retired and was now in his first front-office role. They played in a hockey-mad town where fans had to learn how to watch a basketball game. Looking back, it wasn't just a strange time; it was shocking that it somehow worked.

Prehistoric is the origin story of the Toronto Raptors. It's about the moments that defined the beginning of the franchise, but what it's really about is the story of how a bunch of people from all walks of life and various backgrounds came together with a common purpose: to start an NBA team from the ground up.

Near the start of this project, as I began to conduct what ended up being over 140 original interviews for the book, one of my interview subjects, who worked for the team in the first year, asked me, "Why are you writing about a team that went 21–61?" It was a fair question. But I was never interested in the wins and losses. I was more interested in telling the stories about the first year. The story of a group of twenty-somethings who quit their jobs and helped the team sell season tickets to a city that didn't embrace the sport of basketball. The story of how a designer from Chicago took cues from a Steven Spielberg blockbuster film and the McDonald's Happy Meal to create one of the most talked-about team logos and jerseys of all time. The story of how the first-year Raptors were run by two alumni of the "Bad Boy" Pistons, the most frightening team of the 1980s. The story of the team's many firsts. The first marketing campaign. The first game-day script for a regular-season game. The formation of the first dance team. The first celebrity fan. The first mascot. The first public address announcer. The first public relations team. The first group of reporters to cover the team. The first television broadcast crew. The first community relations team. The first New Year's party. The first trade deadline. The story of a first-year roster led by a rookie from the University of Arizona, a sharpshooter who joined the team at the end of training camp, an overweight big man who everyone counted out, a center from Croatia, a decorated pro from Italy, a former member of the "Fab Five," and an entire group of NBA players who moved to Canada and discovered a new country together.

There were many firsts for the Raptors, but they were not the first professional basketball team to play in Toronto. On November 1, 1946, the Toronto Huskies kicked off the first year of the Basketball Association of America against the New York Knickerbockers at Maple Leaf Gardens. A black-and-white poster advertising the matchup featured a photo of Ed Sadowski, the captain of the home team, with the caption: BIG-LEAGUE BASKETBALL, WORLD'S MOST POPULAR SPORT!

It was a Friday night in Toronto and tip-off was at 8:30 PM. Ticket prices ranged from 75 cents to $2.50. When the Knickerbockers crossed the border the evening before, a Canadian customs officer joked that there weren't too many people in Toronto interested in basketball. It was an accurate assessment. Only around 7,000 fans showed up inside a half-full arena on opening night as city mayor Robert Saunders took part in the ceremonial opening tip, followed by a performance from the 48th Highlanders of Canada Pipes. In the first pro basketball game played in Toronto, the visitors won 68–66.

The Huskies only played in Toronto for one season. The team spent the entire season trying to come up with gimmicky marketing ploys to try to generate any form of sustained fan interest. It started on opening night when the team offered free tickets to anyone who showed up to the arena and was taller than their starting center, George Nostrand, who measured in at 6'8". There was a height shortage in the city, as not a single person arrived to claim the prize.

From there, the team tried to give away Stetson hats, bags of groceries, and even bicycles during games. To encourage more women to attend, they offered free nylon stockings to the first 100 women at a home game, but the promotion was shut down because World War II war-rationing restrictions made it illegal to distribute nylon to the general public. In a hockey-first town, the average attendance of a Huskies game hovered around 2,000 fans, trailing two minor-league hockey teams in the city, the Toronto Marlboros and the St. Michael Pats, who played in the same arena. The team's financial losses reached six figures, and the franchise folded after one season. (The Basketball Association of America would merge with the National Basketball League in 1949 and become the NBA. Today, the league considers the start of the BAA as their first season, which is why we still celebrate the Huskies-Knicks game as the first-ever NBA game.)

When the NBA started considering expanding to Toronto in 1993, the city was still a hockey town, but they were also one of the largest markets in North America. The league had seen the city's recent success in drawing a fan base for the CFL's Toronto Argonauts, who won the Grey Cup in 1991, and the Toronto Blue Jays, who won back-to-back World Series in 1992 and '93.

"It was a pretty prominent view within the league that it had reached a time to have a team in Toronto," Russ Granik, the league's deputy commissioner during that period, recalls. "There was a general agreement that—recognizing hockey was king and there weren't expectations of changing that—under the right circumstances, a team could do well there."

The idea of expanding to Canada was part of the NBA's plans to become a global phenomenon, coming off the heels of the 1992 Summer Olympics in Barcelona, Spain, when the league's biggest stars, led by Michael Jordan, Magic Johnson, Larry Bird, and Charles Barkley, promoted the game of basketball to an international audience as part of the "Dream Team," who became the number one story at the Olympics. It was the culmination of a decade-long transformation for the NBA, which started the 1980s with CBS, their broadcast partner, airing the NBA Finals on tape delay because reruns of *The Dukes of Hazzard* and *M*A*S*H* drew higher ratings. The league was considered an also-ran, filled with players with substance abuse problems, with an on-court product that did not appeal to a younger audience.

After negotiating a drug agreement with the players union, the league started the long road toward cleaning up its public image. An in-house production team named NBA Entertainment was formed to change the perception of the league's product. The team produced a series of television promos that featured the world's biggest stars, including Elton John, Oprah Winfrey, and Gary Shandling, sitting courtside at NBA games. It added a certain cachet to the league. There was also an explosion of modern-day stars on the court. Between Magic's Lakers, Bird's Celtics, and Jordan as a one-person promotional vehicle, the NBA tapped into the growing home video market, putting together superstar highlight reels and championship team videos which helped a new generation of basketball fans catch the bug.

By the start of the 1990s, the NBA had a $600 million national television contract with NBC and was generating billions of dollars of revenue each season from team merchandise. The NBA wasn't just a thriving pro sports league. They were part of mainstream pop culture, and the star players were some of the most well-known celebrities in the world. During this period of extraordinary growth, the league expanded to 27 teams, adding Charlotte, Miami, Orlando, and Minnesota as expansion franchises in the late 1980s.

After the success of the 1992 Summer Olympics, commissioner David Stern decided it was time to expand beyond the United States. The league was taking a risk in expanding to a new country, and they needed an owner who understood the market and had a long-term vision of establishing an NBA franchise in Toronto. There would be a year-long process among three ownership groups to try and convince the NBA to grant them an expansion team.

The first owner of the Raptors was John Bitove Jr., who grew up in the North York neighborhood of Toronto and attended York Mills Collegiate. He was the high school quarterback, ran track and field, and played soccer and rugby, but Bitove was most drawn to one sport. "The one thing about basketball compared to other sports is there's a culture behind the sport," he says. "There's a lifestyle to it, especially in Indiana, where it's just another way you lived. My mother, Dotsa, was from northern Indiana. I would play hoops there in the summer with my cousins."

Bitove went to Indiana University and was a regular at Assembly Hall, rooting on the men's basketball team, who would win the national championship in 1981. Even as a teenager, he would tell family and friends about his goal of bringing an NBA team to Toronto one day. He had visited Madison Square Garden in New York to watch the Knicks play in "the World's Most Famous Arena" and drove to watch Isiah Thomas and the Detroit Pistons at The Palace at Auburn Hills. "I wanted basketball to become bigger in our country," Bitove says. "I didn't understand why it wasn't."

After graduating from Indiana and earning a law degree at the University of Windsor, John landed a junior-level position at the Government of Canada in Ottawa. In 1987, he moved back to Toronto to help with his dad's business. John Sr. ran The Bitove Corporation, a food and catering business that worked with the most prominent vendors in the city (including the Toronto Pearson International Airport and the SkyDome, where the Blue Jays played) and owned two well-known restaurants in the city, the Hard Rock Cafe and Wayne Gretzky's Restaurant.

As the NBA started considering the idea of an expansion team in Toronto, Bitove was working to bring an international basketball tournament to the city. The 1994 FIBA World Championship, the first tournament from the international governing body of basketball to allow NBA players to participate, had initially been awarded to Belgrade, Yugoslavia. But after a civil war broke out in Yugoslavia in 1991, FIBA needed to find a new host country. The NBA was also pushing for the event to move forward, as it was another prime opportunity for the league to spotlight their star players on the global stage. In 1992, Bitove received a call from FIBA head Boris Stanković. "He told me about the civil war between the Serbians and Croatians and said they were going to be moving the tournament and asked if I could get Toronto to put in a bid," Bitove recalls. "I started talking to Basketball Canada and reached out to the NBA. That's when I met David Stern and Russ Granik, who was a USA Basketball official. It started a relationship where I was working with the NBA on a daily basis and building trust with them."

Bitove assembled a local committee that raised $13 million and proposed a plan to host the tournament in Toronto. The games would be played at Maple Leaf Gardens, the SkyDome, and Copps Coliseum in Hamilton. As Bitove waited to hear back from FIBA, he also started to hear talks of a bid process for an NBA expansion franchise in Toronto. "I had a meeting in New York with the league and told them, 'If you guys are expanding to Canada, I want to put together a group,'" Bitove recalls. "They said, 'Go ahead.'" He landed the 1994 FIBA World Championship, and started putting together an ownership group to bid for an NBA team.

David Peterson, the former premier of Ontario, was working at the law firm Cassels, Brock & Blackwell LLP when he met Bitove for the first time. "His father had phoned me and said, 'You should talk to my son,'" Peterson recalls. "So John came to my office, and we met. I said, 'What do you want?' He said, 'I would like you to be counsel and chairman of a group I'm putting together to go for an NBA team.' I said, 'Who's in our

group?' He said, 'If you're in, it's you and me.'" Peterson seemed like an
odd choice considering he had never even watched a single NBA game.
But Bitove needed someone to help him win a campaign. "I sat there
and listened to John," Peterson continues. "I asked him basic questions
like, 'Where do you play? Where do you get the players?' John was cap-
tivating. He was so energetic and full of life. You had to beat him with a
stick to slow him down. He told me, 'There's going to be a point when
basketball will outstrip hockey in this city.' I said, 'Let me think about
this.' I went home at eight that evening and told my kids about it. They
said, 'Dad, this is the best thing you could ever do in your whole life.' So I
phoned John and told him, 'I'm in.'"

After Ted Rogers, CEO of Rogers Communications, and Isadore "Issy"
Sharp, founder of Four Seasons Hotels and Resorts, rejected Bitove's
offer to join the ownership group, Bitove formed a partnership with
Allan Slaight, the broadcast mogul who owned Standard Broadcasting,
the largest privately owned network of radio stations in Canada. Phil
Granovsky, the co-founder of Atlantic Packaging Products and a charm-
ing personality in his early seventies, also joined the group. He had
experience bidding for a sports franchise in the city, having come second
to the CIBC-Labatt conglomerate to land the Toronto Blue Jays two
decades prior. The bid group's name would be Professional Basketball
Franchise Inc.; if they won, Bitove and Slaight would own 44 percent of
the franchise. Granovsky and Peterson would own one percent each, and
the Bank of Nova Scotia, represented by Borden Osmak, would have a
10 percent stake.

The first employee hired by Professional Basketball Franchise Inc.
was David Strickland. Even though Toronto was a predominantly hockey
town, a niche group of people watched, played, and followed the sport
of basketball and believed in its potential. Strickland was one of them.
He was introduced to the game of basketball by his uncle Robert. They
would go sailing together in the summer during the 1980s in Muskoka,
Ontario. In the evenings, they would turn on the television and finish the

day watching an NBA game together. Robert would regale his nephew with stories about how he used to pay $2.50 to watch the Toronto Huskies in 1946. He had joined the Navy, just returned from the Second World War, and studied engineering at the University of Toronto.

Strickland had just come back from the 1992 Summer Olympics in Barcelona as CTV's director of marketing of sports news when Bitove asked him to help with the ownership bid. "I had witnessed the 'Dream Team' and was in admiration of the NBA," he recalls. "I didn't know a lot about John, and I had a really great job. I was going to the 1994 Olympics in Lillehammer, and I asked a friend what I should do with this job offer. He said, 'Tell him a number that it would take for you to give up all the things you have right now.'"

Strickland took only a slight pay raise to leave his job, but he wanted to help bring the NBA back to Toronto. With an arena in place, Bitove wanted to put together a business case to convince the NBA of the viability of a pro basketball franchise in Toronto. He asked Strickland to work with Gord Hendren, the VP of Sports & Entertainment at Decima Research, to develop a comprehensive country-wide market research to identify the long-term potential of basketball in Canada. It was a national survey that included 1,500 interviews with a representative sample across the country. The questionnaire was designed to understand where the sport stood in terms of popularity in fan engagement and participation. The most eye-opening part of the research was the continued rise of participation in basketball across the country and how a basketball team in Canada would create exponential growth in the number of kids who would pick up a basketball and go to the playground and ask their parents to install a hoop on their driveway. When participants were asked to share the likelihood they would attend a pro basketball game in person, Strickland and Hendren found that fans still preferred spending their money on hockey. This did not discourage Bitove from believing there was a long-term audience for basketball. There were immigrants and second-generation Canadians who grew up following the NBA. There were women and children who would attach themselves to an expansion team.

The demographic who Bitove would promote his expansion franchise to would be what he termed "New Canada."

The presentation to the NBA was taking shape, but in the public's opinion, Bitove would not win the bid. The consensus favorite was a bid group led by construction magnate Larry Tanenbaum. He had formed a close relationship with the NBA in 1991 when the Denver Nuggets were considering relocating to Toronto. The Nuggets were trying to get out of a long-term lease with McNichols Arena and called Tanenbaum, who put together a multi-purpose arena plan in the heart of the city's downtown core at the CNE grounds. The long-term vision was to share the venue with the NHL's Toronto Maple Leafs. But the deal fell through, and Denver stayed put. There were other attempts by Tanenbaum to bring an NBA team to the city, including discussions with the New Jersey Nets and San Antonio Spurs about relocation. After those talks stalled, Tanenbaum took matters into his own hands. He submitted a $100,000 non-refundable deposit to the NBA in October 1992 and applied for an expansion franchise, which kick-started the bid process. Tanenbaum had assembled a *who's who* of power players in the city, including SkyDome's chief executive officer Richard Peddie, *Toronto Sun* publisher Paul Godfrey, and former Canadian men's national basketball team head coach Jack Donohue. The group had financing from Labatt Breweries and the Canadian Imperial Bank of Commerce—two groups who helped bring the Toronto Blue Jays to the city as an expansion franchise in 1977.

Himal Mathew still remembers his first meeting with Bitove to discuss the ownership bid. It's a story he's been telling for almost three decades. "People don't seem to tire of hearing it. I'll be at dinner or something, and someone will say, 'We've read about you. Aren't you the guy who helped with the strategy for the Raptors?'" he says. "It was a huge achievement. My family came to Canada as refugees. They couldn't have been further removed from this thing we were doing. But even they understood what we had accomplished."

Mathew grew up in Darjeeling, India, as the son of boarding school teachers. He moved to East Nigeria as a kid after his parents accepted a teaching opportunity there. In 1967, a civil war broke out overnight after the state declared itself to be the sovereign country of Biafra. The government seized the assets of everyone living in the region. Mathew's family, who deposited their life savings at the federal bank, were suddenly penniless. The town transformed into a war zone. Every night, Mathew heard explosions as the Nigerian army advanced into the city. His family was smuggled out of the country on a mercenary plane to Angola before moving to England. At the age of nine, Mathew landed at Montreal-Dorval airport in Quebec City and was driven to his new home in the middle of a snowstorm. His father's best friend, who was French-Canadian, had told him about a shortage of teachers in Quebec.

The immigrant family stood out among the 2,500 people who lived in the small town of Richmond, Quebec. "We were the only non-White people they had ever seen," Mathew recalls. "There was a lot of culture shock and a lot of prejudice. I was routinely beaten up." When he landed a high school scholarship to attend boarding school in Lennoxville, Quebec, Mathew decided academic success would allow him to get a well-paying job and help to support his parents financially. After graduating from Queen's University in Toronto with a political science degree, Mathew extended his stay in the city by three months, living on his friend's couch while plotting his next move. He considered several options: working for the United Nations and helping with third-world countries, applying to law school, or pursuing his Master's degree. While Mathew contemplated what to do next, he grabbed a phone book and started to cold-call marketing firms to learn about what they did.

"I had precious little knowledge of the place we had come to and what life was like," Mathew explains. "I understood what a doctor, a lawyer, and an engineer were. But I had no clue what my friends meant when they talked about working in business." Through those conversations, he learned the function of these companies and became fascinated by the marketing world. "I like to take things apart and put them back together,"

Mathew continues. "That's what they did. They solved problems for a living. They looked at the market, understood the opportunities, and built strategies to capture them." He landed an entry-level role at an advertising firm named Ogilvy before moving up the ladder and becoming the client services director at marketing-communications company Cossette, where he worked with large corporations, including McDonald's, General Motors, and Ikea.

In 1993, Mathew started learning about the potential of an NBA expansion franchise coming to Toronto from reading *The Globe and Mail* newspaper in the morning and listening to Bob McCown on the local sports radio station, "The Fan," in his car. "They were laughing at Bitove. The consensus was, 'Why are these guys doing this?'" Mathew recalls. "Everyone said, 'They don't have the credentials. They don't have the relationships.'" He cold-called Bitove and a meeting was set up at the Cossette offices the following morning.

Mathew stood in front of the boardroom with copywriter Jim Garbutt and art director Brian Hickling and made his pitch to Professional Basketball Franchise Inc. "I told them there's a race to be won here, and you guys can do it," Mathew says. "The mistake was they were focusing on the commissioner, but that's not where the decision would be made. The decision was going to be made by the expansion committee, which was made up of the other owners. I told them, 'Look. Every one of these owners is a self-made person. You can win this by targeting them and making them understand you're just like them. You're self-made people who did it the hard way. You understand them. You share their values and motivations and deserve to be admitted to the club.' John asked for the room, and when I returned, he said, 'We agree with everything you said. It makes perfect sense to us. We'd like you to be responsible for the strategy of the bid.'"

With several months to go until the final presentation, Professional Basketball Franchise Inc. shifted its focus toward winning over the owners. A few weeks after hiring Mathew, a packet was delivered to every owner in the NBA. "The cover looked like a parquet basketball floor," Mathew recalls. "It said, and I'm paraphrasing, 'The NBA is all about pushing, shoving, fouling, and brutal aggression.' When you opened it up, the first page said, 'and that's just to get an expansion franchise.' Within days of sending the package, we got positive feedback from the owners. It had the intended effect of making them stand up and pay attention to who we were. The next question was, 'How do we build on this?'"

On July 29, 1993, Granik and league counsel Joel Litvin flew with Phoenix Suns owner—and chairman of the expansion committee—Jerry Colangelo to Toronto to visit with all three ownership groups. Before the trip, Granik had warned the owners to avoid any over-the-top theatrics. It was a business trip. But Mathew pushed Professional Basketball Franchise Inc. to ignore the deputy commissioner's message. "When these guys leave, they need to talk about us," he told them. "They need to remember us, and they need to remember us with a smile on their face." When the traveling party landed in Toronto, they were greeted by Bitove on the tarmac of the airport runway and whisked onto a private helicopter for an aerial tour of the city. At their two-hour meeting at the Cossette offices, 300 employees waited in the hallways to greet the committee members by chanting "We Want The Ball!" while wearing custom-printed tees bearing the same slogan.

Granik still laughs at the helicopter ride today. "We registered our displeasure with John," he says. But the expansion committee had started considering Professional Basketball Franchise Inc. as a legitimate candidate. "We needed a group that was well-financed and could be good promoters of the sport," Granik says. "It was a new sport in a new country. We wanted ownership that would be actively engaged. As we got to know John, his family, and his partners, we became more and more convinced he would be the right person to spearhead this project."

On September 20, 1993, the three ownership groups flew to New York and gathered inside the Omni Berkshire Hotel in Manhattan to make their final presentations to the expansion committee. Tanenbaum made his presentation and was followed by an ownership group led by concert promoters Michael Cohl and Bill Ballard, who had enlisted the help of Bob Foster, a Bay Street merchant banker, to assemble a group of investors which included Jim Fifield, the CEO of EMI Music; Mark Routtenberg, a former minority owner of the Montreal Expos; and recently retired Lakers star Magic Johnson. Strickland remembers walking into the boardroom after Cohl and Ballard's presentation. "There was enough AV equipment in the room for a rock show," he says. "It was intimidating because we went in with an opposite strategy."

Mathew had recommended a more low-key, personal approach to the final presentation a few weeks prior. "I said, 'I guarantee you Larry will spend at least a hundred thousand dollars, if not more, and it will be a slick production, and there was no point trying to out-Hollywood the largest concert production company in North America,'" he recalls. "At best, we may be just as good as they are, and if we weren't, we would be sending the wrong message." Peterson disagreed. "He screamed at me," Mathew recalls. "He came very close to calling me a fucking idiot. I quietly sat there, looked at the rest of the guys, and said, 'Folks, you've come this far.'"

Professional Basketball Franchise Inc's presentation would open with Peterson explaining their vision for the expansion franchise and providing details on their state-of-the-art arena plan in downtown Toronto. Bitove followed by presenting the business case to the league and explaining the long-term viability of pro basketball in the country. The owners then followed Mathew's advice from their first meeting at Cossette and appealed to the personal values of the NBA owners on the committee. "John talked about his father's business and how he started with a diner with 12 stools," Mathew recalls. "Allan talked about how he ended up building his business. We wanted the committee to say, 'We like these guys. They're just like us.'"

When Granovsky told the story of how his father, Abraham, moved from Romania to Canada and turned a single used packaging machine worth $5,000 into the largest recycling paper packaging company in North America, it moved Philadelphia 76ers owner Howard Katz to tears. He got up from his chair, walked to the front of the room, and hugged Granovsky. "He told Phil, 'That's one of the best stories I've ever heard,'" Mathew recalls.

To wrap up the presentation, the ownership group dimmed the lights and pressed play on a three-minute audio tape featuring New York sportscasters Jim Gordon and Spencer Ross providing commentary of an NBA game in downtown Toronto. "That was the idea of Jim Garbutt, who was part of the creative team at Cossette. He said, 'Let's have some fun with some theater of the mind,'" Mathew recalls. "It was great. We had a really good meeting to this point, and this was the icing on the cake." Even Peterson had to admit Mathew made the right call afterward. "I have been involved in many presentations and campaigns in my life," he says. "This was the most brilliant one I had ever seen."

The presentation was over, and now Professional Basketball Franchise Inc. would have to wait to hear from the league. The group finally sat down for dinner at around nine in the evening at Paper Moon, an upscale Italian restaurant in midtown Manhattan. The party eventually moved to Dangerfield's, a comedy club in the Upper East Side, where Peterson started to heckle an underwhelming comedian on stage. "The guy doing stand-up was terrible," Mathew recalls. "It was cringeworthy."

The comedian looked at Peterson. "Fuck you," he said. "If you think you're so smart, why don't you get up here and do this?" Peterson accepted the challenge and did a five-minute set. "It was pretty bad," Bitove says. "But we all laughed with him." It was past one in the morning when the group strolled into the Plaza Hotel and got a table in the Oak Room. They drank 25-year-old Macallan whisky and smoked cigars to wrap up the night.

When Bitove returned to his Toronto office the following afternoon, there was a message waiting for him from the league.

He had won the ownership bid.

Part One
Beginnings

The Season Ticket Drive

A few months after winning the bid, the NBA and the Ontario government engaged in a four-month staring contest, threatening to take John Bitove Jr.'s dream away. At the center of the debate was the league's insistence for NBA games to be removed from Pro-Line, the provincial sports lottery. The government pushed back against the idea, citing the $6 million in annual revenues from Pro-Line, which went to local hospitals and community programs. The two sides seemed to be making no progress toward an agreement by the end of 1993, when Russ Granik expressed his frustration and set a deadline of February 13, 1994, the date of the NBA's All-Star Game. "If we can't resolve it by February, why should I think we're ever going to resolve it?" he told reporters. "I'm getting concerned that the government doesn't care about getting a team or not. It couldn't be more critical. The whole existence of the franchise hinges on a resolution."

The dispute put Bitove—who had a lengthy to-do list to get the franchise ready for the start of the 1995–96 season—in a holding pattern. "It's very discouraging to hear there's been no progress," he told reporters. "You can imagine where we are with this. There will be no money spent and there will be no job hirings until this is resolved." On February 10, 1994, an agreement was finally reached between the two sides. NBA games would be removed from Pro-Line by October 1, 1995. The league would make a $1.5 million donation to cancer research in Ontario, provide $2 million in television time and advertising space over the next four years to promote tourism in Ontario, and work with the franchise to develop annual television campaigns against drug abuse, child abuse, and domestic violence. The expansion franchise would establish a charitable foundation to support youth programs provincially. The team would contribute $5 million to the foundation over the first three years and help raise a million dollars annually through charity exhibition games and other fundraising initiatives.

Bitove was finally able to proceed with assembling his executive team. He set out to surround himself with people who had previous NBA experience. One of his first hires was Danny Durso, who had previously worked for two teams, the Philadelphia 76ers and Orlando Magic, as their director of finance. He had recently left the Magic to become the VP of sales with Budget Rent-A-Car. In February 1994, Durso flew to Toronto for an in-person interview. "John was very patient," he recalls. "He wanted you to be happy. He wanted you to be sure. He wanted you to work for him and do the best job you could without feeling pressure."

Durso was hired as the team's first VP of finance, living in a downtown hotel for the first three months as he set up the team's finance department. "There were so many things to do," Durso recalls. "We had to review Canadian payroll tax laws. We had to sit down with Revenue Canada. It was intense."

Another major item on Durso's to-do list was helping to come up with a financing plan for a new arena. Bitove had originally worked with Jim Bullock, the president of commercial real estate company Cadillac Fairview, to identify a piece of land next to the Eaton Centre shopping mall downtown at Bay and Dundas. It was a central location with access to the subway line. But the $10 million cost and three-year estimate to tear down a parking garage, reroute underground services, and relocate the movie theater inside the mall was proving to be a challenge, so the team decided to pivot to another location.

In December 1994, the expansion franchise agreed in principle with Canada Post on a 22,500-seat, $130 million basketball facility, which would be developed on a four-acre site at Bay and Lake Shore. The team would pay $30 million upfront, plus 20 years of payments at $1.5 million annually. Waterloo-born architect Murray Beynon unveiled a model of the arena at the press conference. The upper section would feature bars, restaurants, and include the preservation of historic friezes inside the Canada Post building. There would be direct, climate-controlled access to Union Station and an underground shopping complex. Canopies and splash guards would be installed along Lake Shore to protect fans from the outside noise and traffic. The proposed plan was for the team to play at the SkyDome for the first two seasons before moving into the new arena for the 1997–98 season.

The team hired Steve Weber, who had experience in corporate sales with the Phoenix Suns, to oversee the sales department. Weber arrived in Toronto and ran into problems getting corporate sponsors in the city to buy into the new basketball team. "We had way more challenges than I originally expected," he says.

Tom Pistore, another sales executive, helped finalize deals with Ford, Air Canada, and Shoppers Drug Mart, but not every corporation bought in. "For the people writing checks in this city, it was clearly still a hockey town," Pistore says. "There were guys who would hang up or tell me, 'I'm a hockey guy.' There were also some racial connotations I picked up on when I called Bay Street companies. Guys would use racial slurs when they talked about the NBA. I was taken aback a bit. You would just have to move on. But there were people who had no interest in basketball from a racial perspective. It showed the ignorance of the marketplace."

The franchise didn't just have to pitch the idea of a basketball team to corporations around the city. They needed to convince fans to buy in as well. Per the expansion agreement, the team was required to sell 12,500 season tickets for the start of the 1995–96 season by December 31, 1994. To accomplish that goal, a sales team was assembled. The group consisted of people in their early twenties who left their jobs to work for the team. They had MBA degrees, Chartered Accountant licenses, and were leaving their careers in accounting, law, and engineering behind to accept a three-month contract with the team at the start of October

1994. The top five people in sales dollars would get a full-time offer from the team at the end of the season ticket drive.

One of the people hired to join the team was Elaine Quan, a die-hard basketball fan who grew up in Hamilton, Ontario. She spent Fridays playing pick-up ball at the local community center and spent her weekends glued to the television in the living room, rooting for the Boston Celtics. After studying psychology and criminology at the University of Toronto, Quan applied to work with the Metro Toronto Police, where she had interned during school. Graduating in the middle of a recession, she was put on a waiting list as a hiring freeze was in effect at the police department. So a 23-year-old Quan packed up her belongings, moved to downtown Toronto, and looked for a job to help her make rent. She was hired as the front-door hostess for Wayne Gretzky's Restaurant in 1993.

The idea for the restaurant came from Tom Bitove, John's older brother, who met Gretzky through a mutual friend. The Los Angeles Kings center, who wore the number 99 and was considered the greatest hockey player of all time, expressed interest in opening a restaurant. When he showed some trepidation about the many celebrity-themed venues which had recently failed and were critically panned, Tom suggested a restaurant with a more personal touch. He pitched a spot where Gretzky's most cherished hockey memorabilia would be displayed in glass cases and the menu would feature his grandmother's meatloaf recipe, a personal favorite of Gretzky's growing up in Brantford, Ontario. A deal was reached, and a downtown steakhouse owned by the Bitove Corporation was renovated and transformed into Wayne Gretzky's Restaurant.

One final personalized touch would be added to the spot before it opened in the fall of 1993. When Gretzky's agent, Mike Barnett, flew to Toronto for a site visit, he looked at the address for the restaurant. "It would be cool if we got 99," Barnett said. Tom obliged and filed an official request to the mayor's office to change the address to 99 Blue Jays Way. When the media got wind of the story, reporters questioned whether Gretzky had lost touch with the common folk and was now using his celebrity status for an inconsequential address change. After seeing the public backlash, Tom called Gretzky and asked if he wanted to drop the request. "We've already paid the price in the media," Gretzky responded. "Let's see this through." A city hall meeting was held a month later, and the address change was granted.

Wayne Gretzky's Restaurant, located within walking distance of the SkyDome on 99 Blue Jays Way, quickly became the number one hangout spot in the city. "It was the first type of place I can remember in Toronto that brought the who's who to the venue," Quan recalls. "It was casual. It was fun. It was busy. People wanted to be there because they thought, 'Who am I going to run into tonight?'" Celebrities including Martin Short, Rob Lowe, Eugene Levy, and John Candy were spotted there. Local athletes made it their go-to spot. When Gretzky visited the city, he invited friends and family to catch up in the private room. The restaurant drew comparisons to Studio 54, a famous New York disco nightclub. It was described in *The Toronto Star* as "one of the rare places that attracted everyone from business people in suits to sports fans in suits."

Gretzky's wasn't just a landing spot for celebrities and athletes. It was also a meeting place for the most prominent business figures in the city, including Bitove, the new owner of an NBA franchise, who was there several times a week. "If anyone wanted to hand me a résumé, they knew where to find me," Bitove says. "Some people got jobs by being in the right place at the right time."

It was the perfect spot for Quan to meet the most influential people in the city. Directors and executives who worked for large conglomerates, including Labatt Breweries, Nike, and Coca-Cola, frequented the restaurant. "I met tons of people," Quan says. "I was at the front, so I greeted everyone and got to know them."

One of the most memorable evenings at Gretzky's took place on September 30, 1993, when Bitove turned 33 and celebrated his birthday with family and friends with a special announcement. After the final presentation, the league and its board of governors had officially approved his ownership bid. The evening was a celebration of a new era. Quan was not working the front door that night. She was attending a Lenny Kravitz concert at Maple Leaf Gardens instead. Quan had been following the bid process and found out after the show there was a party taking place at the restaurant. "There was one rule for Gretzky's staff," she explains. "You weren't supposed to hang out there after your shift." But this was a special occasion that Quan didn't want to miss, so she took a cab to the restaurant to be part of the celebration. "John had a section of the restaurant booked off," Quan recalls. "At one point, he jumped on his chair and shouted, 'I won the bid!' The whole place erupted. It was so memorable. As a basketball fan, I was freaking out."

Quan quit her job at Gretzky's in October 1994 when she was one of 25 people hired for the season ticket drive and walked into an intense work environment at the team's offices. Each salesperson sat at a desk inside a tightly packed room and started making calls. When they made a transaction, the salesperson would write down the purchaser's personal information and credit card number on a piece of paper and send the data to a fax machine to be processed in the Ticketmaster system. A whiteboard was used to track each individual's sales number in dollars. Quan didn't make too many sales in her first two weeks. "It was a huge learning curve. People didn't understand what we were selling. There was a lot of education on my part in explaining why they should get season tickets," she recalls. "I told people they would love the feel of the game and explained how it wasn't like hockey, where you sat behind a partition. I described the courtside experience of the sneakers squeaking, the dribbling, and the trash talking. I wanted them to understand the energy of the game."

Andrea Smith, who also joined the sales team, grew up in Guelph, Ontario, and was living in Toronto with a friend after graduating from the University of Waterloo. She remembers walking into the office and being handed a list of phone numbers compiled by Dun & Bradstreet, a commercial data company that helped identify prospective ticket buyers in the city. "It was the worst," she recalls. "Half the people on the list were dead." When someone did pick up on the other end of the call, Smith ran into fans who weren't too excited about spending their hard-earned money to watch an expansion team play at the SkyDome. "It was so hard," she says. "We always tried to get them to meet you in person so we could show them the design of the new arena. We were selling a dream."

Justina Klein held a full-time job as a stockbroker at ScotiaMcLeod when she accepted the three-month position. "They were only keeping five people, so I was like, 'Do I quit my job and take a risk?'" she recalls. "The two offices were a block from each other. So I would go in at six in the morning as a broker, then be part of the sales team at nine, before returning to my job at lunch. I wanted to assess the competition and see if I could make the top five." After two weeks, Klein quit her broker job and started moving up the sales leaderboard by tailoring her pitch depending on the clientele. When she called the CEO of a Fortune 500 company, Klein would appeal to their social status by offering courtside seats, where they would be seen on television. Whereas when Klein talked to a father with two kids living in the suburbs, she would pitch a more affordable experience for the family in the upper bowl. She also appealed to customers by pitching them the idea of buying season tickets at the SkyDome as an advance deposit on getting priority access to seats when the new arena opened. "Normally, you could call people back in a month. But it was a tight sales window, so we called them back in a week," Klein recalls. "They were not going to buy on the first call. You had to send them some information and follow up."

The sales manager was Steve Griggs, who grew up at the intersection of Don Mills and Steeles and was living with his parents in Aurora when he joined the team. He had graduated from Wilfrid Laurier University with an arts degree, obtained his Master's in athletic administration at Ohio University, and was looking to work for a pro sports team. Griggs worked as an intern at the 1994 FIBA World Championship and was hired by Bitove after the tournament. "Those three months were the hardest thing," Griggs says. "I didn't know what I was doing. I had never been a manager before. We would be in every mall, from Eaton Centre to Fairview Mall, trying to sell tickets. We were working night and day." Aside from making cold calls, the sales team started setting up pop-up kiosks around the city and handed flyers to hockey fans outside Maple Leaf Gardens. "There was a lot of guerilla marketing," Quan recalls. "It was hand-to-hand combat. We were on the ground."

The top salesperson in the room was Dave Hopkinson. "They told us to sell like hell," he recalls. "So I sold like hell." Hopkinson attended McGill University and studied political science, but he had too much fun and didn't graduate with a degree after failing to meet the school's grade requirements. After moving back home to Toronto, where Hopkinson grew up as a self-described "bicycle-riding nerd who played *Dungeons & Dragons*," he had to become an adult and look for his first full-time job. Hopkinson landed with a marketing company in Scarborough, working with restaurants and golf courses to sell discounted sales packages. ("It was basically Groupon," he says.) One of his clients was the Toronto Argonauts. The CFL team was going through a transition period and needed to increase its sales. Hopkinson used his wit and charm and sold a significant number of ticket packages. When he was later hired to join the Argonauts sales team full-time, Hopkinson called season ticket holders and listened to their concerns. He convinced many of them to renew their seats by establishing close personal relationships with the fan base. When Hopkinson joined the season ticket drive, he thumbed through his Rolodex, calling up corporations around the city he already had relationships with, and asked to speak with the specific people in each company who would be able to sign off on any significant financial transaction. Hopkinson convinced the city's biggest banks, accounting firms, and insurance companies to commit to buying large blocks of season tickets.

The sales team wasn't just pitching a new sport to people, they were pitching a new concept to the fans in the form of a personal seat license. For an extra fee, the license would allow season ticket holders to have *ownership* of the seat, allowing them to transfer the seat to another owner if they wished. It was required for anyone interested in lower bowl tickets, where the fee could cost up to $8,750. Shawn Moscoe, another member of the sales team, remembers trying to explain the fee over the phone. "If you were selling to a huge engineering firm, they didn't really care. It was kind of like, 'Okay. Here's my credit card,'" he recalls. "But if you were pitching to a smaller accounting firm, they would be like, 'Wait, we have to pay $16,000 in fees on top of the seats?'"

The seat license fee was Bitove's idea. He had adopted it from the NFL's Carolina Panthers. Mark Lavaway, who worked as a ticketing manager for the Houston Rockets, was the director of ticketing for the expansion franchise. "We wanted people to feel like they had ownership within the team," he explains. "We wanted to give people a chance to sell the seat to someone else. It was also a way to raise more money." In November, after some public backlash, the team announced they were adjusting the license fees and making it optional in certain sections of the SkyDome. The concept had been criticized as a cash grab by the public, but Hopkinson had already convinced plenty of businesses to pay the fee. The sales leaderboard was measured by the total number of dollars each person sold, and he was leading the way.

Everyone was working towards a common goal of meeting the season ticket target, but they were competing against one another for five full-time positions. The dynamic made the team's offices a very stressful place. "I had good and bad days. We all did," Quan says. "There was one day I sold a suite to IBM. That was 14 tickets. I shot to the top of the leaderboard. That was an awesome day."

Whenever a deal was completed, the salesperson would ring a bell in the office. "You had to hammer it," Smith recalls. "Everyone made a big deal about it. It would be really stressful if you weren't selling and not ringing the bell."

As the December 31 deadline approached, the size of the sales team dwindled. "If you knew you couldn't sell," Griggs says, "you would just stop showing up." Many of the salespeople at the bottom of the leaderboard quit before their three-month contract was up. For the remaining members, the final weeks leading up to the deadline became a bonding experience.

"We were all 20-year-olds," Pistore says, "and having fun was just as important to us." After 16-hour workdays, they would get together for drinks at local bars. (Devil's Martini, My Apartment, and Easy on the Fifth were their favorite hangout spots.) "Some of the guys would go out all night and go back to the office and sleep under their desks," Quan recalls.

At the start of December, the team had sold over 10,000 season tickets but was still more than 2,000 tickets short of the required number. The sales team started to wonder if they would actually make it. For the franchise, falling short would mean there would be no NBA games in Toronto to start the 1995–96 season. For the salespeople who remained, it would mean they would have to find a new job at the end of the year. "It felt like an impossible task," Klein says. "We thought for sure we weren't going to make it."

Bitove showed up to the team's offices every day and never expressed any concern about the deadline. "His passion and enthusiasm trickled down to all of us," Quan says. "It was infectious. We wanted to do it for him." He had designed the office space to be open concept. The team owner would sit in front of the room and occasionally toss a football at salespeople who were dozing off at their desks. Bitove would organize an impromptu company-wide bowling tournament at the office, lining up a series of salt and pepper shakers in the office as bowling pins. He arranged one-on-one lunch outings with employees and allowed them to pick the restaurant. The choices ranged from Morton's, a high-end steakhouse, to Lick's, a popular burger spot in the city.

Doreen Doyle worked in the finance department and would occasionally fill in as Bitove's executive assistant. "We did things as a group. We had our own softball team. We had a golf night every Thursday. It felt like a family," she recalls. "John was energetic, and you felt energetic because of him. He brought that energy to the office every day. It made you want to do more."

He would also help the franchise cross the finish line. Just weeks before the deadline, Bitove met with Stan Thomas, the head of marketing at Shoppers Drug Mart. The local pharmacy chain agreed to buy a block of 4,250 season tickets and would make them available at retail locations across the city during the season. The deal pushed the team across the 12,500-season-ticket target. The three-month push had paid off. On December 21, 1994, the team publicly announced they had reached the league's requirement. "It felt amazing to be part of history," Smith says. "We worked towards something that felt impossible to achieve but we ended up doing it together." A team dinner was organized to celebrate the occasion.

"We all went to The Keg Mansion," Griggs recalls. "That was probably the first time I had a real steak dinner with a glass of wine. It was awesome."

For some of the people on the sales team, it would be a short-lived celebration. Their contracts were expiring, and only the top five in sales dollars would be offered a full-time job. Quan had made a late push up the leaderboard, but the final standings read:

1. David Hopkinson
2. Justina Klein
3. Andrea Smith
4. Shawn Moscoe
5. Mike Ponic

At the start of the new year, the rest of the sales team waited one by one to be called into a boardroom to meet with Bitove. It would be their exit interview with the franchise. When it was Quan's turn, she walked in to meet Bitove with her shoulders slumped. Working for an NBA team over the past three months had been a dream come true. Now, Quan had to return to the real world and figure out her next steps. Perhaps she would go back to Gretzky's. Or maybe she would finally listen to her mom's constant nagging and go back to school to get a Master's degree.

Bitove had another idea. He had been impressed by Quan's work ethic and energy during the season ticket drive and wanted someone with her hustle and passion in the organization. "I have an opportunity for you," Bitove said. "I don't know if you'd be interested. Do you want to work for our community relations team?" Quan could not believe what she was hearing. The lifelong basketball fan was being offered a chance to continue with the franchise.

"I don't know what community relations is," Quan replied, "but I'll do it."

"You can get started tomorrow," Bitove said.

The Toronto Raptors

I n the very beginning, the expansion team was named Professional Basketball Franchise Inc., but that would change when John Bitove Jr. announced a two-month "Name The Team" contest in February 1994. Sponsored by Cineplex Odeon and Sears, fans would get to submit their preferred choice for a team name. Their submissions would be narrowed down by the team to 10 names, and a final fan vote would take place to determine the winner. The contest would result in over 100,000 suggestions. The early entries included some off-the-wall names like Mighty Dunks, Slam Jammers, and Tallboys. There were also a variety of winter-themed submissions including Blizzard, Chill, Flurry, Freeze, and Glaciers. None of these would make the final cut, and neither would the Huskies. The idea of paying homage to the city's original NBA team name had gained some momentum publicly, but the league told the expansion franchise to move in a different direction because the name and logo would have been too similar to the Minnesota Timberwolves, who had joined the NBA in 1989. (It should be noted that while people often confuse huskies for being the same species as a wolf because of their wolf-like pointy ears, they're actually domesticated dogs.)

As the team name submissions came in, the franchise traveled around Canada to seek feedback from elementary and high school students. Focus groups were held to determine what appealed to the younger demographic. A panel featuring Blue Jays second baseman Roberto Alomar, Olympic gold-medal biathlon athlete Myriam Bedard, figure skater Josée Chouinard, and Wayne Gretzky was formed to help narrow the submissions down to the final 10. The extensive research process yielded a major finding: most people found it hard to connect with a team name that referred to an inanimate object, like the Miami Heat and Orlando Magic. So it was decided the team name would be animal themed. After eliminating Beagles, Buzzards, Panthers, Raccoons, Toucans, and Polar Bears, the franchise announced the final 10:

1. Beavers
2. Bobcats
3. Grizzlies
4. Hogs
5. Raptors
6. Scorpions
7. T-Rex
8. Tarantulas
9. Terriers
10. Dragons

Bitove had a very strong preference toward choosing a dinosaur name. He was influenced by his five-year-old son Brett, who loved the Steven Spielberg–directed film *Jurassic Park*, an adaptation of the critically acclaimed novel by Michael Crichton, which arrived in theaters in 1993 and became a global phenomenon. The movie, which followed a group chosen to tour an island theme park populated by dinosaurs created from prehistoric DNA, grossed over $914 million worldwide during its original theatrical run, surpassing Spielberg's *E.T. The Extra Terrestrial* as the highest-grossing film ever. The velociraptor and the Tyrannosaurus rex were two of the most prominently featured dinosaurs in *Jurassic Park*, so it was no surprise to see both the Raptor and the T-Rex make the final cut of fan submissions. The film had brought dinosaurs back into the mainstream and made them a fascination for children and young adults, two key demographics the franchise wanted to reach. Bitove liked the idea of having his team named the Toronto T-Rex, until a lengthy debate about dinosaurs broke out at the team's offices. It was pointed out to Bitove that the Tyrannosaurus rex was considered slow, cumbersome, and a dinosaur that hunted on its own. In contrast, the velociraptor moved at a much quicker pace and usually traveled in packs, which started to make more sense to Bitove in terms of which dinosaur best described a group of basketball players on the court.

When the result of the fan voting was announced, Raptors had finished at the top with 24 percent of the votes, followed by Bobcats at 15 percent, and Dragons at 14 percent. Some in the local media believed the fan vote was a farce, an illusion of making the public feel as though they were involved in the decision-making. They pointed to the fact the team had registered trademarks for the Raptor name before the conclusion of the voting period. The franchise had actually copyrighted several of the final 10 names, and the organization publicly insisted they would have moved in a different direction had the Raptor name not received a favorable result in the fan voting.

The team would be named the Toronto Raptors. The next step was for Bitove to work with the NBA's Creative Services team on a logo and uniform design. The league's merchandising boom of the past decade made it essential for each team to have an appealing design. The NBA sold $2.8 billion worth of licensed merchandise worldwide during the 1993–94 season, a tenfold increase over the previous decade. Bitove would be working with Tom O'Grady, the league's creative director, on the project.

O'Grady grew up in the Belmont Cragin neighborhood of Chicago, Illinois. He enjoyed playing basketball in the summer, and outdoor hockey in the below-zero freezing temperature during the winter. Growing up, O'Grady sat in his room drawing his favorite Blackhawks players on note boards. He would tape illustrations of Bobby Hull, Stan Mikita, and Tony Esposito onto a table hockey rink and play with his friends using an aluminum foil puck. O'Grady attended Columbia

College, where he studied marketing and branding, winning a Society of Typographic Arts award in his senior year. After graduating, he was hired by Saxon Paint & Home Care to design their corporate branding and work on their annual report layouts.

In 1984, O'Grady joined Frankel & Company, a well-renowned marketing agency in Chicago, where he worked with McDonald's as the art director for the fast food chain's first-ever Monopoly promotion and helped the fast food company conceive the marketing campaign for the McDLT, a sandwich which was brought to market in response to Burger King's Whopper. Like many major corporations in the 1980s, McDonald's saw significant marketing potential in sports, allowing O'Grady to merge two interests simultaneously. He helped the company put together a logo design for a gymnastics tournament at McGill University, and later flew to Deerfield, Illinois, to work with Michael Jordan, who was launching a campaign with McDonald's in conjunction with the Muscular Dystrophy Foundation. When the NBA introduced the McDonald's Open in 1987, O'Grady helped design the logo for the exhibition tournament which featured international teams competing against the league's own teams.

Meanwhile, the NBA was going through a transformation in logo and jersey designs. At the start of the 1980s, uniform designs were the responsibility of the team's equipment manager, who would work with the marketing department on choosing fonts, colors, and striped patterns. Hiring a graphic designer to add flair to logos and jerseys was a foreign concept. A turning point came in 1988, when Charlotte Hornets owner George Shinn hired fashion designer Alexander Julian to design the expansion team's jersey. Julian decided to go with his two favorite colors, purple and teal, creating a jersey design that became one of the league's best-sellers. The popularity of the Hornets jersey opened up a Pandora's box of new-age designs. In 1989, the Indiana Pacers turned to three-time Olympic gold medal winner Florence Griffith Joyner to change their team's uniforms. Rebecca Polihronis, an intern with the Pacers, had put together a photo montage of Joyner's most iconic looks, including her signature one-legged one-piece suit, and pitched the idea of having the Olympic sprinter design the new Pacers uniform. The new "Flo-Jo" jersey, with its off-center placement of the jersey number in concert with the team's signature yellow and white colors, which made up the entire left side panel of the uniform, was another hit with the fan base. Teams were no longer looking to play it safe. They wanted their logo and jerseys to be a spectacle and appeal to a younger audience who would go to the department store and ask their parents to buy them apparel. The NBA hired Judy Shoemaker as vice president of marketing to work with third-party design agencies on providing modern updates to jersey designs across the league.

The agencies were not meeting the NBA's standards, so the league asked Shoemaker to move in a different direction. She had previously worked at Frankel & Company, and recommended O'Grady as the right person to be in charge of the league's jersey designs. After a preliminary interview with Rick Welts, the president of NBA Properties (the league's marketing arm which controlled the merchandising and licensing for all teams), O'Grady was flown out to New York. A limousine was waiting for him at LaGuardia Airport to usher him past the Manhattan Bridge to the league's headquarters at Olympic Tower for an in-person interview with commissioner David Stern.

The NBA was hoping for a more streamlined process on logo and jersey updates and wanted to hire O'Grady to oversee an in-house design team. It was a once-in-a-lifetime opportunity, but O'Grady balked at the initial offer. He was relocating his family to New York and needed the NBA to compensate for the increased cost of living. Stern laughed. The commissioner told O'Grady he should be paying the league for all the things he was about to accomplish at the NBA. O'Grady wasn't sure if Stern was joking, until a few weeks later, when the league office called him back and accepted his request for a higher salary. It wasn't a six-figure offer, but it was a lot of money at the time, enough for O'Grady to move to New York and get an apartment in the Carroll Gardens neighborhood of Brooklyn. In the summer of 1990, he arrived at the league office, sat in front of a drafting table with a full set of markers, feeling like Charles Schulz, the creator of the famous *Peanuts* comic strip. O'Grady had a blank canvas to leave his imprint on the NBA as the league's first creative director.

The rest of the North American major professional sports leagues also started investing in their own in-house design teams. O'Grady quickly became friends with Anne Occi, who held the same position with Major League Baseball; National Hockey League creative director David Haney; and Bruce Burke of the National Football League. The foursome would bounce ideas off each other and take advantage of the technological advances in design, including new tools in Photoshop and Illustrator. The rise of dye sublimation also allowed manufacturers to take a design image and cheaply and easily print it onto millions of garments. The possibilities for logos and uniforms were now endless. Leagues were willing to take chances on new colorways and unorthodox designs as the billions of dollars in merchandise sales rewarded them for their daring approach.

After spending his first few months on the new job designing layouts for major trading card companies SkyBox and Hoops, O'Grady received a call from Phoenix Suns owner Jerry Colangelo. The Suns were moving into America West Arena and wanted to pair the arena move with a uniform update. Colangelo wanted something more eye-catching than the team's purple-and-orange jerseys. O'Grady didn't want to tinker with the primary colors but started brainstorming ways to make the team's nickname more of a feature on the uniform. O'Grady convinced Stern to sign off on thousands of dollars worth of equipment to build a Macintosh studio network in the office and was approved to hire three full-time designers to help with the project. Colangelo reviewed several logo concepts from O'Grady and landed on a design that featured a streaking sun, in the form of a basketball, flying across the front of the jersey with a purple backdrop. "I wanted something that was quick moving and fast," O'Grady explains. "I wanted the logo to have some speed and movement." Colangelo wanted the sun to be streaking upward

instead of downward to represent the franchise's forward-moving progress. O'Grady made the change, and the new Phoenix Suns jerseys made
their debut in 1992. The team made the NBA Finals the following year,
and the design became synonymous with a high point in the franchise's
history.

The success of the Suns' project earned O'Grady a significant amount
of trust and goodwill with the league office, so when it was time to help
Bitove with coming up with a brand identity for the Raptors, he had the
autonomy to run wild with his imagination. This was perfect for Bitove,
who wanted something that would stand out from the Maple Leafs and
Blue Jays. In his opinion, the other pro sports teams in Toronto had
played it too safe. "We wanted something global," Bitove explains. "We
wanted something that would stand out in the Canadian landscape."

While the owner preferred a dinosaur-themed name, O'Grady was
rooting for the expansion franchise to be named the Toronto Dragons.
"It's just such a mythical creature. It allows you as a designer to go to
places that can't be wrong," he explains. "As a creative person, I wanted
to continue exploring these different ways of creating a team's identity and breaking some more rules." Before the fan vote on the final 10
names was announced, O'Grady started working with designer Dick
Sakahara and developed a series of preliminary designs for the dragon
name. The two eventually landed on a scowling green dragon with
purple wings breathing fire while spinning a basketball on its finger. The
whimsical design had been inspired by the Mighty Ducks of Anaheim,
whose logo featured a duck-shaped goalie mask on top of a cross of two
hockey sticks, and was a hit among teens thanks to a series of Disney
movies associated with the franchise. The idea was shelved after the fan
vote. (When the New Jersey Nets considered a name change later in
the decade, the sketches were altered and became concept art for the
New Jersey Swamp Dragons, although that name change didn't end up
happening.)

O'Grady had worked with Bitove previously on designing the 1994
FIBA World Championship logo, which featured purple and silver

as primary colors. When he shifted focus to creating a Raptor logo, those two colors became a starting point. Bitove had made it clear to O'Grady that he wanted something that was both brash and memorable. The owner also asked O'Grady to avoid using the color red, which he believed would feel less global, and more of a Canadian-specific design.

O'Grady began by drawing a front-facing velociraptor digging his claws into a basketball. He sketched another raptor from a side profile point of view, with streaking lines next to it to indicate its otherworldly speed. O'Grady would watch specific scenes from *Jurassic Park* to properly reference the speed and movement of the velociraptor in his initial logo sketches. After sending the designs to Bitove for review, O'Grady received mixed feedback. The owner said it was a good starting point, but the raptor he had drawn was too angry looking for kids. O'Grady came back with a friendlier-looking, lime-green raptor wearing a basketball uniform, dribbling a ball with his mouth open, showing a sharp set of teeth, with claws hanging out of his sneakers. The design received Bitove's approval. The league had one problem with the logo when it was submitted for review. They told Bitove there needed to be some reference to Canada in the design. So a final adjustment was made. The raptor was changed from lime green to red.

Bitove wanted to push the boundaries even further when they proceeded to the next step: the jersey design. "He saw what McDonald's had done with the Happy Meal. Kids would walk in, get a crappy burger and apple juice, but their eyes would still light up because of the box design," O'Grady recalls. "That's how he described it. He wanted the Happy Meal box of uniforms." The creative director started by designing the front of the uniform. It would say RAPTORS in an original font which looked as if the words had been ripped and scratched by a dinosaur. Pinstripes in the form of claw marks were added to the jersey. A nameplate with the same arch as the Philadelphia Flyers uniforms was added to the back. The uniform's primary colors would be red, purple, black, and silver. Bitove wanted O'Grady to put the velociraptor logo on the jersey itself. So the final version featured a red velociraptor wearing a jersey dribbling a basketball on the front of the uniform. "We just let it rip," O'Grady says. "It was a great chance as a designer to get in there and do something that no one had seen before."

On May 15, 1994, a press conference was held at Ontario Place. With over 500 high school and public school basketball players in attendance, the expansion franchise officially unveiled its logo. "At our board meeting, when everyone saw the logo for the first time, we did get a bit choked up," Bitove told reporters. "We realized we were putting the stamp on a part of the Toronto scene for the next 100 years."

When reporters asked whether dinosaurs might become a fad, the team's public relations manager, Tom Mayenknecht, pushed back. "Experts assure us dinosaurs have tremendous staying power," he responded. "We all studied dinosaurs in school, our children do, and our children's children will too."

The merchandise rollout started the following day. Over 100,000 t-shirts and over 120,000 baseball caps had been printed out, along with an assortment of jackets, pins, and pennants. Retailers across North America had preordered items in anticipation for a rush of customers. At the Toronto T-Shirt Co. shop on Front Street downtown, 56 limited-edition hats were available for $24.95. They sold out in three hours. At the Eaton Centre Foot Locker, customers asked salespeople whether the raptor ever existed or if it had been a Hollywood invention. The logo design sold really well in the local market, but it wasn't embraced by every fan.

"That looks like Barney on steroids," one Foot Locker customer observed. "If Barney ever pumped iron, that's what he'd look like." The similarity of the team's branding to the famous purple dinosaur on the kids television show *Barney & Friends* was something Bitove became aware of during the brainstorming process.

"We knew people were going to say that," he says, "but we didn't want to give up on the color purple."

O'Grady was surprised when the comparisons to Barney became a go-to critique of the logo. "I always thought what we did was badass and different," he says. "I understand people's reaction because of the purple, but it wasn't a purple dinosaur. It was red, and he had some character to him."

The 1990s is still upheld as a creative high point for sports design. In baseball, the Florida Marlins popularized the color teal with their expansion uniforms. The Tampa Bay Devil Rays wore an eye-popping purple, blue, green, and yellow double-stacked wordmark on their uniforms. A series of futuristic jerseys with over-the-top designs were introduced as part of MLB's "Turn Ahead the Clock" promo. Teams in hockey debuted a series of alternate jerseys which modernized their logo designs. The New York Islanders divided the fan base with a fisherman-themed jersey. When the Quebec Nordiques became the Colorado Avalanche, their jerseys had a striking striping pattern with an unconventional zigzag that went wrist to wrist, with a mix of burgundy, blue, and white colors. An imprint of an abominable snowman's foot was featured on the shoulder of the uniforms.

During the same period, traditional teams added to their logos. The New York Rangers introduced a Statue of Liberty–alternate logo. The Boston Bruins had a giant Pooh bear on their third jersey. In football, the Jacksonville Jaguars leaned into a teal colorway on the tongue of the gold jaguar head featured on their logo, with a black pattern on the animal's skin. The Carolina Panthers introduced a stylish black panther with blue trim.

O'Grady was part of this golden era. He worked with many teams around the NBA and came up with new uniform designs, including an Atlanta Hawks jersey featuring a giant hawk with a sprawling wingspan and a Milwaukee Bucks jersey with an oversized deer on the front of the uniform. He helped reimagine the Detroit Pistons and their red-and-blue uniforms into a teal jersey that featured a Motor City logo paying homage to the city's rich automotive history.

While experimentation and creativity were at an all-time high for sports logos and uniform designs, only one franchise drew inspiration from a popular dinosaur film, referenced the McDonald's Happy Meal box, and had a velociraptor dribbling a basketball on their jersey. The Raptors' brand identity was one-of-a-kind.

"It was one of those rare birds," O'Grady says. "You either loved it or hated it."

Isiah and Brendan

When John Bitove Jr. sought advice on running an expansion franchise, one of the people he leaned on was Paul Beeston, the president and chief executive officer of the Blue Jays, who won back-to-back World Series in 1992 and '93.

"John and I didn't just have one or two conversations," Beeston recalls. "We had 20, 30, 40, or maybe 100 conversations."

The two met when the Blue Jays moved into the SkyDome in 1989, and Bitove was helping with his dad's food and catering business, which provided services at the stadium.

"John was a man about town," Beeston says. "He had this energy. There was a presence to him whenever he walked into a room. Napoleon once said, 'A leader is a dealer in hope.' That was John. He was a dealer in hope. He doesn't give up."

But the success of the NBA franchise in Toronto would require more than just optimism and a high-energy act from the owner. Aside from meeting the season ticket requirement and finalizing the team's branding, there was one other task that made Bitove lose the most sleep in 1994. It was the hiring of the team's first general manager.

"It was the hardest thing," Bitove says. "I had to find a basketball mind who could also help sell the team in Toronto and help grow the sport in Canada."

Beeston was the ideal person to talk to because he had been with the Blue Jays since they were an expansion team. The Welland, Ontario, native graduated with an economics and political science degree from the University of Western Ontario in 1967 and became a chartered accountant. He worked at Coopers & Lybrand, the accounting firm that would later become PricewaterhouseCoopers, until the Blue Jays called. Beeston became the team's first employee when the franchise joined Major League Baseball in 1977.

The talking points about the Blue Jays at the very beginning reminded Beeston of the narrative that was taking shape about the Raptors among the local media. "First of all, we played in Exhibition Stadium. It wasn't just the worst stadium in baseball. It was the worst stadium in sports," Beeston explains. "People also said, 'You have to show us you'll be good.' There were very few teams in sports like the Toronto Maple Leafs who could be bad and still draw large crowds and raise ticket prices."

The Raptors were in a similar spot heading into the first season. They would play at a baseball stadium, and the product would likely be subpar. Few expansion teams won many games in pro sports. The Blue Jays were a perfect example. It wasn't until 1983 that they recorded their first winning season. But Beeston remembers the skepticism going away once the Jays became a perennial contender and made three American League Championship Series appearances in seven years. The only way to win people over, he told Bitove, was to put a winning product on the court. But it was also important to block out the noise and not make decisions to please the media. Beeston saw Bitove as the right person to run a first-year team.

"John was always prepared to take chances," he explains.

On April 19, 1994, over 60 friends and family members gathered inside The Palace of Auburn Hills to watch Isiah Thomas play in his final NBA home game. A series of injuries started slowing down the Hall-of-Fame point guard in his 13th season with the team. After suffering a hyperextended knee, a broken rib, a broken hand, a strained arch, a calf injury, and a cut left hand, which forced him to miss significant time on the floor, the 32-year-old announced he would be retiring at the end of the 1993–94 season.

Thomas grew up in the inner city on the West Side of Chicago as one of nine siblings, raised by his single mother, Mary, who worked at the local church, provided food at the school cafeteria, and ran the youth center in the neighborhood. When Thomas was 12, his family moved to the suburbs after Mary landed a job working for the Department of Human Services. The youngest of the nine, Thomas played basketball at the Boys' Club and honed his skills at Gladys Park. His family lived under the poverty line. There were weeks when Thomas would feel blessed to have three meals a day, even if it meant getting by on Hamburger Helper and Quaker Oats granola boxes. While other kids wore fresh clothes and new kicks, Thomas needed a pair of sneakers to last him the entire school year.

Isiah looked up to his older brother Larry. He was a basketball phenom whose NBA dreams were cut short after he suffered an ankle injury just days after landing a tryout with the Chicago Bulls. Larry became a hustler on the streets. He drove a 1971 powder-blue Cadillac; wore wide-brimmed hats with tailor-made clothes; and made money by shooting dice, dealing heroin, and working as a pimp. Larry wanted to keep his younger brother off the streets, so he drove Isiah to St. Joseph High School and convinced their head coach, Gene Pingatore, to provide the family with financial aid. It allowed Isiah to enroll at the school and play on the basketball team.

The high school was 10 miles from home, so Thomas woke up every day at five in the morning, took three bus transfers, and walked a mile and a half afterward to make it in time for first period. On the court, Thomas became one of the best point guards in the nation, leading the school to a second-place finish in the state tournament in his junior year and finishing his four seasons at St. Joseph with a 73–15 record. At Indiana University, Thomas made the All-Big Ten team in his freshman year and led the school to the national championship in his sophomore season. After scoring 23 points in the national championship game against North Carolina, Thomas was named the Most Outstanding Player of the Tournament. As Hoosiers fans ran onto the floor to kick off an evening-long celebration, Thomas spotted Mary wearing a red suit jacket with a button on her lapel that read "ISIAH THOMAS' MOM, MRS. MARY THOMAS," in the middle of the chaos. The two embraced at center court and cried tears of joy together.

The Detroit Pistons selected the 6'1" point guard from Indiana with the second overall pick in the 1981 draft. Thomas joined a team with a 21–61 record and a losing record in 21 of their previous 24 seasons. Magic Johnson's Los Angeles Lakers and Larry Bird's Boston Celtics were the two marquee NBA teams in the 1980s, but another team would take ownership of the decade. The Pistons were a blue-collar squad. They wore down opponents on defense with their physical approach. They pummeled superstars into submission on the floor. They were the bully on the playground who set their own rules and pushed everyone around. They were the NBA team most likely to turn a basketball game into a barroom brawl. The team became known as the "Bad Boy" Pistons, and at the center of their rise to prominence was their starting point guard. Thomas was a respected leader in the locker room and one of the most fearsome players on the court. His creativity at the point guard position was second to none. He had excellent court vision, a wonderful touch around the basket, and a burst of speed on the perimeter, which left defenders helpless.

He was also one of the toughest players in the league. Up 3–2 in the 1988 NBA Finals with a chance to clinch his first championship in Game 6 against the Lakers, Thomas limped around on a sprained ankle in the second half and managed to put up 25 points in the third quarter. He finished with 43 points in 44 minutes and almost single-handedly carried the Pistons past the finish line. But a questionable foul call on center Bill Laimbeer sent Kareem Abdul-Jabbar to the free-throw line in the closing seconds, where the Lakers center hit both shots to even the series. After being hooked up to a portable cold compression unit for almost 20 hours, Thomas stepped onto the court for Game 7, but was limited to just nine minutes in the second half because of his ankle, as the Lakers clinched the championship with a 108–105 win. The 1987–88 Pistons were considered one of the best teams to have never won it all. A year later, Thomas exacted revenge on the Lakers, sweeping them in the Finals. The "Bad Boy" Pistons cemented themselves as one of the best teams of the decade after defeating the Portland Trail Blazers in the NBA Finals the following year. The two championships pushed Thomas into the greatest point guard of all-time conversation.

Four years later, the "Bad Boy" Pistons era was a distant memory when Thomas walked into the banquet room at The Palace of Auburn Hills to greet his family before his final home game. The team was rebuilding and moving in a new direction. The evening would be one last chance for the home crowd to celebrate the franchise's all-time leader in points, assists, steals, and games played. Thomas could not recall ever being nervous before a game. This night was different. His career was coming to a close, and the idea of life after basketball was frightening.

The evening would begin with a four-minute tribute from teammates and coaches before the game, as the home crowd greeted Thomas with a standing ovation. At halftime, a special video presentation featuring Thomas' greatest moments was played on the Jumbotron. But the night took a turn in the second half. In the third quarter, as Thomas tried to dribble past Orlando Magic guard Anfernee Hardaway, he felt a snap in his foot and fell to the ground. The arena went quiet. Thomas got up and hopped on one leg to the bench. The crowd gave Thomas one more ovation as he was taken to the locker room, high-fiving courtside fans on his way off the floor. Thomas had suffered a torn right Achilles tendon. His final home game would also be the final game of his NBA career. Afterward, a solemn and dejected Thomas tried to put everything in perspective. "If this is my last game, I have no regrets," he told reporters. "As a basketball player, you gave everything to your sport, gave everything to the organization and to the team you played for. You leave it all out on the floor. So It's not disappointing to me at all." Even though his playing career was over, the expectation was for Thomas to remain with the organization after retiring.

Three months earlier, a report surfaced that Thomas had been offered a $55 million contract by team owner Bill Davidson to remain with the team. He would have a role in basketball operations and receive an ownership stake in the franchise. However, when the season was over, Thomas never received a formal offer from the team.

After announcing his retirement, Thomas reached out to Bitove over the phone. As the organizer of the 1994 FIBA World Championship, the Raptors owner had some input on the selection of players on each roster, and Thomas wanted to say thanks to Bitove for playing a small role in getting him selected to the Team USA roster. The Achilles injury would prevent him from participating in the tournament, but Thomas was grateful, especially after he didn't make the "Dream Team" at the 1992 Summer Olympics. The conversation soon turned to Bitove's search for a general manager.

The list of candidates for the position included Del Harris, who had head coaching experience in Houston and Milwaukee; Gary Fitzsimmons, the director of player personnel in Cleveland; Brad Greenberg, Portland's vice president of player personnel; David Twardzik, Charlotte's director of player personnel; Rick Barry, a former NBA star; and Butch Carter, an assistant coach in Milwaukee. But after a round of preliminary interviews, another name emerged as an early favorite for the role. It was Chuck Daly. He had won a gold medal with the "Dream Team" at the 1992 Summer Olympics and was the head coach of the "Bad Boy" Pistons, an NBA franchise Bitove wanted to model the Raptors after.

"I was very close to hiring him," he says. "But a part of me said, 'You're just copying what everyone else does.' I also wondered if he had the energy level for it."

At the same time, Bitove was exploring the idea of hiring Joe Dumars, the starting shooting guard on the Pistons.

"I had a lot of discussions with Joe," he recalls, "but he was still con-templating retirement and wasn't sure if he wanted to do it."

Thomas offered his perspective. He told Bitove the person running basketball operations for the expansion franchise had to be for-ward-thinking. Thomas explained that the NBA was growing on the business side, but front offices were still lagging behind when it came to international scouting and how they assembled a coaching staff. When he got off the phone after a two-hour chat, Bitove realized he had just talked to the perfect person for the job. Thomas was a recognizable figure in the basketball community, a recently retired player who under-stood the modern-day game and had his own ideas on building a roster from scratch. Bitove started talking to executives around the league for a second opinion on Thomas. The feedback he received was overwhelm-ingly positive. The one drawback was Thomas' lack of experience as an executive, but Bitove believed he could translate his leadership qualities on the court to the front office.

A meeting was set up in Windsor, Ontario. The two discussed the general manager role and agreed to meet again at the Park Hyatt in Chicago, where John and his wife, Randi, met Isiah and his wife, Lynn, to talk about what it would be like to move to Toronto. As the two sides engaged in more serious conversations about the job, Bitove became more and more convinced he had found the right man. There was one final step in the contract negotiations. The ownership offer from the Pistons never came, but Thomas wanted the same terms with the Raptors. In addition to running basketball operations for the franchise, he wanted to become a part-owner. Bitove talked to David Peterson and Allan Slaight, who agreed to give a 10-percent ownership stake to Thomas as part of the deal. The Raptors called a press conference at Wayne Gretzky's Restaurant on May 24, 1994, to introduce their general manager.

In the days leading up to the announcement, the local media in Toronto had been tipped off about Thomas' hiring. To maintain the element of surprise at the introductory presser, Tom Mayenknecht, the team's public relations manager, decided to get creative. "I was a proponent of a visual photo-op," he explains. "This one worked out better than I imagined." Thomas was an easily recognizable figure, especially since he was still limping on crutches after surgery to repair his Achilles. Walking through the front door at Gretzky's into the presser was not an option. Mayenknecht grabbed a uniform from the kitchen of the restaurant, and when Thomas arrived, he escorted the team's new general manager to the back, where he was given a room to change. Dressed as a kitchen staffer, Thomas managed to evade the horde of media gathered at the venue and positioned himself behind the podium, where he waited to be introduced.

At 10:00 in the morning, Thomas, wearing a leather jacket bearing the team's logo, cradling a Spalding basketball in his left hand, ripped through the giant Raptors logo banner hanging on the podium and walked on stage with a massive grin on his face. "This is a dream of mine," Thomas told reporters. "It's a dream of a lot of players. I'm just thankful that the ownership group had faith in me."

Bitove was ecstatic to welcome Thomas, whose official title would be executive vice president of basketball operations, into the fold. "Number one, we've got a proven winner," he told reporters. "Number two, we've got someone who has been involved in judging talent in his leadership role with a successful organization. And number three, he has a desire to work. Of all the factors we considered, he was the most capable in the league."

When reporters asked Thomas about his surprise break-up with the Pistons, he was diplomatic. "I've learned to never look back," Thomas said. "I welcome the challenge of leading the Raptors to a championship someday, of building a team that people in Canada will be very proud of."

The hiring drew criticism from those who expected the Raptors to go with a more experienced front-office hire, but Thomas pushed back. "My job is to get the job done, and your job is to evaluate that," he told the media in attendance. "I'm very confident that when all is said and done, you'll be pleased with the way the Raptors organization runs itself and how the players perform."

After the presser, Thomas hopped on a plane with Mayenknecht to New York, where the two sat in the green room of CBS's *Late Show with David Letterman* with model Cindy Crawford and comedian Louie Anderson. In the afternoon, Thomas taped an episode of the late-night show, appearing in front of a national audience wearing his Raptors leather jacket, providing the franchise with their most significant exposure to an American audience to date.

Thomas started his search for a head coach right away. He consulted two people in pro football: Tex Schramm, the general manager of the Dallas Cowboys when they were an expansion team, and Don Shula, who spent 26 years as the head coach of the Miami Dolphins. He wanted to understand the challenges of running a first-year team and to gain insight into how a head coach could spend two-plus decades with one franchise. As he started to gather more information, Thomas realized the Raptors needed a head coach who could be patient with a younger group of players in the first few seasons and help lay the groundwork for a winning program. He wanted to make sure his first head-coaching hire was the start of a long-term partnership.

"I think when you have a lot of change, a lot of upheaval and turnover, it doesn't breed the type of consistency that it takes to win," Thomas told reporters. "So I don't expect to change coaches in a year or two or three years. I expect this to be a long-term situation. If we can get through the pain and misery and suffering that we're going to have in the next couple of years and all live with each others' sins and ups and downs, I think in the long term this will be a happy marriage for all of us."

The list of candidates included Phoenix Suns assistant coach Lionel Hollins; retired Lakers legend Kareem Abdul-Jabbar; Kevin McHale, a special assistant with the Minnesota Timberwolves; and Dallas Mavericks assistant Randy Wittman, Thomas' former teammate at Indiana. The consensus favorite was Jim Cleamons, an assistant coach in Chicago who was credited with the player development success with the Bulls. He was a top coaching candidate around the league, and the Raptors believed he had all the necessary ingredients to help guide an expansion team. It appeared to be a foregone conclusion, and negotiations were at the one-yard line, but Cleamons changed his mind at the last minute. "He bailed on us," Bitove says. "He was Isiah's first choice, but he didn't want to go to an expansion team, so he backed out."

After Cleamons passed on the job, the coaching search came to a sudden halt. Thomas told reporters he wanted to survey the landscape and see who might be available in the open market. It was now May 1995, and with opening night just six months away, the Raptors remained without a head coach as the team prepared to open free agency camp at Seneca College, where a group of players was invited to be scouted as potential end-of-roster signings during the summer. Thomas needed three coaches to help run the camp, and reached out to Mike Woodson, John Shumate, and Brendan Malone, who spent seven years with Thomas in Detroit as an assistant coach, where they won two champion-ships together. A month earlier, the Pistons had fired Malone as part of a larger house-cleaning move after the 1994–95 season. Malone canceled a family vacation as a favor to Thomas and booked a flight to Toronto for the free agency camp.

It would be a career-changing decision. At the three-day showcase featuring 23 players hoping to land an invite to the Raptors' summer league team in July, Thomas started to see his former assistant coach in a new light. He came prepared for camp and brought professionalism and accountability to the gym. "I never considered Brendan as anything but an assistant coach before this weekend," Thomas told reporters. "He's had command of the team in practice. He's been very organized and thor-ough." As the general manager gave more thought to what he wanted from a head coach, he started to see all those qualities in Malone. He was a smart Xs and Os guy and an authoritative voice who could bring a defensive emphasis to the first-year franchise. After the camp, Thomas and Malone started engaging in more in-depth conversations about the role, and an agreement was reached a few days later.

On June 2, 1995, the Raptors held a press conference to officially announce Malone as the franchise's first head coach. At age 53, the long-time assistant finally landed his first NBA head coaching gig, signing a three-year contract that would run through the 1997–98 season. Malone's coaching staff would include Darrell Walker, Bob Zuffelato, and Shumate, who also helped run the free agency camp. "This is a great challenge," Malone said. "The slate's clean. It's us against the world. We'll be a bunch of guys who will be playing and people will say, 'Oh, he can't play in the NBA or he can't coach in the NBA,' or whatever. That is a tremendous motivator for everyone involved in this organization."

He envisioned the Raptors as a roster of guys who would play hard for 48 minutes with a focus on defense and rebounding. "An expansion team is going to take a while, it's going to take three to four to five years. It's going to take losing, it's going to take maturity, it's going to take imagination as far as improving your roster," Malone continued. "But I'm realistic. I know it would be Pollyanna of me to suggest that we're going to win the NBA championship next year, but we are going to be competitive."

After a year-long search, Thomas had finally landed his head coach. "He's a principled man with great character," the general manager said of his hire. "You get an honest day's work every day from Brendan, win or lose. His qualities hopefully will translate into coaching players on the floor."

The Expansion Draft

Maybe the Raptors didn't actually need to go through an elaborate ruse to conceal Isiah Thomas' identity at his introductory press conference. While his hiring sent shockwaves around the NBA, when Thomas arrived in Toronto, he quickly realized many people in the organization had no idea who he was. It started when Thomas went for dinner with the ownership group and was introduced to David Peterson. "So John brought Isiah over to meet me, and I introduced myself," Peterson recalls. "I said, 'I'm embarrassed to tell you, but I have never heard of you.' He said, 'I've never heard of you either.'"

Once Thomas settled into the team's offices, he realized people working for the team didn't know much about the NBA. When Pistons teammate Joe Dumars called to congratulate Thomas, the general manager's executive assistant Ruth McFarlane asked Dumars what company he worked for and the purpose of his call. "I'm here to create a framework where a basketball team can perform," Thomas told Michael Farber of *Sports Illustrated* in November 1994 when the writer traveled to Toronto to write a profile. "But first, it starts with educating your staff. I feel like a professor sometimes."

One of the employees to receive a lesson was Kelly Gianopoulos, who worked in the advertising department. The first marketing campaign she worked on was to devise a billboard slogan that would hang above the team's proposed new arena location at the Canada Post office next to Union Station. After brainstorming with a local creative agency, Gianopoulos came up with a billboard that said, "The New Home of the Toronto Raptors." When Thomas saw the ad, he shook his head. "He said, 'The NBA has their own language and culture,'" Gianopoulos recalls. Thomas explained how the NBA's fan base differed from other popular leagues in the city, like the NHL. He told Gianopoulos the team's marketing needed to be more snappy and hip, in line with how the league was moving into a more personality-driven product with star players who appeared in cool commercials, filmed Hollywood movies, and sold their own hip-hop albums. When the billboard went up, the tagline changed to "Brand New Spanking Digs."

But the NBA wasn't foreign to everyone who worked with the Raptors. Inside the team's offices, there was a group of employees for which basketball had been a huge part of their lives growing up. One of them was Sandra Hamilton, who worked in the community relations department with the newly hired Elaine Quan. Hamilton still remembers seeing the general manager at the team's offices for the first time. "The day Isiah walked in, my jaw dropped," she recalls. "He was just in the kitchen getting coffee, and it was no big deal to anybody else. Nobody knew who he was. Meanwhile, I was like, 'That's Isiah Thomas. He's in the building right now getting coffee.'"

Hamilton grew up playing high school basketball in Sudbury, Ontario, and was one of the top-ranked players in the country. After playing overseas, she returned to Toronto with a bachelor of education and wanted to become a teacher. Hamilton's career path changed when she turned on the radio and heard a call for volunteers for the 1994 FIBA World Championship. She worked at the tournament and was hired by the Raptors afterward. When Hamilton finally got to sit down and chat with Thomas, the general manager expressed his desire to become more involved in the local community. "He spoke with me about getting into the Black community," Hamilton recalls. "He would do speaking engagements there and make sure they received autographed items from the team."

Thomas was the most prominent basketball figure associated with the Raptors. His name gave the expansion franchise credibility, and Thomas was happy to use his stature to help promote the sport of basketball to a new fan base in Toronto. He went door-to-door during the season ticket drive, knocking on doors and trying to convince locals to buy into the team. He regularly appeared on local television and radio stations and always made time for reporters. The job he was hired to do was to run basketball operations, but Thomas was also playing an ambassador role in a new country.

Another employee who understood the importance of Thomas' hiring was Matt Akler, who worked in public relations. He grew up at the intersection of Bathurst and Lawrence and became a basketball fan at the age of nine. "It was the 1970s and I loved the Lakers. I remember seeing in the newspaper they had acquired Kareem Abdul-Jabbar," Akler recalls. "We used to get one NBA game a week on CBS. Nobody in my family watched it. I didn't have any friends who talked about it. They would show the playoffs games after a *M*A*S*H* rerun. I remember being up until two in the morning watching Magic Johnson in the 1980 Finals."

After graduating with a degree in analytical chemistry, Akler worked for the Ontario Ministry of Government. The job did not inspire much joy. In 1992, Akler quit and backpacked through Southeast Asia before returning home a year later. An expansion franchise was coming to Toronto, and Akler decided he needed to work on something he was passionate about. As he attended a sports management program at Durham College, Akler followed the ownership bid process. Even without a media credential, he managed to sneak into Gretzky's when John Bitove Jr. held a press conference to chat with reporters about landing the franchise. "It was in the backroom and they had a row of chairs set up," Akler recalls. "Nobody checked anything, so I just sat in the back. But I was too intimidated to introduce myself to anybody." He would be one of the many volunteers at the 1994 FIBA World Championship and joined the Raptors in November of the same year.

One of Akler's favorite memories was helping Thomas with the expansion draft, which would take place in June 1995, just four days before the NBA draft. The expansion draft was the NBA's version of bargain-bin shopping. Every team had to submit a list of eight protected players who would not be available in the expansion draft. The rest of the roster, which was left unprotected, would comprise the talent pool available for the Raptors. Teams prioritized their star players and young, developing talent, which they envisioned as part of their future. So what was left for Toronto were overpriced veterans, bad contracts, end-of-roster players who rarely got off the bench, and second- and third-year guys who had worn out their welcome.

Teams around the league looked for every loophole to protect their most valued players. One way to do so was by making players with injury history available. The Charlotte Hornets protected their core group of Larry Johnson, Alonzo Mourning, Scott Burrell, Muggsy Bogues, Hersey Hawkins, and Dell Curry but left Michael Adams (who had missed 53 games during the 1994–95 season with a knee injury) unprotected. The Atlanta Hawks were allowed to make center Blair Rasmussen available because he held a spot on the roster as an injured-list player, even though he had not played in an NBA game in two years. Because unrestricted free agents were exempt from the list, teams like the Phoenix Suns, who had a roster filled with players headed to free agency, were only required to leave one player unprotected in restricted free agent Trevor Ruffin. Other teams used the expansion draft to dangle star players who had become overpriced contracts. Dominique Wilkins, once known as "The Human Highlight Film" for his earth-shattering dunks, was now a 35-year-old forward with the Celtics. The Raptors could sell tickets with a marketing campaign centered around someone like Wilkins, but his salary figure ($2.8 million for the upcoming season with several years left on his contract) would hamper their salary cap. They could bet on Cleveland center Brad Daugherty, a five-time All-Star, to recover from a back injury which kept him out for the entire 1994–95 season, but it would be a $3.8 million gamble.

In the week leading up to the expansion draft, Akler reached out to every team and asked their media relations team to provide any information on their available players. The first person he contacted was Tommy Sheppard of the Denver Nuggets. They had made a player named Arvid Kramer available, but Akler could not find any newspaper clippings or stats about him. When Sheppard heard the name, he laughed. Kramer was a third-round pick in 1979 by the Utah Jazz. The center played eight games for Denver in 1980 and was selected in the expansion draft in the same year by the Dallas Mavericks. Kramer had signed a contract with Antonini Siena of the Italian League the week before the draft and decided to spend the next three years playing overseas. In 1988, the Mavericks still had the rights to Kramer when the Miami Heat joined the league and had their expansion draft. Dallas didn't want to lose a player off their active roster, so they sent a first-round pick to Miami in exchange for the Heat agreeing to select Kramer with the first pick in the draft. Sheppard was appalled when Akler called. He knew it would be a problem if the Raptors went ahead and selected someone who the Nuggets didn't actually have the rights to. "He was like, 'Oh shoot, if you guys draft Kramer, I'm going to come up there and shoot you,'" Akler recalls. "He was kidding, of course."

The Raptors would be one of two first-year teams participating in the expansion draft. On the same day Bitove and his ownership group flew to New York to make their bid presentation and land the Raptors, a group from Vancouver had also met with the expansion committee. They were led by Arthur Griffiths, the president of Northwest Sports Enterprises, which owned the NHL's Vancouver Canucks. After briefly considering Tampa-St. Petersburg, the league had moved forward with two Canadian cities as potential expansion candidates. They would listen to three bids from Toronto and consider a single ownership group from Vancouver.

The 37-year-old Griffiths was introduced to pro sports when his father, Frank, purchased a controlling interest in the Canucks two decades earlier. When the hockey team, playing in a 15,600-seat rink called Pacific Coliseum on the city's east end, announced they were constructing a new arena for completion in 1995, Griffiths realized he needed to add another significant tenant to make it financially feasible. He assembled an ownership group for an NBA team that included his wife, Joanne; his sister Emily; John McCaw and Bruce McCaw, owners of a cellular communications company and part owners of the MLB's Seattle Mariners; and Vancouver glass magnates Allan and Tom Skidmore.

In New York, the group made a 90-minute pitch for an expansion team in Vancouver, centering their pitch on the new downtown arena, the city being the fourth-fastest-growing city in North America, the high economic spending demographic which existed, and the ethnically diverse fan base who would be drawn to a pro basketball team.

But while Bitove and his ownership group were celebrating in the city, Griffiths flew home empty-handed. He had assumed the expansion fee would come in around $80 to $90 million, had balked at the $125 million asking price, and told the NBA he needed to crunch some numbers before proceeding. It wasn't until April 1994 that a deal was finalized to bring a second expansion franchise to Canada. Vancouver would join the NBA for the 1995–96 season and had to meet the same requirements as Toronto, including the 12,500 season tickets by December 31, 1994. "The city came out like gangbusters," Griffiths recalls. "But then we stalled, partly because we were asking people to step up in the summertime and because it was a crowded marketplace with the Canucks." With five months to the deadline, Vancouver remained 5,000 season tickets short of the goal.

David Doroghy, the team's director of sponsorship sales, remembers when Tod Leiweke joined the sales campaign as the vice president of marketing and created a "Drive for Five" slogan to help push the team across the finish line. "We were going nowhere fast until he got there," Doroghy says. "He devised all kinds of nutty advertising campaigns and created a fun atmosphere. We had people standing on bridges with signs. We made it a grassroots movement with local universities, schools, service clubs, and churches."

At the bid meeting, Griffiths had passed around red leather-bound binders to members of the expansion committee featuring the Mounties name on the cover. His initial preference was for the team name to pay homage to the Royal Canadian Mounted Police. The ownership group arranged a meeting at the RCMP headquarters in Ottawa to discuss a licensing arrangement and offered to contribute part of the merchandising revenue to crime prevention and bike programs, but the idea fell apart when the team ran into problems with trademarking the name. Tom O'Grady says the NBA would not have approved the name anyways. "I don't think they loved the police and government connections," he explains. "It was very military."

A province-wide naming contest was held, and names including Rain, Ravens, Orcas, Dragons, Storm, Eagles, Venom, Vultures, and Vampires, were in consideration. The Vancouver Vipers was another name that gained some momentum, but it happened to be the name of a Dodge car, which created a problem since the team was playing in an arena sponsored by General Motors.

Griffiths wanted a name that resonated with the city of Vancouver. The grizzly bear, which populated western Canada and was a totem symbol for the local Indigenous community, became the ownership group's first choice. O'Grady met with a Haida chief to help incorporate a deeper meaning to the team's color scheme. "He told us the turquoise was the sea and the sky, the red was the passion and the blood and the soul of the grizzly bear," he recalls. "The brown was the color of the wood omnipresent throughout the region." Those would be the primary colors of the team. The logo would feature a crouched, snarling bear with an outstretched front paw clutching a red basketball. Professional volleyball player Gabrielle Reece was on hand to model the team's new uniform when the Vancouver Grizzlies officially unveiled their name, logo, and jerseys inside an Indian longhouse at the UBC Museum of Anthropology.

The design did not receive universal approval. "If you want a team with staying power in the 21st century, you don't pick a shade that will become the joke color of the '90s," wrote Mike Beamish of *The Vancouver*

Sun. "Peach, purple, puce. Anything but tired-out teal. You know teal. The Charlotte Hornets. The San Jose Sharks. Blue-green. It is to the '90s what avocado green was to the '70s. It's the hottest, hippest, but most overworked hue in professional sports marketing. It seems to me the Vancouver Grizzlies are copycats, afraid to try something new."

While many people referred to the team's primary color as teal, it was, in fact, turquoise. Larry Donen, who worked in the marketing department for the team, told reporters: "Teal is bluey-green. Turquoise is greeny-blue. It's distinctly not teal. We wouldn't put another teal uniform in because the Hornets already have it."

When it came time for the Grizzlies to hire a general manager, their short list included assistant general manager of the Los Angeles Lakers, Mitch Kupchak, along with two names the Raptors had considered, Chuck Daly and Gary Fitzsimmons. When Griffiths traveled to the NBA's offices for a meeting, David Stern recommended Stu Jackson, a 39-year-old who had just finished his second year as head coach at the University of Wisconsin. Jackson had extensive experience coaching in the NCAA and became the second-youngest head coach in NBA history when the New York Knicks hired him in 1989 at the age of 33. Griffiths flew to St. Louis, where Jackson was coaching a USA Basketball collegiate team, for a face-to-face interview. After chatting for several hours, Griffiths decided he had his man. Jackson was hired to be Vancouver's first general manager. He would pick Brian Winters, who had worked as an assistant coach for Cleveland and Atlanta in the past decade, to be the Grizzlies' first head coach.

A week before the expansion draft, the Grizzlies won a coin flip over the Raptors and were given the option to pick first in the expansion draft or one spot ahead of Toronto in the NBA draft. Vancouver decided on taking the higher pick in the NBA draft. Toronto would select first in the expansion draft.

On June 24, 1995, the Raptors' front office gathered on the 17th floor of their Bay Street office for the expansion draft. A telephone line was set up inside the room for Toronto to relay their selections to the NBA

Entertainment offices in Secaucus, New Jersey, where the event was tele-vised. At 4:30 PM, the Raptors were officially on the clock. They had three minutes to make their first selection. Thomas looked around the room and broke the tension. "So," he said, "who are we going to pick here?"

In the weeks leading up to the draft, it had become clear who the team would use their first selection on. B.J. Armstrong was only 27 and had just finished his sixth season in the league, where he started all 82 games as the point guard of the Chicago Bulls. Armstrong did not have an injury history, was a starter on a contending team, had won three championships, and was considered one of the best three-point shooters in the league. He made $2.8 million per year, a reasonable salary for a dependable starter entering his prime. A player like Armstrong wasn't supposed to be available in the expansion draft, but after the Bulls lost in the second round to the Orlando Magic, the front office decided they needed to address the team's frontcourt, who had no answer for Shaquille O'Neal in the playoffs.

To upgrade the roster, the team needed to shed salary. With Michael Jordan having returned after a year-and-a-half sabbatical to pursue a pro baseball career, the Bulls, who viewed Armstrong as a below-average defender, decided they would move forward instead with Steve Kerr, who was making a significantly lower salary at $620,000. After failing to land more than a late first-rounder in trade talks, the Bulls decided to make Armstrong available for the draft. On the night before the expansion draft, Armstrong was resigned to the fact he would be joining a team in Canada. "When I came into this league I was blessed with the sense of this being a business and I'm looking forward to the challenge," he told reporters. "It's a chance for me, if I do get drafted, to see other places, see how they do things, and a chance for me to go out and prove myself all over again in a new setting. So it's very positive for me. I've had wonder-ful years in Chicago. It's been great. I love it here and it will always be a part of me."

Another name had emerged as a potential first pick in the months leading up to the expansion draft. It was San Antonio forward Dennis

Rodman. He had been a key contributor on the "Bad Boy" Pistons and was the best rebounder in the league. Rodman had worn out his welcome in Detroit and was traded to San Antonio in October 1993. The Spurs had built a contending team around center David Robinson and saw Rodman as the missing piece to push them over the top. Spotting a new blond hairdo inspired by Wesley Snipes' blond-haired character Simon Phoenix from the 1993 science fiction action film *Demolition Man*, the man known as "The Worm" had made a flashy introduction to his new fans in San Antonio. The feel-good vibes were short-lived. At the start of the 1994–95 season, Rodman decided to take a sabbatical from the Spurs and returned to his home in Detroit. During this time, he confided in Brendan Malone, his former assistant coach in Detroit. Rodman would return to the team but continued to clash with head coach Bob Hill, who benched him during the 1995 playoffs after the forward refused to join a team huddle during a timeout in the second round. After losing in the Western Conference Finals, San Antonio appeared ready to move on from the 34-year-old forward, which made everyone wonder whether he would be made available in the expansion draft. And if so, reporters believed Thomas and Malone were open to a reunion with Rodman in Toronto. The speculation would be moot by draft night. The Spurs had decided to protect Rodman in hopes of finding a trade partner over the summer. The Raptors went ahead and selected Armstrong with their first pick.

Because each team was only allowed to lose one player via the expansion draft, the options started to dwindle immediately. When the Grizzlies selected New York Knicks guard Greg Anthony with their first pick, it took Doug Christie, an intriguing, young, low-cost prospect for the Raptors, off the board. The team used their second pick on 27-year-old forward Tony Massenburg from the Los Angeles Clippers, then added several low-cost, low-upside players in Andrés Guibert, Keith Jennings, Dontonio Wingfield, and Doug Smith, which drew a laugh from the local reporter covering the team who shared the same name. The Raptors also picked up forward Ed Pinckney from the Milwaukee Bucks and swingman Willie Anderson from the San Antonio Spurs to add some veteran presence to the team. The team also took a swing at two young prospects, Acie Earl from Boston and B.J. Tyler from Philadelphia. After the Grizzlies took Utah's Blue Edwards off the board with their 13th pick, the Raptors were on the clock again with their final selection.

The only team remaining who had not given up a player was the Detroit Pistons. Because of the number of free agents on their roster, they had maneuvered around the expansion draft rules and managed only to leave one player on the unprotected list. It was Oliver Miller, a center making $1.5 million, near the league average for an annual salary. Miller was considered lazy, a malcontent, and his physical conditioning was a question mark every year. The ownership group wasn't thrilled about being forced to take on such an unfavorable contract. Bitove viewed it as a circumvention of the rules by Detroit. The owner was so upset he flew to New York and had a meeting with league officials at the head office. (The Raptors also expressed their displeasure with having to pick up the contract of Miami Heat forward John Salley with their second-to-last pick.) "I told them we weren't going to do it," Bitove recalls. He was considering forfeiting the expansion draft process, was assessing his legal options, and decided to ask Glen Grunwald, the team's assistant general manager, for advice.

"The draft was about minimizing costs," Grunwald says. "Oliver was a good player, but his contract far exceeded his value."

An All-American player at East Leyden High School, Grunwald grew up on the West Side of Chicago and joined Indiana University as a freshman recovering from an Achilles tear suffered during a summer pick-up game. The injury limited Grunwald during his first two years in college. He redshirted his junior season and returned to the team the following season when the Hoosiers won the national championship. On the day of the 1981 NBA draft, Grunwald had already moved on from pursuing a pro career.

When the phone rang, he was back in Illinois, preparing to study for his law degree. Grunwald's mom wasn't sure if someone was pulling a practical joke on her. Earlier in the day, someone had called the house and

introduced himself as a front-office rep for the Boston Celtics. Grunwald
contacted a friend who worked at *The Chicago Tribune*, who confirmed
the Celtics had selected him in the fifth round. The prospects of playing
in the NBA were too tempting, so Grunwald skipped a week of law
school and took his chances as a training camp invite. When he failed to
make the opening day roster, Grunwald passed on offers to play overseas,
a decision he regrets today, and landed a job at the law firm Winston &
Strawn, where he met Peter Bynoe and Bertram Lee. The two became
owners of the Denver Nuggets and hired Grunwald to be the team's legal
counsel in 1990. When an ownership change took place a year later,
Grunwald landed at a media company named Reiss Media Enterprises,
which was helping a mixed-martial-arts league called the UFC to launch
their first pay-per-view event. In the fall of 1994, Grunwald received
a phone call from Thomas, his former Indiana teammate. The general
manager needed someone to help draft legal agreements and contracts
and help the franchise navigate the salary cap. He offered Grunwald the
role of assistant general manager and vice president of legal and business
affairs.

Bitove had hired lawyers from Winston & Strawn, Grunwald's former
employer, and was exploring his legal options in the days leading up to
the draft. The league was not thrilled at a potential controversy involving one of their expansion franchises before the start of the 1995–96
season. On draft day, when Grunwald walked into the office, Bitove was
still determining whether the Raptors would proceed. He would end up
reaching a compromise with the league. In exchange for having to pick
up Miller and Salley's contracts, the NBA agreed to provide $2 million in
financial relief. The expansion draft would proceed.

The Raptors would use their final pick on Miller and finished the
evening with the following 14 players on their roster:

B.J. Armstrong, Chicago, G
Tony Massenburg, LA Clippers, F
Andrés Guibert, Minnesota, F

Keith Jennings, Golden State, G
Dontonio Wingfield, Seattle, F
Doug Smith, Dallas, F
Jerome Kersey, Portland, F
Žan Tabak, Houston, C/F
Willie Anderson, San Antonio, G
Ed Pinckney, Milwaukee, F
Acie Earl, Boston, C
B.J. Tyler, Philadelphia, G
John Salley, Miami, F/C
Oliver Miller, Detroit, C

Two days after the expansion draft, Armstrong landed in Toronto and found Elaine Quan waiting at the arrivals gate at the Toronto Pearson International Airport. He hopped in her 1990 Honda Civic hatchback to visit the team's offices. "I wanted to come up here and see what's going on. I wanted to see everything for myself. I didn't want to talk over the phone," Armstrong told reporters. "I wanted to get a firsthand view for myself of what Toronto is all about, not what people tell me. I want to see the people in this organization. I want to get out and walk around the city, enjoy it and see what Toronto is all about."

At the introductory press conference, it was all smiles. Bitove presented Armstrong with a white home Raptors jersey with his name stitched onto the back. Thomas called him the "perfect guy to start an expansion team" with. In front of the cameras, everyone said the right things. Armstrong put on a Raptors cap, posed for pictures with local photographers in team apparel, and walked to the SkyDome for a personal tour of the stadium.

Armstrong saw how excited the locals were about the new basketball team and had great respect for Thomas from their playoff matchups during the height of the Bulls-Pistons rivalry, but he wasn't looking to be part of an expansion team who would take several years at the minimum to become a contender. "The biggest thing for me was having an opportunity to play and compete at the highest level," Armstrong explains. "I understood where Toronto was and where I was in my career. It was an expansion team, and there were going to be tough times. I went from winning a championship just a few years ago, and now we were going to lose 60 games a year."

Armstrong did not want to squander the prime of his career on a rebuilding team. He sat down with Thomas and requested a trade. "I asked Isiah to see if there was a way to get me to a team that was further along in the journey," Armstrong recalls. "Isiah was incredibly honest with me. He said they couldn't promise anything, but they would look into it, and if there were something that would help the team, they would do it."

While Thomas maintained a strong public stance and said he would be happy to start the season with Armstrong on the roster, the trade discussions had started even before the expansion draft. Several teams expressed their interest in Armstrong, and Thomas was weighing all the offers, including a deal with Charlotte for sharpshooter Dell Curry and a first-round pick. With the NBA draft looming, the general manager was now trying to find a new home for the team's first pick in the expansion draft.

The Rookie

T he Orlando Magic joined the league in 1989. Three years later, they landed center Shaquille O'Neal with the number one pick in the NBA draft. With a franchise cornerstone in place, the Magic paired O'Neal with guard Anfernee Hardaway at the draft a year later, vaulting them right into championship contention. With the most promising young duo in the league, Orlando won 57 games during the 1994–95 season and made the NBA Finals in the franchise's sixth year in the league. Meanwhile, the Minnesota Timberwolves joined the NBA in the same year as Orlando but found themselves as a perennial basement-dweller in the Western Conference. The Wolves' spotty draft record included spending top-10 picks on: point guard Pooh Richardson, who became a journeyman role player; big men Felton Spencer and Luc Longley, who did not live up to their draft billing; Isaiah Rider, an all-world talent who failed to become a franchise player; Donyell Marshall, who was taken fourth overall and traded after 40 games; and Christian Laettner, who couldn't translate his stellar college résumé to the pros. When the Magic reached their first NBA Finals, the Wolves finished the 1994–95 season with a 21–61 record. It was their sixth straight losing season since entering the league.

Each year, the NBA determined the order of the draft with a lottery, where ping-pong balls numbered one through 14 were placed into a machine, which would spit out a four-digit number combination. Each non-playoff team held a number of four-digit combinations allocated based on their regular-season record. The team with the worst record would hold the most four-digit combinations, giving them the highest percentage to land the number one pick. The team with the four-digit number drawn from the machine would get the first overall pick. Two more four-digit combinations would be drawn to determine the second and third picks. The rest of the draft order would be ranked based on win-loss records.

The team entering the 1995 draft with the highest odds of landing the first overall pick was the Los Angeles Clippers, who finished 17–65 and held 25 percent of the lottery combinations. They were followed by Washington and Minnesota, who both finished 21–61 and had an 18.3 percent chance to win the lottery. None of those teams won the lottery. Instead, with a 9.4 percent chance to land the number one pick, the Golden State Warriors jumped ahead of four teams and would draft first. As part of the expansion agreement, Toronto and Vancouver were not eligible to win the draft lottery in their first four years. The clause, another point of contention for Bitove, who at one point unsuccessfully lobbied the league to lift the restriction, came from the rest of the owners wanting to limit the competitive advantage for first-year teams and prevent another O'Neal-to-Orlando scenario. The Raptors and Grizzlies would have the sixth and seventh picks in their first year. Vancouver won a coin flip before the expansion draft and decided to go with the higher pick in the NBA draft, meaning they would select one pick ahead of Toronto.

A year earlier, when the 1994 NBA draft took place at the Hoosier Dome in Indiana, Isiah Thomas had rounded up the team's chief scout, Bob Zuffelato, who had 33 years of scouting experience, and his brother Larry, and sat inside a hotel boardroom across from where the draft was taking place and ran a mock draft. It would begin a year-long process of preparing for their first draft. Zuffelato and the rest of the scouting department traveled across the United States, visiting high school and college gyms and talking to coaches and executives to gather intel on prospective first-round picks. There were overseas visits to identify international talent who might fit what the Raptors were trying to build. Thomas would travel with the scouts when his schedule allowed, bringing a tape recorder and recording audio notes while scribbling down in-game observations on his legal pad. The team had developed a computer program that helped the scouting department input all their data to analyze each prospect based on their physical and psychological attributes. It was a tedious and extensive process to pick one single player, but Thomas understood the importance of the franchise's first draft pick. The right selection would help the Raptors chart a course toward contention, like the Magic. A miss would set the team back and potentially send them into a lengthy rebuild, like the Wolves. As he narrowed down the team's options with the number seven pick, Thomas kept returning to a player he had seen several times with the University of Arizona.

He was a point guard named Damon Stoudamire.

Liz Washington still remembers raising her son as a single mom in Portland, Oregon. Her husband, Willie, had moved to Milwaukee, Wisconsin, to take on a new job, leaving Liz; Stoudamire's uncles Charles and Anthony; his baseball coach, Terry Tims; and Julian Cowan, the father of his close friend Erin, to be parental figures in Stoudamire's life. Liz worked overtime as a bill collector at a local trucking company to help the family make rent. But every Christmas she would hand Stoudamire a JCPenney catalog so her son could make a wish list. He would wake up on Christmas morning and find a large bundle of gifts in the living room under the tree. "I thought we were rich because she made me feel rich," Stoudamire recalls. "My mom wasn't a hugger. She never said, 'I love you.' But I knew she loved me because of the things she did." Working long hours, Liz would drop Stoudamire at his grandmother's house in the morning and pick him up in the evening after school. Stoudamire loved visiting his grandmother Wanda. She lived across from Albina Park. Stoudamire would grab Wanda's kitchen alarm clock, wind it down to 10 seconds, and pretend to hit game-winning jumpers at the park every day.

Stoudamire fell in love with basketball at Matt Dishman Community Center, where he played on organized teams starting at the age of eight. "That's where I learned everything," he says. "It holds a special place in my heart." The community center was also where Stoudamire was humbled for the first time, when, as a fifth grader, he lost a game by 40 points going up against a sixth grader named Terrell Brandon, who would go on to become a first-round pick in the 1991 NBA draft. Stoudamire tended to remember the losses more than the wins. "It made me practice harder than everyone," Stoudamire says. "It made me play harder. It made me want to be the best."

Liz didn't mind all the hours her son spent playing basketball at the community center. It was a way to stay out of trouble in their inner-city neighborhood. Stoudamire remembers having to end pick-up games at the park early because of shootouts growing up. He would run into child-hood friends who had grown into teenagers and were now making ends meet on the streets. They would say no when Stoudamire asked them to join him at the gym. "They signed up for something they couldn't get out of," he explains.

One of the first coaches who helped Stoudamire develop into the player he would become was rec league coach Vedi Simington, the demand-ing type who would scream and swear at his players and make parents wonder whether he was pushing their kids too hard. It was the exact kind of tough love Stoudamire needed. "I allowed him to coach me like that because after each practice, he would pile all the kids in his car. He would feed us and then drop every single one of us home," Stoudamire explains. "There was shit going on at different cribs. He wouldn't leave until each of us got in. If somebody couldn't get into their apartment, he would wait until their parents got home. He did that every Monday and Wednesday. That's how I know he loved us."

Stoudamire landed at Wilson High School, and expected to be handed a starting position on the team. When the point guard was still barely coming off the bench in his sophomore season, he asked head coach Dick Beachell for an explanation. Sophomores are to be seen, the coach told him, not heard. "Man," Stoudamire replied. "I can't be seen or heard sitting on nobody's fucking bench." He would go home in tears, begging his mom to transfer him to another school. Liz wanted his son to stick it out, so Stoudamire started treating practice like games, going at his teammates and forcing Beachell to take notice of him.

Toward the end of the season, Stoudamire was finally inserted into the starting lineup against rival school Jefferson High School. "If you don't do shit in this game," Beachell told him, "you will sit your ass over there for the rest of the year."

"Coach," Stoudamire replied. "You might as well tell whoever you're taking out of the lineup to sit their ass over there because you're about to look like a genius." Stoudamire hit two three-pointers to start the game and never left the starting lineup, leading the school to two state championships and becoming one of the most prized college prospects in the country.

Liz remembers her son as a straightforward high school kid to deal with. He would sometimes skip curfew to hang out with the older kids and missed a few basketball games in his freshman year because his grades weren't up to par, but Stoudamire largely stayed out of trouble.

Well, except for the phone calls.

One day, Liz returned from work and saw a phone bill for more than $300. She was confused and called the telephone company, thinking it was a billing error. The operator told Liz the extra charges were coming from a series of calls to a 1-800 number. Since he was a five-year-old kid, Stoudamire loved reading the sports section in the newspaper. He would study photos of the players and scan the box scores to memorize their stats. Entering his senior year, where he would average 26 points per game, Stoudamire found a number in the paper which you could call to hear a list of top-ranked high school players in the nation. He thought it was a free service, called it every day, and started to rack up hundreds of dollars in charges. Stoudamire initially denied he had made the calls when Liz confronted him but did eventually fess up to his mistake. A block was placed on all 1-800 numbers in the household from that day on.

During high school, Stoudamire's father, Willie, had returned to Portland after Damon's grandmother, Wanda, was diagnosed with cancer. She passed away six months after Willie's return. It was a challenging time for the family. Stoudamire had lost his grandmother, who he was close to growing up, and was also working on accepting his father back into his life. "It was harder on me than I let on at the time," he says. "You want to know your dad, but you also have a lot of resentment. He hadn't been around, so you feel a certain type of way. We had our good days, and we had our bad days."

Willie saw the chance to travel to Wisconsin for a new job as an opportunity to grow as a person but understood why his son would be upset. "It was something we both had to work through, and to some degree, it's something we're still working through," Willie says. "He just wanted to know why I left. He would ask me questions, and I would tell him, and sometimes he didn't like the answers."

A top-ranked college prospect in his senior season, Stoudamire narrowed his choices to Oregon, Louisville, and Arizona. Liz sat down with her son, and the two decided it was best for him to go somewhere far. "I needed to get away from home to grow up a little bit," Stoudamire says.

The first few months at the University of Arizona were challenging. Stoudamire, who majored in media arts with a minor in sports broadcasting, was homesick. During Christmas, the campus was empty. Most of the students had gone home to spend the holidays with their family, but Stoudamire had to stay behind for a basketball tournament. He was coming off the bench as a freshman, averaging only 18 minutes per game, and second-guessing his decision to pass on Oregon's offer to stay closer to home. Stoudamire called his mom.

"He was crying on the phone," Liz recalls. "I said, 'If you want to transfer, go ahead, but believe me, they're going to promise you a lot of stuff that you might not get when you get there.'" After the holidays, Stoudamire started developing a trust with head coach Lute Olson, and eventually became the team's starting point guard in his sophomore season. Arizona entered the 1993 NCAA tournament with a 24–3 record and were a popular national championship pick. They were 20-point favorites in the opening game, but the number-two-seeded team would fall to 15th-seeded Santa Clara in the first round. Stoudamire had six turnovers in the 64–61 upset and went 0-for-7 from the field. The crushing defeat stayed with him for the entire summer. Stoudamire spent each day in the gym, promising to return for his junior year, ready to erase the memories of the disappointment.

In his third season at Arizona, Stoudamire increased his scoring average from 11.0 points to 18.3 points and formed one of the best backcourts in the nation with Khalid Reeves, who averaged 24.2 points in his senior season. The school was first in the Pac-10 conference with a 14–4 record and finished 29–6 overall. Arizona was the number two seed in the tournament once again and would erase the previous year's first-round embarrassment, recording double-digit wins in the first three games of the tournament. In the West regional final, Stoudamire scored 27 points and grabbed 10 rebounds in a win over number one seed Missouri, sending Arizona to the school's second Final Four appearance.

Stoudamire's outstanding season made him an NBA prospect, but he didn't want to sit on the bench and wait for his opportunity in the pros. If he was going to enter the draft, Stoudamire wanted to make sure he was a lottery pick. So he played for Team USA at the 1994 Goodwill Games in the summer and decided to return for his senior season at Arizona. Stoudamire averaged 22.8 points and 7.3 assists, finished as a finalist for the Naismith College Player of the Year award, and was a top-10 prospect entering the 1995 NBA draft.

On June 28, 1995, Stoudamire arrived at the SkyDome in a gray-pinstripe suit and sat at a table near the podium where the draft picks would be announced. He was joined by his mom and dad, his close friend Erin Cowan, and his girlfriend, Rene Evans.

Golden State started the evening by using their first overall pick on Maryland center Joe Smith, who won ACC player of the year, averaging 20.8 points and 10.6 rebounds on 58 percent shooting in his sophomore season. The Clippers took Alabama forward Antonio McDyess second and traded him to Denver for forward Rodney Rogers and the 15th pick. North Carolina swingman Jerry Stackhouse, who averaged 19.2 points and 8.2 rebounds, went third to Philadelphia. The Washington Bullets were now on the clock.

Thomas had explored every option leading up to the draft to acquire Washington's pick. The player he most coveted was Kevin Garnett, a Greensville, South Carolina, native who played basketball at Mauldin High School in a nearby town. Garnett and his family then moved to Chicago, where he transferred to Farragut Academy on the city's West Side for his senior year. The 19-year-old became the number one high school prospect in the country at Farragut and decided to forgo college and enter the 1995 draft. Garnett was a 6'11" power forward who could run the floor like a point guard, shoot threes like a shooting guard, and defend on the perimeter and in the low post.

When Thomas was hired as the general manager, he had explained to Bitove his vision of assembling a roster filled with interchangeable pieces. He wanted players who could play and defend multiple positions. The concept was for all five players on the court to be capable of slowing down the speed of quicker guards around the league, while also being physical enough to bang with the bulkier forwards and centers. This forward-thinking approach was one of the reasons why Bitove chose to hire Thomas, who started to refer to players who fit this description as a "Raptor Two." Thomas was so enamored with Garnett, the perfect embodiment of a "Raptor Two," that he had lobbied the NBA to see if he could sign the high schooler after his junior season but was told it would not be allowed under the league's collective bargaining agreement.

The buzz around Garnett had become so considerable leading up to the draft he landed on the cover of the June 26, 1995, issue of *Sports Illustrated*, where he was photographed in a black-and-white tracksuit holding a basketball in his hands with a curious look on his face, staring at the camera. The cover line read: READY OR NOT... A second, smaller cover line below said: THREE WEEKS AGO KEVIN GARNETT WENT TO HIS HIGH SCHOOL PROM. NEXT WEEK HE'LL BE A TOP PICK IN THE NBA DRAFT.

"Garnett represents the most elusive of commodities for the bottom feeders of the NBA—hope," wrote Jack McCallum in the cover story. "He runs the floor like a sprinter, he shoots 20-foot jumpers with ease and perfect rotation, and he's the best passing big man in the draft. Most teams believe he'll eventually be a do-everything small forward, but for now let's give him a new handle. Call him a faceup 4, a power forward who can hurt you from anywhere, a cross between Reggie Miller and a kinder, gentler version of Alonzo Mourning." Garnett had left everyone in the gym slack-jawed with his athleticism at an individual workout during predraft camp in Chicago. According to eyewitnesses, the high schooler was stationed at center court and asked to put the ball on the floor and finish at the basket. He used the drill to show off his skills, dribbling behind his back, then between his legs, while running towards the rim at full speed.

Washington general manager John Nash was one of many people in attendance for Garnett's workout. He walked away convinced he had seen a franchise player in person. There was a significant risk to any team using their first-round pick on Garnett. Very few players had successfully made the high school-to-pros jump. There were also concerns about the high schooler's maturity and whether his 220-pound skinny frame would develop and translate at the pro level. When Nash recommended using the number four pick on Garnett to Abe Pollin, the owner of the Bullets rejected the idea. He didn't want to bear the risk of drafting a high schooler and instructed Nash to pick a more established college player instead.

Thomas had made it clear before the draft that Garnett would not slip past the Raptors at number seven. He was also aware the Timberwolves, who had the number five pick, were strongly considering taking the high schooler. In the days leading up to the draft, Thomas engaged in trade talks with Washington. At one point, he offered to swap first-round picks, which would allow the Raptors to move up to four and draft Garnett, in exchange for including B.J. Armstrong in the deal. The two sides could not come to an agreement, and the Bullets ended up using the fourth pick on North Carolina starting power forward Rasheed Wallace, who finished his NCAA career as the leading field-goal percentage shooter in ACC history.

Minnesota was next, and now Thomas knew his chance at landing the high schooler was slim to none. Wolves head coach Flip Saunders also witnessed Garnett's legendary workout in person. He had actually walked into the gym that day with another idea. Saunders was going to talk up the high schooler to reporters afterward regardless of how he fared in the drills in hopes of convincing a team ahead of them in the draft to take Garnett, so the Timberwolves could swoop in and take a more established college player. Instead, the workout had convinced Saunders he was watching the best prospect in the draft. He told general manager Kevin McHale it was the best workout he had ever seen. The Wolves had a poor draft history up to this point and were ready to take a swing on the high schooler. They selected Garnett with the number five pick.

After Vancouver took Oklahoma State center Bryant Reeves with the sixth pick, the next two picks belonged to Toronto and Portland. Sitting inside SkyDome, Stoudamire knew he was headed to one of those teams. The point guard had blown the Raptors away at a predraft workout, making 22 consecutive jumpers to open one shooting drill. When the training staff asked him to do 40 push-ups, he did 80. He impressed the coaching staff with his level-headedness and maturity in a post-workout interview. His competitive nature, conditioning, and work ethic appealed to Thomas. Over and over again, Stoudamire talked about his desire to spend every day in the gym to continue improving his game to become a superstar at the NBA level. Even though his 5'9" frame made scouts wonder whether he could defend in the pros, Thomas walked away convinced Stoudamire would be able to be the point guard of an expansion team. The Arizona guard had also caught the attention of the Trail Blazers' front office after he dominated two other first-round prospects, Brent Barry and Bob Sura, at a private workout. Two days before the draft, Portland traded up from the 19th spot to eighth, right behind the Raptors, with an eye toward landing Stoudamire if he was still available. The point guard had been intrigued by the idea of returning home to start his NBA career but also saw a strong mentor in Thomas and an opportunity in Toronto to continue growing as a player and person without the pressure of being in Portland. "It wasn't the right time," Stoudamire says. "It was better for me to be somewhere else."

As the anticipation built among the home crowd, commissioner David Stern walked to the podium and stood in front of 21,268 fans inside the SkyDome to announce Toronto's pick. A chant started inside the stadium. "We want Ed! We want Ed!" The home fans wanted their team to select Ed O'Bannon, the UCLA forward who had led his team to a 31–2 record in his senior year. O'Bannon scored 30 points and grabbed 17 rebounds in the national championship game, leading UCLA to their first championship in 20 years, and was named the Final Four Outstanding Player of the Tournament. On paper, he had a much more established résumé than Stoudamire and was a much more recognizable name to the average basketball fan.

"In the long shot event that he is available when the Raptors have their number called seventh in next week's college draft, Thomas should have the net ready," wrote Chris Young in *The Toronto Star.* "O'Bannon is a rarity in an NBA draft group that contains far more questions than answers: a finished product, a legitimate NBA small forward at 6-foot-8 and, it seems, mature beyond his 22 years. No one has to wait on him, either in terms of basketball development or pampering." Despite his accolades, there were significant concerns from teams in the draft lottery about how O'Bannon's surgically repaired left knee might hold up in the NBA. As a result, he slipped on draft night and was now surprisingly available to the Raptors.

As the chants continued, Stern adjusted the microphone on the podium. "With the seventh pick in the 1995 NBA draft," he said, "the Toronto Raptors select Damon Stoudamire from the University of Arizona."

Stoudamire leaned back in his chair, fighting tears from his eyes, thinking of his journey from the playgrounds in Portland, Oregon, to realizing his dream of making it to the pros. He stood up and embraced Liz as fireworks went off inside the stadium to mark a special occasion for the expansion franchise. "I had a hundred things flashing through my head," Stoudamire says. "The process of getting to that point. It was a culmination of all the hard work. It was the biggest moment of my life."

But the lasting memory from the draft will forever be the boos that rained down from all over the stadium when the pick was announced. The Raptors fans in the building voiced their displeasure at the franchise's decision to draft Stoudamire instead of O'Bannon as the Arizona guard walked to the podium to shake hands with the commissioner. It was an awkward start for the team's first draft pick.

Training Camp

Brendan Malone was eager to get started at his new job with the Raptors, but just three days after the NBA draft took place at the SkyDome, the basketball world came to a stop after owners and players failed to reach a new collective bargaining agreement. A lockout started on July 1st, and the start of the Raptors' first season was suddenly in jeopardy. As he waited for the two sides to come to an agreement, Malone woke up every day with a nervous energy. He would keep busy by watching tapes of old NBA games and going for a round of golf in the afternoon, but the coaching lifer just wanted to get back to work.

Malone grew up in the Astoria-Queens neighborhood of New York. The son of Irish immigrant parents, he watched his dad unload railway boxcars while his mom worked as a nanny. From an early age, Malone was instilled with an appreciation for hard work. His family didn't own a bike or a car, so Malone spent most of his childhood hanging out at the playground across the street from his tenement building. He was the tough kid in the neighborhood, getting into fistfights and winning the respect of his peers. Malone lived a simple life with his parents and three siblings. "We made the best of what we had," he recalls. "We didn't even know what we were missing. We were happy, and I liked all the kids in my neighborhood."

At 13, he made the Pee Wee hockey team and spent every Sunday afternoon playing at Madison Square Garden during the intermissions of New York Rangers games. Malone traveled across North America, including his first trip to Canada, where he competed in a tournament in Halifax, Nova Scotia. After starring as a forward in a metro hockey league at 16, Malone gave up his dreams of playing professional hockey and turned his attention to basketball. After riding the bench in his senior year at Rice High School in Harlem and playing briefly at Iona College, Malone realized he wasn't going to make the NBA, so he joined the Army before returning home and landing a job as a writer with the *New York Daily Mirror* while working with the police service at the Empire State Building. "I didn't have any direction. I didn't know what I wanted to do," he says. "I was a log just drifting down the river."

Everything would change after Malone got his Master's degree in Physical Education at NYU. He reached out to Robert McMullen, the principal at Power Memorial Academy, an all-boys Catholic school in New York. The school had become a basketball powerhouse thanks to a high schooler named Lew Alcindor, who earned the nickname "The Tower from Power," while leading the school to a 71-game winning streak and three straight New York City Catholic championships. Malone was hired as the director of physical education and coached the school's basketball team for a decade, leading them to two state championships. "It was my most satisfying time as a coach," Malone said of his time at Power. "You were with the kids all the time and helped them get scholarships. You could become their surrogate father. Helping other people achieve success is what makes me happy."

Malone was a three-time New York high school coach of the year, and college programs had started to pay attention. In 1976, he accepted an offer to become the assistant coach at Fordham and later moved to Yale before spending six years at Syracuse. Malone got his first college head coaching job in 1984 with Rhode Island and was hired by the New York Knicks two years later, joining Hubie Brown's coaching staff as an assistant. After Isiah Thomas and the Detroit Pistons lost in seven games to the Los Angeles Lakers in the 1988 NBA Finals, assistant coach Ron

Rothstein was hired by the Miami Heat to be their head coach. Chuck Daly called Malone, who joined the Pistons as an assistant coach.

After winning two championships with the team and developing a reputation as a defensive mastermind, Malone was now looking to import the same identity he built in Detroit to an expansion franchise in Toronto in his first opportunity as an NBA head coach after 27 years of coaching. He would finally be able to get back to work when the lockout ended in September. The two sides reached a six-year agreement which would include a significant increase in the salary cap and average player salary over the term of the deal. When the league opened for business again, the Raptors announced they had traded B.J. Armstrong to Golden State for Victor Alexander, Carlos Rogers, Dwayne Whitfield, Martin Lewis, and Michael McDonald. (The trade had been agreed upon before the lockout but was now official.)

Training camp would start in October at Copps Coliseum in Hamilton, Ontario. Malone had a month before opening night to find a roster capable of competing during the franchise's first season. "We have never been together before, and it takes time to build up team chemistry," he told reporters. "I want guys who'll show up in boxing gloves, who'll kick butt. I don't like soft players with finesse."

The expansion agreement allowed the Raptors to invite up to 30 players to camp, higher than the 20 players permitted to other teams. On the eve of training camp, Damon Stoudamire flew to Toronto and signed his first NBA contract, a three-year, $4.6 million deal, before hopping on a bus to Hamilton. It did not take long for the rookie to recognize Malone was an old-school, no-nonsense head coach who wanted to establish a blue-collar, defense-first identity for the expansion franchise.

On Day One, the team started a two-a-day practice schedule which would become the norm during camp. "It was so tiring," Stoudamire recalls. "We practiced for like three hours twice a day for two weeks straight. It was a different grind, man. My body was struggling to recover. I never did anything after practice. I just went straight to my room to get my body right."

Players started complaining to reporters on the second day. When Malone was made aware of the complaints, the head coach snapped. "This is a tryout camp," he said. "If you don't think you can practice twice a day, you don't belong on this team." Malone had granted a one-on-one interview with *The Toronto Star* during the lockout and explained his lack of tolerance for laziness. "Some guys are paid a lot of money who don't play hard all the time," he said. "Teams should make a thorough background check of players they draft, to see what makes them tick." After a week in training camp, Malone made it clear there weren't enough players meeting his standards. "I see a lot of good things and a lot of bad things," he told reporters. "There are times I walk out depressed and other times I walk out happy."

The salary cap for the 1995–96 season was set at $23 million, a jump of nearly $8 million from the prior year. But under the terms of the expansion agreement, the Raptors were only allowed to use two-thirds of the salary cap, putting them at a handicap versus the rest of the league. When free agency opened shortly after the end of the lockout, teams were able to use the extra salary cap space to bid for coveted players like Chris Webber, Dana Barros, Anthony Mason, Sean Elliott, and Dennis Scott, but the Raptors only had $15.2 million to spend on their roster. They allowed three of their expansion draft picks, Andrés Guibert, Keith Jennings, and Doug Smith, to leave via free agency, and waived Jerome Kersey after failing to find a trade partner for the veteran forward. The team's most prominent free agent pick-up was Alvin Robertson, a 33-year-old shooting guard who had been out of the NBA for two years after a back injury ended his 1992–93 season with the Detroit Pistons. After the Denver Nuggets traded for him and waived him at the start of the 1994–95 season, they remained responsible for most of his $2.5 million salary, meaning the Raptors were able to sign Robertson for a bargain price of $200,000.

Robertson, a four-time All-Star and a former Defensive Player of the Year, was well past the prime of his career and still recovering from two herniated discs. But the 6'4" guard walked into training camp and set the tone on the court right away. Stoudamire can still hear Robertson's voice in his head today. "Man, you guys don't compete," he would shout at his teammates. "You gotta compete. You gotta compete." Robertson pushed the players in camp, including Tony Massenburg, to start accepting Malone's hard-nosed approach.

"He was the oldest guy on the team, but he was also the hardest-working guy on the team," Massenburg says. "He had all these years in the league, and he still showed up every day to practice. He was not sitting over there with ice bags on his knees and taking it easy. If he could give it his all, that would challenge you to step up and do it as well."

Robertson embodied what Malone wanted to see from his first-year team, so the head coach nicknamed him "The Raptor."

The lockout prohibited teams from having official contact with their players, so Stoudamire spent the summer back home in Portland, working out every day. He hit the weight room for an hour each day, followed by an hour of shooting drills, and scrimmaged against college and NBA players at the River Place Athletic Club. In the summer, Stoudamire had also gotten a tattoo on his right arm. It was an illustration of Mighty Mouse, a superhero version of Mickey Mouse created by Terrytoons Studio in the 1940s, to complement a Gothic letter tattoo of the name DAMON on his left shoulder and a photo of his grandmother Wanda and her address on his left arm. "Mighty Mouse was always saving people, always coming to the rescue," Stoudamire says. "He was the man. He could get you out of any jam. That's what I always wanted to be."

The rookie had arrived at training camp with something to prove, which was nothing new to Stoudamire, who had always been the smallest player on the court. "I've always been slighted," he says. "I've always had to prove myself. Nothing has ever been given to me. I've always had to beat down the door myself."

Stoudamire impressed his head coach, who was already letting his interest in old Hollywood classic films slip in during his interviews in camp. "Damon doesn't think he has any limitations," Malone said. "He's like Sophia Loren. I was reading a story about her the other day; someone mentioned to her that she's 61, and she said, 'Really?' She doesn't think about her age. Damon's the same way. I don't think he realizes how small he is. And you know what? I'm not going to be the one to tell him."

Players in the locker room saw a rookie who appeared ready to lead an NBA team in his first season. "When I got to training camp, I saw how dedicated he was and how much he truly loved the game," Massenburg says. "Damon was a special little man. There weren't many little guys who impacted the game the way he did. He was also a good teammate. When you see a guy who has his character, his leadership, and his commitment to the game, it makes it easy to embrace a guy like that."

Even Robertson, who did not dole out too many compliments, praised the rookie. "Damon's tough. He's relentless. He doesn't care who you are or how big you are. He just keeps pounding away at you," he told reporters. "The basketball skills are obviously there, but what sets him apart is what's in his chest. You can't put a tape measure around his heart."

Stoudamire earned the respect of the locker room right away, and the vets on the team even made an exception for the first-year guard when it came to having to perform rookie duties. Generally, NBA teams subjected rookies to performing menial tasks during their first season as a rite of passage. The tasks included grabbing laundry for teammates on the road, getting breakfast and a box of donuts for everyone before morning shootaround, or getting a call at four in the morning on a road trip from a teammate who needed toothpaste, mouthwash, and an extra box of condoms. John Salley recognized the first-round pick would be doing a lot of heavy lifting on the court, so he stepped in and relieved Stoudamire from rookie duties. "He hasn't had to pick up my luggage one time, and I'm not happy about that at all," Salley told reporters. "But I guess it makes sense, because you can't ask a guy to carry the team and carry the bags."

On October 14, 1995, the Raptors played their first exhibition game against the Philadelphia 76ers. The matchup took place in front of 9,367 fans at the Metro Convention Centre in Halifax, Nova Scotia. A number of preseason games had been scheduled across the country as part of the team's long-term plans to promote the sport of basketball to a national audience in Canada. Stoudamire would impress the home fans, scoring 15 points in the first quarter and finishing with 25 points in a 120–107 win.

In the victory, Willie Anderson had come off the bench and scored a team-high 26 points. The 29-year-old swingman was soft-spoken but had become a mentor to the younger players in camp. "Willie helped me understand the league," Stoudamire recalls. "He had a high IQ and an understanding and feel for the game. It was big just being able to pick his brain." The vet had been selected 10th overall by the San Antonio Spurs in the 1988 NBA draft after finishing as the school's eighth-best all-time scorer at the University of Georgia. In his rookie season, Anderson averaged 18.6 points and drew comparisons to San Antonio legend George "The Iceman" Gervin for his athleticism and explosiveness at the basket. After a stress fracture injury that required multiple surgeries and metal rods being inserted in both legs, Anderson entered a different phase of his career and arrived at training camp as a question mark. He quickly became another strong presence in the locker room.

Two weeks into training camp, the early sketches of the Raptors' regular-season rotation started coming together. Malone envisioned a starting backcourt of Stoudamire and Robertson, with Anderson coming off the bench to provide some secondary scoring.

Two nights after their preseason debut, the Raptors and Sixers played at the Harbour Station in Saint John, New Brunswick. Malone wanted to get a closer look at Victor Alexander, the 26-year-old center acquired from Golden State in the B.J. Armstrong trade. Alexander was the 17th pick in the 1991 NBA draft and entered the league having been a dominant low-post scorer at Iowa State. The 6'9" center averaged 23.4 points and 9.0 rebounds in his senior year in college but struggled to establish himself in four seasons with the Warriors. Malone had become increasingly frustrated with the big man and singled him out to the

media in the first week of camp after the two had a heart-to-heart conversation about his work ethic. In search of a big man he could trust, the
head coach decided to insert Alexander into the starting lineup against
the Sixers. He responded by scoring just four points in a blowout loss.
Afterward, the team announced they had traded Alexander to Cleveland
in exchange for Harold Miner.

Before he even played a single game in the NBA, Miner was given
the nickname "Baby Jordan" for his ability to soar at the rim for high-
light-reel dunks. He averaged 26.3 points in his junior year at USC and
was selected 12th overall by the Miami Heat in 1992. His otherworldly
athleticism did not translate into results on the floor. After he was
traded from Miami to Cleveland in the summer of 1995, the Cavaliers
decided to move on from the 24-year-old in training camp. Miner joined
the Raptors in Winnipeg, Manitoba, where the team was preparing to
play the Vancouver Grizzlies. The preseason matchup between the two
expansion franchises was promoted as "The Naismith Cup," named after
James Naismith, the Almonte, Ontario, native who invented the game of
basketball in 1891. The two teams had agreed to donate a portion of the
ticket sales proceeds to Basketball Canada and the Naismith Foundation.

Malone was excited to inject Miner's athleticism into the lineup. But
on the morning of the game, the team discovered Alexander's physical in Cleveland revealed a ruptured tendon in his right leg. The trade
was called off. Miner expressed his disappointment before rejoining the
Cavaliers. "It was going to give me a chance to play a lot," he told reporters. "Isiah was really excited to try and get me up there. I would've played
a whole lot of minutes." In front of 11,000 fans inside Winnipeg Arena,
the Raptors claimed the Naismith Cup with a 98–77 win. The following day, Alexander rejoined the team. Malone demoted him to the third
team of the practice squad.

As the days remaining until opening night dwindled, Malone was still
trying to fill out his frontcourt rotation. At the start of training camp, he
had tried to be optimistic about 7'2" center Thomas Hamilton, who had
grown up in the same neighborhood in Chicago as Isiah Thomas, and was

once a top-50 national high school prospect. Hamilton was ruled academically ineligible after signing a letter of intent to attend the University of Illinois. He was later recruited by the University of Pittsburgh but failed out of school after his first semester and never played a single game in the NCAA. After going undrafted in 1994, Hamilton remained on the radar of NBA scouts, who still remembered him as a highly touted prospect. He was invited to training camp by the Raptors. The big man showed up at 370 pounds. "There's a player inside that body," Malone insisted to reporters at the start of camp. While Hamilton occasionally displayed a soft touch around the basket, it took a lot of work to overlook his conditioning. The Raptors waived him after two weeks in camp.

In the meantime, another big man had surprised everyone and jumped to the top of Malone's depth chart. Žan Tabak grew up in Split, Croatia, and turned pro at age 15, leading Jugoplastika Split to three straight European championships and winning the Yugoslav Cup twice. He was part of the Croatian national team which finished runner-up to the "Dream Team" at the 1992 Summer Olympics. The seven-footer was a second-round pick of the Houston Rockets in the 1991 NBA draft but chose to continue his pro career overseas. After averaging 15.5 points and 10.3 rebounds with Recoaro Milano in the Italian Series A league in 1994, he finally decided to make the jump to the NBA.

In his rookie year, Tabak only played 182 minutes in 37 games during the regular season and only saw the floor for 31 minutes during the playoffs. "At the time, European players weren't looked at like they are now," he explains. "As soon as you came from Europe, they would say you needed to learn how to play the right way."

Tabak would get his reps in practice, going up against Hakeem Olajuwon every day. The Rockets starting center had the best footwork of any big man in the league and would use a series of shoulder moves and pump fakes to shake his defenders in the low post. Those series of moves became known as the "Dream Shake." In an era where he had to go up against the likes of Patrick Ewing, David Robinson, and Shaquille O'Neal, Olajuwon was considered the best center in the league, and he was helping to mentor Tabak every day. "He had an unbelievable talent for teaching," Tabak says. "There are a lot of stars when you ask them, 'How do you do this?' They say, 'I don't know. I just do it.' Hakeem was different. He could explain how to do something. He was passionate about teaching me every day."

When the expansion draft arrived, the Rockets made their young center available. Tabak had played such limited minutes in his rookie season that they didn't think he was on Toronto or Vancouver's wish list. The 25-year-old was waiting at the Houston Airport with his newborn daughter, Ella, to board a flight back home to Croatia when he looked up at a television screen and saw his name on ESPN on the night of the draft. He was now a Toronto Raptor. "I didn't know much about the city," Tabak recalls, "but I knew there was going to be a possibility to play after spending a year backing up the best player in the world."

The big man impressed Malone so much at training camp that the team tossed away their initial plan to have Tabak return overseas to further develop his game. "I loved Žan," Malone says. "He was a kid who would set screens, roll to the basket, and score. He was a solid basketball player."

There would be another surprise addition to the rotation. Malone was disappointed when Oliver Miller, the 25-year-old who the Raptors reluctantly selected in the expansion draft with the final pick, arrived at training camp out of shape. The two had spent time together in Detroit and often butted heads. "If Oliver decided to get himself in the best shape of his career, he'd be one of the best big men in the game," Malone told reporters at camp. "He's talking about losing 10 more pounds. I wish he'd just settle for one. That would be a start."

Miller also drew the ire of his teammates. Robertson stopped a scrimmage once to single out the big man. "O, you just leave so much on the table," he shouted. "You out here always fucking around. You don't wanna do shit. You don't wanna get in real shape. You don't fucking compete."

As training camp progressed, Malone recognized he would have to arrange a marriage of convenience with Miller. The big man had the best all-around game on paper compared to the other players on the roster, and the head coach needed his skillset to start the season. The two sides slowly reached a mea culpa. "Talent-wise, he's the best center we've got and I want to win," Malone told reporters. "But I expect him to work." In the final game of the preseason, Miller scored 16 points and grabbed four rebounds in 19 minutes, securing his spot on the team. He had sat down with Malone and promised to improve his conditioning as the season went along.

But the big man would not be available for the first game. In the third quarter of the Raptors' first preseason game, Sixers center Shawn Bradley had caught John Salley with an elbow to the face. The Raptors forward responded by putting his shoulder into Bradley's chest, drawing his fist up, and preparing to land a punch on the Sixers center before Philadelphia forward Clarence Weatherspoon stepped in. As players circled each other, Miller had come off the bench and walked onto the floor to get into Bradley's face, picking up a technical foul in the process. Because he left the bench and stepped on the floor during the altercation, the NBA suspended Miller for one game and fined him $5,000. He would miss opening night.

One more round of cuts would take place before opening night. At the start of camp, the team had looked to find a capable backup to Stoudamire, who had won the starting point guard job. They had picked up Chris Whitney in free agency. The 24-year-old guard spent two seasons with the San Antonio Spurs after being selected in the second round in 1993 and had just won Rookie of the Year in the Continental Basketball Association. He had shown enough during camp to be the first point guard off the bench, someone Malone could trust to run the second unit. Whitney had outplayed the competition, including Jimmy King, the team's second-round pick; Vincenzo Esposito, a 6'3" guard from Italy slowly adjusting to the NBA; and B.J. Tyler, who fell asleep with an icepack on his leg and ended up missing the entire preseason. But the front office was facing a salary cap crunch and did not want to waive players with multi-year contracts who would take up cap space even if released, so they decided to make Whitney one of the final cuts.

Malone was visibly upset when he heard the news. He called Jim Lynam, the head coach of the Washington Bullets, and recommended Whitney, who would end up signing with the team. "Chris is a quality kid," Malone told reporters. "He can shoot the ball, he can pass the ball, he can penetrate, he can run a team on the court. He's a great person who just got caught up in the numbers game and the business of the NBA."

The roster was set.

The Raptors would be led by a rookie point guard and several vets nearing the end of their careers. They had a big-man rotation filled with question marks. It wasn't a perfect roster, but Malone was ready to see how his team would compete to start the regular season.

The Sharpshooter

Tracy Murray is challenging himself to make more than a thousand three-pointers every day. From the left corner, he's rising up, in perfect rhythm, draining another jump shot with a follow-through most shooters could only dream of. He's running to the top of the key, the sweat dripping from his face onto his practice jersey. He catches the ball and nails another jumper. Now he's running into the opposite corner, catching passes right into his shooting pocket, and watching his high-arcing shot drop perfectly through the basket. The sound of the ball swishing perfectly through the net has become a metronome inside the Los Angeles, California, gymnasium. It's days before the start of the 1995–96 season, and not a single NBA team has reached out to Murray.

Is this the end of my NBA career?

The thought kept running through the 24-year-old's head every day as he made a thousand threes.

Should I consider going overseas?

He could continue being a pro in Europe, but going overseas usually meant you weren't returning.

His agent had been coming up empty-handed, and Murray was running out of time.

He decided to give Isiah Thomas a call.

Tracy Murray has been practicing his jumper since he was old enough to pick up a basketball. His father, Robert, used to take his son to the gym when he was just a baby. He had just gotten married and didn't want to miss his weekend run, so a young Tracy would be in the corner of the gym, crying hysterically in his stroller until someone handed him a basketball. That's when the tears would stop, and everything calmed down. Robert would retell this story to his son as he grew up as if he was destined to become a basketball player one day. When Tracy was five, he sat in his living room watching the Los Angeles Lakers and asked his dad how he could become just like Kareem Abdul-Jabbar and be in the NBA. "If you listen to everything I tell you and do what I say," his father told him, "maybe we can make it happen."

The practices started shortly after. Soon, Murray was getting more than a thousand shots up every day at the gym and improving rapidly as a shooter. He would set a rule for himself. If Murray didn't make 75 percent of his shots at the gym, he would stay behind and put up five hundred more shots before going home. At age 10, Murray started playing in an organized league against kids twice his age and was beginning to develop a reputation as a marksman from beyond the arc.

Growing up in Pasadena, California, Murray remembers the gang activity, the drug dealers, the gunshots, and the break-ins. They were deep in the hood. His father was a well-known figure in the neighborhood, so everyone left Tracy and little brother Cameron alone. They were Robert's two kids who just wanted to hoop. Tracy's parents worked for Southern California Edison, an electrical company, and received a job offer to move to the Glendora neighborhood when he was 15. Tracy had plans to play at John Muir High School in Pasadena and team up with another local basketball phenom named Stacey Augmon, who would become a college star at UNLV and go on to have a 15-year NBA career. Most of all, he had already made a group of close friends as a teen and didn't want to start over again.

Before starting his first year at Glendora High School, Murray traveled with an AAU team over the summer and put up scoring numbers that made him one of the top eighth-grade prospects in the country. He was going to the gym every day, getting shots up, and preparing to start anew in a new school in a new neighborhood. But something wasn't right. The shots weren't falling like they used to. Murray started to feel some discomfort throughout his lower body. He began to develop a limp when he walked. When his parents finally took him to the doctor, Murray discovered he needed major hip surgery and would have to learn how to walk again after the procedure. The doctor told him to prepare to never play basketball again.

When the school year started, Murray showed up on crutches. The sharpshooter had been grounded, and the daily visits to the gym had stopped. Murray had opted against hip surgery and wanted a second opinion before proceeding with a potential career-altering procedure. A visit to a second doctor, a third doctor, a fourth doctor, and a fifth doctor came back with the same conclusion: Murray needed surgery to repair his hip, and he might not ever step on a basketball court again.

It wasn't until Christmas when Murray would receive an unlikely gift. During a visit to Los Angeles Orthopaedic Hospital for another opinion, Dr. Noel promised he would have Murray back on the floor and fully recovered in nine months. It was the news the entire family had been searching for. Murray went under the knife for a successful procedure and returned to school, itching to play basketball again. While Tracy was recovering, Robert brought his son to the gym. It wasn't to get his usual thousand shots up. Instead he made Tracy watch every single Glendora High School game and started whispering in his ears about what the people were saying. There were players and coaches who didn't think Tracy would come back as the same player. He wasn't going to have the same rhythm with his jumper. He wasn't going to have the same physical advantage on the court. He wouldn't be the same kid who dominated the AAU circuit and became a top prospect in the nation. Robert made Tracy hear all of it, and all the negativity turned into motivation.

Murray created a hit list of players and schools. He was going to prove everyone wrong when he returned to the floor. After five months off, Murray was recovering and back in the gym. He spent the entire summer rediscovering his jumper. Murray rejoined the team the following school year, beginning a three-year-long revenge tour at Glendora High School. Whether it was a scrimmage in practice, workouts, or a game, he shot the ball every time to prove a point. He was on the basketball court to get his respect back. Murray became the all-time career scoring leader in California high school history, scoring 3,053 points at Glendora, and averaged a staggering 44.3 points in his senior year, the highest scoring average in the country.

As a McDonald's All-American and considered one of the best pure scorers in the country, the kid from Pasadena was recruited by major NCAA programs, including Arizona, New Mexico, and Louisville. Murray sat down with his parents and narrowed his choice to two schools: UNLV and UCLA. The UNLV Runnin' Rebels were coached by Jerry Tarkanian and led by Augmon, who Murray wanted to play together with in high school until he moved to Glendora. They had a roster that was primed to compete for a national championship. Murray was close to committing until he started to hear whispers about the NCAA potentially coming down on the men's basketball program for recruiting violations.

UCLA emerged as his number-one choice. It would allow Murray to remain close to home and continue mentoring his brother Cameron. The two had become best friends and were pursuing their dream of playing in the NBA together one day. Murray was also enamored by the prestigious history of their basketball program, which had coach John Wooden, center Kareem Abdul-Jabbar, and fellow sharpshooter Reggie Miller as their alumni. UCLA had also impressed Murray by recruiting other local California talent, including Darrick Martin and Mitchell Butler, two guys he had competed with growing up. The decision was made. Murray was staying home and becoming a UCLA Bruin.

In his three seasons at UCLA, Murray became a top-five scorer in school history, scoring 1,792 points in 98 games and leading the program to three straight NCAA tournament appearances, including a trip to the Elite Eight. After his junior season, where he averaged 21.4 points, 7.0 rebounds, and led the Pac-10 in three-point shooting at 50 percent, Murray declared for the 1992 NBA draft.

The evening started with the Orlando Magic selecting LSU center Shaquille O'Neal as the first overall pick. Georgetown center Alonzo Mourning went next to the Charlotte Hornets. The Minnesota Timberwolves picked Duke forward Christian Laettner with the number three pick. Murray waited patiently in the green room. He had worked out for several teams in the lottery and expected to hear his name soon. He was already envisioning the walk up to the podium and the handshake with commissioner David Stern. It was something he had dreamed of his entire life.

Murray perked up in his seat when it was the Atlanta Hawks' turn at number 10. They were looking for a shooter, and the UCLA forward had heard the Hawks might have an interest in him. Instead Stern took the podium and announced they were selecting power forward Adam Keefe from Stanford. Murray was not discouraged. The Houston Rockets were on the clock, and he had a great individual workout with them before the draft. It was one of those workouts where he was shooting off-the-dribble, left-handed jumpers, just showing off in the gym. Murray was convinced he was going to Houston and was shocked when they decided to go with Alabama forward Robert Horry instead.

The night was taking a turn as more names started to come off the board while Murray remained in the green room. USC guard Harold Miner went to Miami. Bryant Stith, a guard from Virginia, went to Denver. St. John's forward Malik Sealy went to Indiana. Then it was the 15th pick and the Lakers were on the clock, followed by the Clippers. Before the draft, both Los Angeles teams had told Murray they would select him if he were still available when their spot was up. The surprises kept coming. The Lakers picked Missouri shooting guard Anthony Peeler instead. The Clippers nabbed La Salle point guard Randy Woods. Seattle was up next and drafted Pepperdine guard Doug Christie. Murray was the only player remaining in the green room.

Draft night had become a nightmare. He decided to go for a walk to clear his mind. Murray was pacing back and forth in the hallway when his brother Cameron sprinted over at full speed. While he stepped away, San Antonio had selected him with the 18th pick. There was more relief than joy for Murray. It had been a dream come true to make the NBA that evening, yet he had felt slighted again. His night wasn't done. After walking off the podium, Murray discovered he had been traded to Milwaukee for guard Dale Ellis. His draft rights would be traded from Milwaukee to Portland. The sharpshooter would begin his NBA career in the Pacific Northwest.

With his first NBA contract, Murray took care of his mom and dad, buying them a new 11,000-square-foot house inside a gated community in La Verne, California. A year prior, Murray was playing for UCLA against USC at Pauley Pavilion in the Westwood Village district of Los Angeles when a team staffer walked into the locker room at halftime of the game. His father, Robert, could not make it to the game, and his uncle would pick him up from the arena afterward. Murray knew something was off in the first half when he looked in the stands and didn't see his dad cheering him on in his usual seat. After scoring 24 points in a loss, Murray rushed to the locker room, showered, changed, and met his uncle outside. The 30-minute drive was quiet. Murray knew something was wrong as his uncle sped across town to their Glendora home. When they finally arrived, Murray's suspicions were confirmed.

There were fire trucks parked on the driveway. Earlier in the day, a fire had started in the kitchen and spread toward the attic, burning the roof of the house. Robert and Candy managed to exit through the back door and escaped without significant injuries. When the firefighters arrived, the interior walls had been burned and soaked. Murray got out of the car, saw his childhood home in flames, dropped to his knees, and started crying. His parents had worked for years to provide for their kids, and now their house was up in smoke. The damage ended up being around

$125,000. While the roof, carpeting, and wallpaper were being replaced, Murray's family stayed at a temporary home nearby.

With their son in the NBA, Robert and Candy could settle into their new dream home and start thinking about retirement. Murray asked his parents to manage his life. So his father started running errands for him, and his mom would organize his basketball camps and help with his finances. While his parents were adjusting to their new life, Murray had trouble settling into his first year in the NBA. In his rookie season with the Blazers, he appeared in only 48 games, playing 10.3 minutes and averaging 5.7 points. The Blazers had a crowded roster, and Murray struggled to find shots on a team led by Clyde Drexler, Terry Porter, and Rod Strickland. He complained to his teammates and expressed frustration to the front office and the coaching staff. The college star had become a benchwarmer in the pros. It was always raining in Portland, and he missed the sunshine in Los Angeles and didn't get to see his family much. The second year wasn't much better. Murray occasionally came off the bench and would display his sharpshooting skills, making a league-leading 45.9 percent of his three-point attempts, but he remained at the end of the rotation, averaging only 12.4 minutes.

On February 14, 1995, Murray arrived at Reunion Arena in Dallas to get some shots up a few hours before tip-off. Even though he wasn't getting much playing time, Murray kept to his routine and stayed ready. As the shots swished through the net from every part of the court, a team staffer sitting courtside waved at Murray. "What are you doing here?" he said. "You just got traded."

Murray ran to the locker room, grabbed his flip phone, and saw several missed calls from teammate Clyde Drexler, the franchise star drafted 14th overall in 1983 who had spent his entire career with the Blazers. Portland had agreed to a deal to send Drexler and Murray to Houston for Otis Thorpe and a first-round pick. Drexler was already at the Dallas Fort Worth International Airport waiting to board a flight and was wondering where his teammate was. Murray said a series of quick goodbyes in the visitor's locker room, hopped in a cab, and sprinted through the airport terminal, barely making it onto his Southwest Airlines flight before takeoff. As he boarded the plane, sweating through the suit he had changed into, Drexler was slumped in his seat, relaxed, laughing at the entire scene.

The trade was the change of scenery Murray had been hoping for. In the middle of his third NBA season, he joined the defending champions. The Rockets were led by center Hakeem Olajuwon, who was now reunited with Drexler, his former University of Houston running mate. Murray showed up to his first practice with his new team, hoping to use the final stretch of the regular season to showcase himself as a serviceable role player on a contending team before he hit free agency.

On the first day, Mario Elie, who had been Murray's teammate in Portland, pulled him aside. Elie let Murray know this was a fresh start for the young sharpshooter. "Clear your head," he said. "We've got something good here. Calm down, chill out, and get ready to work." Murray took those words to heart.

Showing up to the gym was fun again, like when he would get a thousand shots up as a kid with his father watching on the sideline. Murray was still only playing sparingly, but was looking forward to getting an opportunity to prove himself in the playoffs. After finishing the regular season with a 47–35 record, head coach Rudy Tomjanovich organized a team retreat in the town of Galveston, a coastal city in Southeast Texas an hour drive south of Houston, for final tune-ups before the start of the playoffs. When Murray arrived at the mini-camp, Tomjanovich pulled him aside for a chat. He had devastating news. The Rockets were putting Murray on the inactive list, making him ineligible for the playoffs.

Murray was heartbroken. He was angry. He was hurt. In his third season in the NBA, he was told by his head coach he wasn't good enough to help his team in the playoffs. Growing up, he had dreamed of competing for an NBA championship, and now he had been relegated to practicing with his team every day and cheering them on from the bench during games. Before the start of the playoffs, Olajuwon and Drexler sat down and chatted with Murray. The two stars understood his frustration and wanted Murray to know they still considered him a part of the team. Even though he was not playing, Murray became an integral part of the scout team in practice, where he would play the role of opposing players the Rockets were playing in the playoffs. There were sharpshooters on the other side, including Phoenix's Dan Majerle and Orlando's Dennis Scott. Murray continued putting work in at the gym every day as the Rockets embarked on one of the most memorable championship runs in the history of the NBA.

It started with an upset of the Utah Jazz in the first round. Next, Houston stormed back from a 3–1 deficit to defeat Charles Barkley and the Phoenix Suns to advance to the Western Conference Finals, where Olajuwon resoundingly ended the "best center in the league" debate, dominating David Robinson and defeating the San Antonio Spurs in six games. After sweeping Shaquille O'Neal and the Orlando Magic in the NBA Finals to win their second straight championship, becoming the first sixth seed in NBA history to win it all, Tomjanovich grabbed the microphone after the game and told everyone in the world: don't ever underestimate the heart of a champion.

As the celebration began in the locker room, Murray could not help feel bittersweet as he put on his championship hat and congratulated his teammates. He had watched other role players on the team, including Robert Horry, Sam Cassell, Kenny Smith, and Elie, cement their postseason legacy by delivering huge individual moments during the title run. And there he was, spending hours on the court warming up before each game, getting thousands of shots up, only to change back into street clothes at tip-off every night. Murray knew he played a role in helping the team during the playoffs, but he wanted a bigger role. So the sharpshooter did what he's always done. He went back to the gym in the summer to get some more shots up.

It was the final week of October and Murray was still in the gym. He had hired a trainer to stay in tip-top shape, was running the sand dunes outside every day, and hitting the weight room with Cameron.

But Murray was still waiting for an NBA team to reach out. He became a free agent in the summer and did not receive a contract offer from the Rockets. His agent had been calling teams around the league but wasn't registering much interest. Murray had started to explore his options of playing professionally in Europe. He knew leaving the NBA at age 24 would narrow his chances of ever coming back.

A year earlier, Murray had walked into the Pistons locker room after a game to catch up with his cousin Allan Houston, who was on the team. Isiah Thomas had noticed the two chatting and walked over to join the conversation. Murray expressed his frustration at his lack of playing time with the Blazers. Thomas stood and listened and told Murray he would get him to Detroit. The Pistons didn't end up trading for him. Murray remembered the conversation, and now he was on the phone with Thomas, looking to see if the expansion franchise needed a shooter. The dismal shooting from beyond the arc had become a worrisome trend for the Raptors during the preseason, and Thomas desperately needed a three-point shooter. The general manager was working within the constraints of the salary cap. He wanted to sign Murray but could only offer him a one-year contract for the minimum.

He had been written off after hip surgery at Glendora. He had been passed over by more than half the league on draft night. He was never given a chance in Portland. He was left off the playoff roster in Houston. Murray was finally going to prove everyone wrong in Toronto.

"Send me a plane ticket," he told Thomas over the phone. "I'm coming."

Part Two
The First Season

Ted Stepien and the Toronto Towers

On March 15, 1983, Ted Stepien held a press conference at Maple Leaf Gardens in downtown Toronto. Standing at the podium with his well-coiffed hair, tinted glasses, a perfectly fitted patterned suit, and a wide grin on his face, the owner of the NBA's Cleveland Cavaliers officially announced he was moving his team to the city.

Stepien grew up in Pittsburgh, Pennsylvania, where he was raised by Polish immigrant parents and became an all-city football and basketball player. Stepien embodied the American Dream. He founded National Advertising Services, an ad agency that helped corporations place recruitment ads in newspapers nationwide for a fee. The company grew to 35 office locations across North America and made more than $70 million in revenue each year. Stepien's wealth afforded him a 17-acre estate in the Cleveland suburbs, a six-figure condo in Florida, and a 36-foot power boat. He drove a 1979 Cadillac and a late-model Mercedes-Benz, and collected gold watches and large diamond rings. In 1980, Stepien also purchased an NBA team.

The worst ownership reign in league history began before the ownership transfer was even official, when Stepien talked about his preferred racial make-up of the roster in a 1979 *Rave* magazine interview. "This is not to sound prejudiced, but half the squad would be White," he explained. "I think people are afraid to speak out on the subject. White people have to have White heroes. I myself can't equate to Black heroes. I'll be truthful. I respect them, but I need White people. It's in me, and I think the Cavaliers have too many Blacks—10 of 11. You need a blend of White and Black. That draws, and I think that's a better team." The comments drew significant backlash, but Stepien pushed back after the Cavaliers picked nine Black players in the NBA draft. "Is that the draft of a racist?" he asked reporters.

The exchange at the draft was just a preview of what was to come. Stepien surprised everyone and fired respected head coach Stan Albeck and started bringing in sales personnel from his advertising company to help prepare scouting reports during the season. He also asked the sales team to provide input on incoming trade proposals, which might explain why the Cavs traded four first-round picks in Stepien's first year on the job. The picks turned into Derek Harper, Sam Perkins, Detlef Schrempf, and Roy Tarpley, four players with lengthy and productive NBA careers. In exchange for mortgaging nearly a half-a-decade's worth of first-rounders, Cleveland received Mike Bratz, Richard Washington, Jerome Whitehead, and Geoff Huston, a bounty of low-upside players who logged a combined 438 games with the team. The transactions were so egregious the league had to step in. They made the unprecedented move of prohibiting Cleveland from making any more trades without the league's approval. A new rule was also introduced where teams were no longer allowed to trade their first-rounders in consecutive years. It is commonly known today as "the Stepien Rule."

With a roster stripped of any long-term potential, the Cavs were predictably horrible on the court. They finished 15–67 in 1982, a year where Stepien cycled through four head coaches, including Don Delaney, who coached the owner's pro softball team. The home crowds dwindled to a couple of thousand people a game, and that was after accounting for the complimentary tickets handed out by the Cavs to avoid playing in an empty Richfield Coliseum. Stepien had to start dipping into the money he was investing into his advertising empire to keep the basketball team afloat. He concluded there was no future in Cleveland and held a press conference in Toronto, officially announcing his intentions to relocate the franchise up north.

Stepien's bold proclamation to move an NBA franchise was no surprise to anyone covering the team in Cleveland. The chatter about the Cavs relocating to another city had been an ongoing storyline since the owner took over. Leo Roth, who covered the team for *The Lake County News-Herald*, remembers it well. "It was always a threat," he recalls. "Whenever the media, fans, or the city got critical of him, that would be his threat." There had been previous reports of potential moves to Pittsburgh and Cincinnati. At the press conference, the Cavs owner was his gregarious self, standing in front of reporters in Toronto and selling a dream. Stepien held up a logo design that drew inspiration from the city's most recognizable landmark, the CN Tower. The plan was for the newly named Toronto Towers to start selling season tickets for the 1983–84 season, pending approval from the league's board of governors. Stepien had crunched the numbers and found a way to be financially viable after relocation. The team, he said, would generate $6 million of income in their first season in Toronto. Stepien had also reached an agreement with Maple Leafs owner Harold Ballard to play at the Gardens. Before the presser was over, Stepien revealed one more piece of his grandiose plan. The team had acquired a first-round pick in 1983 and was going to use it to select a hometown star.

His name was Leo Rautins.

Leo Rautins was born and raised in Toronto, on the city's west end, one block north of Oakmount Park. He started picking up the game of basketball thanks to his older brother, George, who would later become a star at Niagara University, and who was tough on his little brother. He wouldn't let Leo play on the main court at the playground at first. It was his way of pushing his younger brother to work on his game. From the very beginning, Leo wanted to prove his older brother wrong. He wanted to be better than him. He wanted to be better than everyone else. Their mom and dad were from Latvia and Lithuania, respectively, and had met at a prison camp after they fled their native countries in 1940, when the Soviet Union invaded the Baltic States. After that, they escaped to Canada to start anew.

"Our house was one of no excuses," Leo explains. "You don't let setbacks stop you. You don't cry about silly things. You just kept going."

George's younger brother kept coming back to the basketball court every day, and soon he was invited to play on the main court, holding his own against players twice his size and age. Rautins started playing in an organized league in eighth grade. Teammates of drinking age would take him to Bar Lokys, a local Lithuanian establishment, where he would hang out until two in the morning on school nights. Rautins became a regular at pick-up games across the city, from late-night runs at York University to games at George Brown College. He became known in local basketball circles by the nickname "the Kid from Keele Street."

Rautins attended St. Michael's College, a private Catholic high school in the city, and still remembers sneaking into the priests' residence, tip-toeing through their private cafeteria, and making a three-foot drop from the balcony onto the school's gymnasium. Once he was there, Rautins would walk towards the catwalk and lower the baskets. His friends would join him for late-night pick-up games. When it came time for exam week, they would remove all the tables and chairs on the court and then rearrange them before leaving the gym through the back door before the first period.

The first time Rautins attended an NBA game in person was at the age of 11. He was sitting in a local hospital with a giant scar across his lower back. A few months earlier, Rautins started to feel a pain that spread through his legs. He couldn't even sit through Sunday Mass. The discomfort was too much whenever he sat or stood for long periods. When his left leg started to atrophy, his mother took him to the doctor, who couldn't figure out what was wrong. Another doctor recommended therapy. A later visit to The Hospital for Sick Children would finally reveal a compression in Rautins' spine. He underwent surgery to remove a portion of his vertebral bone to open room for the spinal column. The procedure took eight hours. The rest and recovery in the hospital would take much longer. Doctors recommended bed rest for 10 days. The Buffalo Braves were in town, and Rautins wasn't going to miss a chance to attend his first NBA game. He had watched the game's biggest stars on television, listened to playoff games on the radio, and scanned the box scores in the newspapers, but he wanted to witness the sights and sounds in person. Rautins managed to get a permission slip to leave the hospital, paid two dollars for upper-level seats, and made it to the arena to watch Braves star Bob McAdoo in person. He left the Gardens determined to one day play for a pro basketball franchise in his hometown.

Doctors had warned Rautins he might never play sports again after the surgery. They also said he might never walk again. Two months after the procedure, "the Kid from Keele Street" started going for jogs to get back in shape, even though he was told not to run. He would pick up a basketball and get some shots up when no one was looking. Soon, Rautins was healthy enough to continue pursuing his hoop dreams. At the age of 16, he became the youngest player ever to represent Team Canada.

Television camera crews started following him around at school. He appeared on the front page of the local newspaper sports section. After a stellar high school career at St. Michael's College, Rautins received recruiting letters from prestigious NCAA Division I programs, including North Carolina and UCLA, but decided to attend the University of Minnesota instead. He spent a year there before transferring to Syracuse. The injury woes continued. Rautins had knee surgery in college but kept improving on the court. The 6'8" forward became the first player to record a triple-double during Big East conference play, accomplishing the feat twice in one month during his senior year. Rautins averaged 14.2 points, 7.3 rebounds, and 6.2 assists, which earned him an honorable mention on the All-American Team and a spot on the All-Big East Third Team. He entered the 1983 NBA draft as a first-round prospect.

Rautins watched Stepien's press conference and was excited at the thought of playing for a hometown team at the Gardens, where he attended his first NBA game. "It would have been a dream come true," he says. "I kept thinking about how unbelievable it would be to play at home."

Very few people in the city shared his enthusiasm. A day following Stepien's announcement, columnist Jim Proudfoot of *The Toronto Star* offered his opinion on the matter, which reflected how everyone felt at the time. "Some of Cleveland's smelliest garbage is dumped into Lake Erie, floats down the Niagara River into Lake Ontario, and ultimately washes up on the Toronto waterfront. There isn't much we can do about that, unfortunately. Water insists on flowing downhill," he wrote in the sports section. "But can't we do something to prevent Clevelanders from shipping us their malodorous National Basketball Association team? This is rubbish we don't need. We as a city have done nothing to deserve the Cadavers, arguably the worst franchise in pro sport."

A few weeks after the presser, Stepien's lawyer Kent Schneider got wind of the owner's grand plan to sell his successful advertising company and use the funds from the sale to move the franchise to Toronto and keep it afloat. As a close friend to Stepien, Schneider was appalled. "It would have been a disaster," he explains. "No matter how much money he got from Nationwide, he would have pissed it all away in three years and ended up with nothing." Schneider called Dick Watson, lawyer of George and Gordon Gund, who owned Richfield Coliseum, and proposed a deal for them to purchase Stepien's ownership share and National Advertising. After 24 hours of boardroom meetings, phone calls, and several rounds of negotiations, the Gund brothers agreed to pay $22 million to complete the transaction. The headline of the following morning's edition of the *Akron-Beacon Journal* read: FOR CAVALIERS' FANS, THE NIGHTMARE IS OVER. The league would also award four first-round picks to the new Cavs owners to compensate for Stepien's mistakes. The team would remain in Cleveland.

Rautins' dream of playing for the Toronto Towers was dead.

On June 28, 1983, "the Kid from Keele Street" became the first Canadian to be taken in the first round of an NBA draft when the

Philadelphia 76ers selected him 17th overall. A record five Canadians were chosen in the draft, including Stewart Granger, who became the first Black Canadian player ever taken. It was a landmark day for the sport of basketball in the country. Even though he wasn't going to be a hometown hero, it was still a special night for Rautins, who had a giant smile on his face as he addressed reporters that evening. "Growing up, Canada wasn't the easiest place to find a pick-up basketball game," he said. "You could probably get a pick-up hockey game in a matter of seconds. I feel I now give other kids something to shoot for."

Rautins breathed a sigh of relief after the draft process was over. He had been dealing with back spasms in college and never shared in-depth the pain he was dealing with at Syracuse. Rautins showed up to the draft combine and worried a physical would reveal the extent of his injuries and move him down the draft board. Instead, the physical consisted of a doctor bending his knee back and forth and asking him how he felt. Injuries would become a dominant theme of Rautins' pro career. His rookie season was derailed after he tore ligaments in his foot, limiting him to 28 games with Philadelphia, who traded him to Indiana after the season. Rautins was released by the Pacers and signed with the Atlanta Hawks before the start of the 1984–85 season and was waived after just four games.

As he considered his overseas options, Rautins received a call from Gerald Oliver, a former assistant coach in Cleveland who was now the head coach of the Toronto Tornados, a minor-league basketball team playing in the Continental Basketball Association. The team was owned by Stepien, who had taken $100,000 from his sale of the Cavaliers and purchased the Tornados a month after he left the NBA. Strangely, Stepien did end up bringing basketball to Toronto. But Rautins wasn't interested in their pitch at a homecoming. "It wasn't the same thing as playing for an NBA team in Toronto," he says. The Tornados would move to Pensacola, Florida, in 1985. Stepien cited low attendance, negative coverage from the media, and a general lack of interest in basketball as reasons for the relocation.

Rautins would make the jump to playing overseas in the same year. Across seven seasons, he was an All-Star in professional leagues in Italy, France, and Spain. Injuries would make him call it quits in 1992, when Rautins sat on the operating table in Lyon, France, waiting for doctors to perform the 14th knee surgery of his career. The most promising pro basketball prospect from Canada would finish his career with just 32 NBA games played and without a single Olympics appearance with the national team. The closest Rautins came to representing Team Canada at the Olympics was in 1980, but the country decided to boycott the Games, which were being held in Moscow, Russia, to protest the Soviet Union's invasion of Afghanistan. After the final knee surgery of his playing career, Rautins downed a few beers, went to sleep, and woke up the following morning to plot his next move.

When he graduated from the Newhouse School of Public Communications, a renowned broadcasting program at Syracuse, a professor named Dwight Jensen had pulled Rautins aside. He offered a piece of advice. "Your degree doesn't mean anything," Jensen told him. "It's all about what you have on your résumé." Rautins took those words to heart. Before he traveled overseas to continue his pro career after leaving the NBA, Rautins worked as a CBC commentator at the 1984 Summer Olympics. When he played in the Italian Professional League, Rautins wrote feature articles for *Corriere dello Sport*, a national sports magazine. A day after his retirement, Rautins called a few people at Syracuse and landed a job at a local Fox television affiliate covering the university's games. The résumé continued to build when he worked as the color commentator at the 1994 FIBA World Championship in Toronto, alongside Dan Shulman, a talk-show host at "The Fan" radio station.

"The tournament was a big deal," Shulman recalls. "The Raptors hadn't started yet, and we were just two years removed from the 'Dream Team' in Barcelona. We called six games in eight days. We had a fantastic time."

The 1994 FIBA World Championship showcased the NBA's new crop of stars. Michael Jordan, Larry Bird, Magic Johnson, and the "Dream

Team" had moved on after the 1992 Summer Olympics. The USA team that arrived in Toronto featured a brand-new roster headlined by Shaquille O'Neal, Larry Johnson, Derrick Coleman, Reggie Miller, Shawn Kemp, and Kevin Johnson. Nicknamed "Dream Team II," the NBA stars went 8–0, winning by an average of 37.8 points, and beating Russia by 46 points to win the tournament in front of a crowd of 32,616 at the SkyDome, the largest basketball crowd in Canadian history.

Team Canada, which featured Boston Celtics forward Rick Fox and a point guard entering his junior season at Santa Clara named Steve Nash, finished in seventh place. Despite the disappointing result, the event had been a preview of what basketball in Toronto would look like the following year when the Raptors started the 1995–96 season. Bitove would hire many volunteers and employees involved with the tournament to join the organization. Rautins was hoping to be one of them. He had gotten a chance to showcase himself to a sizable television audience and was angling to catch the attention of one of the NBA expansion teams. In hopes of landing a full-time broadcasting job, he started appearing on radio stations regularly, ensuring his voice was heard. "I wasn't getting paid," Rautins says. "But I wanted people to know my name."

After Isiah Thomas was hired as Toronto's general manager, Rautins decided to reach out. The two had played against each other when Atlanta and Detroit had an exhibition game at Maple Leaf Gardens in 1984. Rautins' mom had kept a scrapbook of his son's accomplishments, and inside it was a newspaper ad from the game which promoted a showdown between the hometown kid and the Hall-of-Fame point guard. Rautins photocopied the LEO vs. ISIAH ad and faxed it to Thomas. The two started to chat about potential roles with the team. John Bitove Jr. had agreed to a national television deal with CTV. The network wanted to hire someone who could explain the game of basketball to the viewers and was a recognizable face to Canadians at home. Rautins checked all the boxes. He was the favorite to land the color commentator job and flew to the NBA Entertainment studio in Secaucus, New Jersey, for a formal audition.

His play-by-play partner was Rod Black, who had grown up playing basketball in Winnipeg, Manitoba, and dreamed of becoming the next Leo Rautins one day. After garnering some interest from NCAA schools, Black stayed home and enrolled in a communications program at Red River Community College to pursue a sports media career. A job opened up at the local CTV station a year later, and an 18-year-old Black, with his signature Afro and a cheeky mustache, was hired to edit sports highlight packages. Black landed his first on-air appearance three months later and became a local broadcaster. In 1990, he moved to Toronto and became CTV's go-to national host for sporting events, covering everything from the Olympics to figure skating championships to college football bowl games. Black was traveling in Africa doing charity work when his phone rang in the summer of 1995. His executive producer wanted to know if he would be interested in auditioning to become the Raptors' play-by-play voice for CTV. Black caught the next flight home and introduced himself to Rautins at the audition. The two were a perfect pairing on air and were hired for the national broadcast.

"I thought I knew a lot about the game, but I learned so much from Leo," Black says. "He liked to have fun, but he also knew the game."

The duo arrived on opening night at the SkyDome to call the first game in Toronto Raptors' history. "It was a life-changing moment because I loved the game," Black says. "I used to be a kid back in Winnipeg, at the playground by myself doing play-by-play. Now we had perfect courtside seats. I was like, 'We don't have to pay for this?' It was like, 'Pinch me, man. Are you serious?'"

Standing next to him courtside was Rautins. The kid who grew up dreaming of playing for an NBA team in Toronto would have to settle for the next best thing: being the color commentator of an expansion franchise in his hometown.

The First Game

I t's November 3, 1995, and popular country singer Tim McGraw is performing at Maple Leaf Gardens. On any other night, it would be the biggest event in the city. But nearby in downtown Toronto, over 33,000 people are crowded inside the SkyDome to watch the first regular-season game in Toronto Raptors' history.

As the 9:00 PM opening tip drew near, Sharon Edwards, the team's special event and game operations coordinator, was greeting guests inside the Sky Lounge at the SkyDome. She had organized a kick-off party and invited season ticket holders and corporate sponsors to mingle in the lounge. There was also a lot of star power in the room. The plan was to play up the glitz and glamor of opening night for everyone watching at home. In the weeks leading up to the game, Edwards prepared a special invite to an exclusive VIP group who she wanted to sit courtside for the opener. The celebrity row for the first game included Blue Jays designated hitter and 1993 World Series MVP Paul Molitor, supermodel Kathy Ireland, Canadian figure skater Kurt Browning, actor David Hasselhoff, and Mike "Pinball" Clemons of the Toronto Argonauts. The most notable absence was prime minister Jean Chrétien, who canceled last minute with a scheduling conflict.

Everyone was enjoying themselves a little too much at the open bar in the lounge when Edwards realized tip-off was just minutes away. She could not afford to have the game start with a bunch of empty seats courtside. The Raptors were here to make a first impression, and they didn't want to give anyone a reason to think nobody cared about basketball in the city. So Edwards started to walk around the lounge and frantically ushered the celebrities into an elevator. She brought them to the floor level of the stadium and walked them to their seats. The arena was officially at capacity, and the courtside seats were filled as public address announcer Herbie Kuhn grabbed his mic at 8:50 PM to address the crowd.

Kuhn grew up in The Beaches neighborhood in Toronto and attended Malvern Collegiate in the city's east end, where he was a rugby and hockey player. Kuhn participated in school plays and musicals and enrolled in a theater performance program at Humber College. After giving up on his dreams of becoming an actor, Kuhn talked with the college's sports complex administrator. He was a fan of Kuhn's booming voice and recommended him for an announcing role with the school's football team. Kuhn enjoyed being the master of ceremonies at sporting events and would later venture into covering hockey, soccer, and volleyball games. He took German and French classes in his free time to expand his vocabulary and improve his pronunciation. Kuhn was one of 24 announcers hired to work at the 1994 FIBA World Championship and beat out 40 other applicants to become the Raptors' first public address announcer.

"Good evening, ladies and gentlemen, and welcome to SkyDome for tonight's game between the New Jersey Nets and your Toronto Raptors," Kuhn said. "We ask that you please rise as we honor both Canada and the United States of America in the singing of their national anthems."

At 4:30 PM in the afternoon, the Canadian rock band Barenaked Ladies arrived at the stadium for their sound check. They had been handpicked to sing the Canadian national anthem on opening night. (The Temptations would perform the American anthem.) The Scarborough-based band was a trendy group, becoming an international sensation after releasing their debut album *Gordon* in 1992. The album featured several hit singles, including "If I Had $1,000,000," a catchy tune that contemplated the myriad of ways life would change if one suddenly came upon a seven-figure fortune.

Meeting the Barenaked Ladies for the sound check was Kenny Solway, the team's event coordinator. He was responsible for preparing a game-day script for the game operations and entertainment team. The script would include pregame announcements, the introduction of the halftime entertainment, the timing of in-game performances and contests during timeouts, and any required sponsorship reads. On opening night, Solway wanted to make sure the singing of the Canadian national anthem—a moment of national pride which would be replayed over and over again as a sports highlight—would be executed without any problems. He walked the Barenaked Ladies through where they would stand on the court, who would hand them the microphone, and made sure their audio levels were proper. Solway also asked the band to practice the anthem to confirm that they knew all the words.

Tyler Stewart, a member of the Barenaked Ladies, remembers opening night. "You don't spend all that time woodshedding and playing in base-ments, garages, and bars and say, 'Hey, one day, I'm going to sing the anthem at a sporting event,'" he says. "But it was a natural step for us to get into the anthem thing, and there was a real sense of excitement in the building that evening."

Wearing purple-and-white Raptors windbreakers, Stewart and his bandmates walked toward center court and received a rousing applause. In the middle of performing "O Canada" the Barenaked Ladies made a seamless transition from singing in English to French. The home crowd, already standing on their feet, started to cheer even louder. Opening night took place just several days after 50.58 percent of voters in the French-speaking Canadian province of Quebec had voted against the province becoming an independent country. Hearing the national anthem in French seemed especially poignant at that moment.

"We always made our own version of the anthem," Stewart says. "We always tried to do a different version of a song to make it more challeng-ing and exciting."

On opening night, Ryan Bonne was trapped inside a dinosaur egg.

A one-time Canadian junior trampoline champion, Bonne was finishing up his final year at the University of Winnipeg when he received
a call from his grandparents. They had been watching *Wheel of Fortune*
earlier and had to stop the program midway to make the senior special
at a local restaurant. They taped the rest of the episode on their VCR.
When the two returned home from dinner and played the tape, it had
also recorded *Prairie Pulse*, a news program that aired after *Wheel of
Fortune*. There was a television ad about the Toronto Raptors. Auditions
were being held for the team mascot position. They called their grandson
to let him know. Bonne had a background in cheerleading. He had also
worked as a mascot for the Winnipeg Thunder, a local semi-pro basketball team, where he dressed up as Kaboom the Polar Bear. Bonne was
also Wild Wild Wes, the university's mascot.

After hearing the news, Bonne borrowed his aunt's handheld cam-
corder and put together a quick audition tape, which he mailed to the
Raptors. When the team called back and invited him to Toronto for an
in-person audition, Bonne borrowed money from his parents to book
a flight and got a room at the Quality Inn on Jarvis Street. He landed
in Toronto and arrived at Harbour Collegiate Institute for a five-minute
audition, showing off his personality-driven shticks and acrobatic skills.
At age 22, Bonne became the first Raptor mascot. He would dress up in a
velociraptor costume. The initial design of the outfit had a scary-looking
raptor instead of a more playful and friendly look which was more appropriate for the kids who would see the team mascot at the arena. So the
design team returned with a more age-appropriate costume by carving
an upward smile on the mascot's face.

When Bonne put on the costume and made his debut at the team's
first preseason game in Halifax, Nova Scotia, he seemed nervous and
was a step behind. Brian Cooper, who ran the team's game operations
department, was not impressed. He pulled Bonne aside and told him to
step his shit up. Bonne started to relax after the first game. He watched

Charlie Chaplin growing up and admired what the actor was able to convey during the silent-film era. Bonne's favorite film at the time was *Ace Ventura: Pet Detective*, starring Jim Carrey. He studied how Carrey could use mannerisms to express feelings to an audience, something Bonne needed to do under his mascot uniform. Before the season, Bonne had flown to San Antonio to pick the brain of the Spurs' official mascot, the Coyote, and also studied other mascots around the league, including the Gorilla in Phoenix and Hugo the Hornet in Charlotte. For the rest of the preseason, he would start tapping into these inspirations and found a perfect balance of slapstick humor and physical entertainment, blending in a unique persona behind the costume and becoming a welcomed presence every game.

For opening night, the team decided to make a very symbolic and somewhat on-the-nose introduction of the mascot as a way to give birth to the franchise. Bonne was placed inside a dinosaur egg made of plastic and wheeled out to center court by three actors dressed as *Flintstones*-era cavemen. After a 20-minute wait, Bonne heard a knock. It was his cue to crack through the egg and greet the home crowd as the *2001: A Space Odyssey* theme song played.

The Toronto Raptors were born.

It was time to introduce the starting lineup, which featured Damon Stoudamire and Alvin Robertson as the starting backcourt, Carlos Rogers and Ed Pinckney at forward, and Žan Tabak at center. As the two teams walked onto the floor, Kuhn had one more announcement. "Fans, please focus your attention to center court," he said. "This historic game marks a proud moment in Canadian sports and heritage." The person being escorted to center court was Jeffrey Naismith, the great-great-grandson of Dr. James Naismith, who conducted a ceremonial opening tip between Tabak and Yinka Dare of the Nets.

The first regular-season game in franchise history was finally ready to begin.

The opening tip would belong to Pinckney. As the crowd roared in unison, the ball landed in Tabak's hands. The Raptors center handed it over to Stoudamire. The rookie stood at the top of the key and started dribbling toward the right block. Stoudamire saw Tabak in the low post and threw him a perfect entry pass. Two Nets defenders converged on the big man. Tabak threw a pass to the other side of the floor, where Robertson had shaken his defender and was now open from beyond the arc. The shot swished right through the net. "There is the first-ever basket scored by a Toronto Raptor!" exclaimed Rod Black on the national broadcast. "A three-pointer!"

Rick Kaplan's tenure with the Raptors wasn't even a week old, but he couldn't help but shake his head at the sequence that had just unfolded on the court. Five days earlier, Kaplan was woken up by a phone call in his hotel room at six in the morning. He had just flown into Toronto the evening before, after leaving his public relations job with the Orlando Solar Bears of the International Hockey League and accepting a role in the public relations department with the Raptors. Now his boss was giving him an early wake-up call. John Lashway had replaced Tom Mayenknecht and was now in charge of public relations. He had dialed Kaplan and told him the team needed to distribute a press release to reporters before noon. Lashway calmly explained the situation. In the wee hours of Sunday morning, Robertson had been charged with common assault after getting into a physical altercation with a woman at the SkyDome Hotel. They needed to get ahead of the story and prepare a statement before it became public.

For a second, Kaplan thought his new boss was pranking him.

"That's very funny," he said.

There was silence on the other end of the phone.

That's when Kaplan realized Lashway was serious.

He got up from his hotel bed, put together an acceptable wardrobe from the clothing in his suitcase, and headed to the team's offices, where he drafted his first press release with the Raptors.

Lashway arrived at Old City Hall to post the $3,000 bail for Robertson and was denied because he wasn't a Canadian citizen. He decided to place another call.

The person on the other end of the line was Robin Brudner, who grew up in a midtown neighborhood in Toronto. Brudner collected hockey cards and watched the Maple Leafs with her dad, Jack, who would take her to the neighborhood rink where they often skated together and passed the puck back and forth. She loved to play sports, but as a self-described tomboy growing up, Brudner was often called names and made fun of for being the only girl who played in an organized hockey league with the boys. It wasn't until high school that Brudner finally got to play on an all-girls team. At Osgoode Hall Law School, she played flag football, hockey, and basketball, and competed against other lawyers in recreational leagues. The school recognized her as their female athlete of the year. After working at a small boutique law firm, Brudner took a job at CBC. She worked in business affairs and later became the business manager of *The Paris Crew*, an independent television show.

In 1995, Brudner cold-called the Raptors in hopes of getting a job. When no one responded, she faxed her résumé and cover letter to Glen Grunwald, who was looking to add a lawyer to the team. The two met for a formal interview. Brudner was offered a six-month contract and joined the expansion franchise in 1995. She reported to Grunwald, helped draft sponsorship agreements, and worked on other legal matters. Brudner sat with the basketball operations department and regularly chatted with the team's scouts. After her six-month contract expired, the Raptors hired her full-time. Brudner was promoted to become the team's director of legal affairs. "It was really exciting," she says. "They were building. They were creating. They were trying new things. There was no playbook on how to do anything."

After Lashway explained the situation, Brudner withdrew the money, went to Old City Hall, and posted the bail. "I had never done that before," she says, "and thank god, I've never had to do it since."

Robertson appeared in court on the morning of the first regular-season game. Crown Counsel James Atkinson asked the case to be held until December 8, 1995, when a trial date would be set. Later in the evening, Brudner sat in the lower bowl at the SkyDome and watched Robertson score the first basket in Raptors' history.

With under three minutes remaining in the first quarter, the Raptors had jumped out to a six-point lead. After a timeout, Brendan Malone looked over to the end of his bench and pointed at Tracy Murray. It was time for the sharpshooter to make his debut. After talking to Isiah Thomas over the phone, Murray packed his bags and took a red-eye flight from Los Angeles, landing at Toronto Pearson International Airport at seven in the morning the following day. Murray took a cab to the SkyDome for a team physical, signed his one-year minimum contract, and was on the court practicing with his teammates before noon. "I was laser-focused. I came up there with a kill-at-will mentality," Murray says. "I was coming in with guns blazing. The roster was wide open. Damon was the guy. But there was no second guy. I wanted to be the second guy. I knew I was gonna play. So I was ready. I was coming here to take what's mine."

Murray's first three-pointer would come in the second quarter. He ran the floor, parked behind the three-point line, and received a cross-court pass from Willie Anderson. Murray took one dribble to the left to avoid his defender and drained the shot, holding his follow-through to appreciate the moment an extra second longer. The week had started with daily workouts in Los Angeles. Now he was playing in front of a sold-out crowd in Toronto. Murray's NBA career had been given a second life.

The three-pointer would help spark a 15–4 run by the Raptors in the second quarter. They went into halftime with a 13-point lead. "It was a gettable game," Murray says. "We wanted to win the game and start the franchise off on a good path. You couldn't start a brand-new franchise off better than that. It was important for us to pull it off."

The Raptors came out of the locker room and maintained their double-digit lead in the third quarter as Murray stepped to the free-throw line for the first time.

Whenever a Raptor player went to the free-throw line, Kuhn would announce the player's name and how many free throws he was shooting. He would repeatedly emphasize the *"shhhh"* part of the word "shooting" (for example, "Damon Stoudamire to the line, *shhhh*-ooting two") to remind the home crowd to remain quiet during the attempts. It was a subtle way to educate the new basketball fans in the audience on the basic etiquette of a game. Another rule of thumb was for the home crowd to try and distract the visiting players when they shot free throws.

At halftime, Solway used his headset and walkie-talkie and spoke to the 30 in-arena volunteers, reminding them to hand out thundersticks to fans sitting in the section behind the Nets' basket for the second half. Something got lost in translation. When Murray stepped to the line and prepared to shoot his first free throw, he looked up at the basket and saw a group of fans deliriously waving their thundersticks in his direction. He smiled and laughed. The volunteers had handed out the thundersticks on the wrong end of the floor.

Murray missed both free throws.

Nine months before opening night, John Bitove Jr. stood in front of a podium at The Canadian Club in Toronto to deliver a speech and shared his plan for the franchise. He explained his two primary goals: success on the court and success in the community. He wanted to build a championship contender on the floor and make an impact through community programs and initiatives to grow the game locally. Bitove wanted the experience of taking kids to a Raptors game to compare to a Disneyland trip. He wanted the team to become a model franchise in the NBA. The first season would be about laying down a blueprint for these goals.

Bitove passed on having courtside seats during the first season. "I didn't want to be in the spotlight," he explains. Instead, he was seated in row J in the lower bowl, across from the players' bench on opening night. Seated next to him was David Stern, who had flown to Toronto to be on hand for the special occasion. When he saw the thundersticks, the commissioner nudged the Raptors owner. "Are you trying to teach us something new?" he joked.

During a television interview that evening, Bitove had been asked to describe what it was like to finally see the NBA return to Toronto.

"The reality is better than the dream, to be honest with you. It's going better than expected," he said. "When I was a kid, I always dreamed of one day maybe having a franchise, especially dreaming of an NBA team in Toronto, and now it's reality. It's happening."

After he won the ownership bid, Bitove started to hear a narrative forming around the expansion franchise. Media members wondered aloud whether the city was ready for an NBA team given the history of pro basketball in Toronto and the space the Maple Leafs and Blue Jays occupied.

"People viewed it as an experiment. I understood what they were saying, but I knew they were wrong," Bitove says. "It would bother me, but it also drove me to prove them wrong."

The only person who was more upset at the coverage was his wife, Randi. They were studying together at Indiana University when John convinced the All-American cheerleader from Chicago, Illinois, to play tennis with him and share a picnic lunch on their first date. The two got married in 1984.

"There was always negative press about the team. It was a hockey town, and basketball had a derogatory connotation," she says. "John would tell me they would learn. But I took things personally whenever anything was said about him and the team."

Behind the scenes, Randi saw how much her husband cared about building the franchise.

"That was his lifeblood," she explains. "He lived it. He breathed it. He was thinking about it every moment. He would come home and see the kids. We would have dinner and put the kids to bed. And he would be on the phone at 10:00 at night."

On opening night, Bitove allowed himself a few hours to soak in every moment.

"It was as much a celebration as it was the beginning of something," he says.

Liz and Willie had flown to Toronto to attend opening night to watch their son make his NBA debut. In the afternoon, hours before tip-off, Liz was busy cooking and cleaning in Stoudamire's downtown condo. He had moved in with two close friends, and his mom was learning to trust her son, who was growing up before her eyes. "I stopped worrying about him too much," Liz says. "He had matured after college."

Despite an impressive preseason, Stoudamire couldn't shake the nerves in the hours leading up to opening night. "My heart was pounding," he admits. "I wasn't even thinking about it being the first game in franchise history. I was more concerned about it being my first NBA game."

New Jersey was coming off a disappointing 30–52 season, but second-year head coach Butch Beard was optimistic about his team. The opening night matchup would pit Stoudamire against Kenny Anderson, the starting point guard of the Nets, whom the rookie idolized. Anderson was in the final year of his contract, and the other franchise cornerstone, Derrick Coleman, had demanded a trade before the start of the season. So the Nets pinned their hopes on Ed O'Bannon, who was taken ninth overall in the 1995 draft, two picks after Stoudamire. "He's something special," Beard described his rookie during training camp. "First, he's a great athlete. But when you talk to him you realize there's something different. He's the type of player and person who's going to help this team both on and off the court. I don't want to put any undue pressure on Ed. But if he can just be himself he'll make a difference."

While Stoudamire already started swaying the fans who booed him on draft night in the preseason, O'Bannon was still finding his footing. He averaged 8.6 points in the preseason and shot 38.5 percent from the field. "I thought I'd come in really comfortable," he said. "But that wasn't the case." O'Bannon was disappointed to see his draft stock plummet because of his injury history and vowed to prove every team who passed on him wrong, which included the Raptors. The much-talked-about narrative about the two rookies, the one who was booed by the home crowd and the one who the home crowd clamored for, would turn out to be a disappointment on opening night. Stoudamire finished with 10 points and three steals on 4-of-14 shooting. O'Bannon came off the bench and scored four points in 16 minutes.

The night would instead belong to Robertson. The man nicknamed "The Raptor" finished with a game-high 30 points, grabbing seven rebounds and making five steals. The Nets never threatened in the second half, as the Raptors became the sixth expansion team in the history of the NBA to win their first game, beating New Jersey 94–79. As the final buzzer sounded, John Salley grabbed a rebound off a Nets' miss and handed the ball to Bitove. Even Malone, who rarely smiled in public and hated taking pictures, allowed himself to enjoy his first win as an NBA head coach.

Malone did notice something strange that evening. As he roamed the sidelines on opening night, he kept hearing a familiar voice heckling him courtside. When he finally stopped to get a closer look at the culprit, Malone realized it was Leo's older brother, George Rautins. The two had met at Leo's wedding, where they shared a couple of drinks and formed an instant bond. George had a few drinks on opening night too, and was shouting at Malone throughout the game. Afterward, the head coach went to Leo, who had finished the first Raptors' broadcast of his career, and made him aware of George's antics.

"It never happened again," Leo laughs.

Solway was relieved to see the night come to an end. It had been a rewarding evening. It wasn't perfect. It was impossible to have a perfect night at the arena, even if you tried your best to script every single moment and plan for everything. It was a night he had been looking forward to for a long time. There were still days when Solway would pinch himself. He was working for an NBA franchise. "It was the coolest job in the country," he says. "My friends had MBAs. They had corporate jobs. They were lawyers and doctors. But anytime we would go out, everyone just wanted to talk to me about working for the Raptors."

Solway grew up in Toronto. After graduating with a psychology degree from the University of Western Ontario, he booked a one-way flight to Australia. Upon landing in Cairns, a city in the Far North Queensland region of the country, Solway met a man from Tasmania who was sailing around the entire continent on a 32-foot wooden sailboat. He hopped on his boat and ate peanut butter and jelly sandwiches three times a day for the next three weeks, embarking on the journey of his life. After traveling abroad for a year, Solway flew back and lived with his parents, earning a paycheck every two weeks working for an advertising firm. When he saw news of an NBA team coming to the city, Solway was determined to land a job with them. "At that stage of my career, I didn't think of myself as someone who went to one company and would work my way up the corporate ladder," he explains. "But I saw this as a really interesting opportunity. I could get in on the ground floor and be part of a professional sports franchise as it grew. That's what appealed to me personally and professionally." Even before Bitove won the ownership bid, Solway built relationships with all three owner groups. He attended events around the city, introducing himself to anyone who might be involved with the expansion team. "I wasn't picking a favorite," Solway says. "I was betting on all the horses."

In 1994, he volunteered at the FIBA World Championship. The evening before the start of the tournament, Solway was at a hardware store. FIBA saw the court design for the tournament and decided the herringbone pattern of the court needed to be painted over. Solway spent the evening painting the key. It didn't dry overnight, so fans were brought in to blow-dry the court. The paint had dried enough for the games to be played. At the tournament, Solway met Brian Cooper, who was hired to run the game operations department for the Raptors. Solway submitted his résumé to Cooper and interviewed for a role with the team. He made several follow-up calls and didn't receive an answer, so Solway traveled to Vancouver to visit some friends. Cooper finally called back. Solway still remembers standing in a payphone booth in Vancouver, where he accepted a job offer to join the Raptors.

Now, it was opening night, and he was the event coordinator in charge of the game-day script.

It's an evening Solway still cherishes today. "It was monumental. You think of all the work that led up to it. It was a culmination of so many people's collective hard work and dedication," he says. "There were so many sleepless nights leading up to it, and before you knew it, the night was done."

Fab Five

Jimmy King grew up in Plano, Texas. As a kid, he would go to the playground and mimic Michael Jordan's signature dunks to the awe of his childhood friends. At Plano East High School, King once took off from the free-throw line, jumping over a defender for a dunk, which caused the entire gym to rush the court. There was so much buzz about the young phenom that out-of-towners started making the half-hour drive from Dallas to watch King in person. High-profile NCAA coaches—including Kentucky's Rick Pitino and Roy Williams of Kansas—began to make the pilgrimage to Plano, too.

The days of being the star of his hometown was a simpler time. King was living the typical life of a teenager: chasing girls, taking a trip to Mexico during spring break, hanging out with his friends at the local roller rink on the weekend, and spending evenings at Bullwinkle's Bistro & Pub with the locals. King even got his ears pierced without his mom's permission. His close circle of friends all loved to play basketball. Plano was a town filled with transplants from across the country. It was where King made lifelong friends with kids from Virginia, Georgia, Michigan, and Indiana. Khary Scott was one of them. "We just spent all day at the gym," he recalls. "Our whole day was built around whose mom cooked the night before so we could eat the leftovers in the morning. Our parents would give us five bucks and we would go to McDonald's during the day."

After averaging 25.5 points and eight rebounds in his senior year at Plano, where he was named Mr. Basketball in Texas, King's basketball journey took him to the University of Michigan. On his first day on campus, he met up with Chris Webber, Juwan Howard, Jalen Rose, and Ray Jackson. The five incoming freshmen players were the most-talked-about recruiting class in NCAA history. They moved into their dorm in the South Quad, dropped their luggage off, and went to an outdoor court on the campus to shoot around. The chemistry was instant. "We were playing around just to get a feel of one another," King says. "But you could tell it was going to be magical. It was like we had played together for a long time." After 15 minutes, a crowd gathered around them on the court. Students on campus were hanging out their dorm windows, trying to catch a glimpse of the commotion.

The five players would spend every day of their NCAA careers in the national spotlight. They had initially wanted to call themselves "Five X," pronounced "Five Times," to signify how together they were. "You see one, you see us all," King explains. "It was a strength in numbers thing." The media started calling them "the Fab Five" instead. The national conversation about the five players was less about *what* they were doing on the basketball floor and more about *how* they were doing it. Reporters and commentators did not appreciate the baggy shorts and black socks combo, the trash talking and showmanship on the court, and the anti-establishment approach, which ran counter to the buttoned-up, blue-collar college basketball environment. There was a lot of criticism about "the Fab Five" and if they were setting a poor example for kids watching at home. "They just didn't understand," King says. "It was 'shut up and dribble.' You had people saying we were bad for basketball. They wanted us to make the play, turn around, run down the court, and not say anything. I thought it was funny. The criticism never had anything to do with our game. They criticized us on our appearance and the personality we brought to the game. We were five Black kids from the inner city representing Detroit. You were either going to love us or hate us. But the love came from the streets. The love came from the hood. And that was enough for me. That's why we were unapologetic."

The personalities of "the Fab Five" were starting to mesh away from the basketball floor. Webber was the most recognizable star of the group. A Detroit, Michigan, native, he was the most recruited high school player from the state since Magic Johnson. Webber was named Mr. Basketball at Detroit Country Day School and the McDonald's All-American Game MVP. Rose, who was also from Detroit, was the most vocal. Howard, who grew up in Chicago, Illinois, was the funniest one in the group. Jackson, who came from Austin, Texas, came up with the idea for the group to wear black socks as a fashion statement on the floor. He was the Swiss Army Knife of "the Fab Five," who could be serious and introspective when needed, but would also not be afraid to crack a joke at the drop of a hat.

King was the quiet one. He would sit back, observe, and never be the person to say too much. But teammates saw the competitive spirit which burned inside him early in his freshman year, when King found himself behind teammate Michael Talley on the depth chart. The first-year guard could not believe he was coming off the bench and showed up to practice with a point to prove. He hustled after every loose ball in practice and pushed Talley around during scrimmage. Teammates still remember King swatting Talley's finger-roll layup on the fast break so hard the ball bounced off the backboard and landed on the other side of the court. King walked off practice and told head coach Steve Fisher he was quitting. His "Fab Five" teammates found him in the locker room afterward and talked King into changing his mind. A few weeks later, he was inserted into the starting lineup.

"The Fab Five" would become the first team in NCAA history to make the national championship game with five freshmen starters, losing 71–51 to the Duke Blue Devils. The defeat was a bittersweet end to a magical first season for the group, but they would build on it in their sophomore year, returning to the national championship game for a second straight season. Today, the 1993 NCAA championship game between North Carolina and Michigan is remembered for one single play. With the Wolverines trailing by two in the final minute, Webber, who had nearly been called for a traveling violation before dribbling the ball up the court, found himself trapped in the corner, double-teamed by two Tar Heels defenders. He decided to signal for a timeout instead of risking committing a turnover as the seconds ticked down on the game clock. There was one problem. Michigan had no timeouts remaining. The resulting technical foul would help North Carolina clinch a 77–71 victory. King stood on the sideline next to Webber at the Michigan bench after the timeout and noticed Webber slumping his shoulders in disbelief. The entire team was in shock. The television cameras were panning in, and King knew millions across the country were watching how the team would react. For two years, "the Fab Five" had each other's backs, and King wasn't going to turn on his friend now. He hit Webber in the chest. "Stand up," King told him. "We're with you. Hold your head up. We've been through so much. We'll get through this too."

The loss ended their dreams of winning a championship together. After the season, Webber entered the NBA draft. After losing in the Elite Eight the following year, Rose and Howard left for the pros too. Now, the spotlight was on King and Jackson to lead the team by themselves. Their senior year was a disaster on the court. The two remaining members of "the Fab Five" never got on the same page with the incoming freshmen class. "They thought it was going to be easy," King says. "Ray and I tried to bring along the young guys. They thought it would be easy because they saw our success, but they didn't see the hard work we were putting in. The only reason we made it look easy was because we worked at it and we listened." King averaged 14.7 points and 5.0 rebounds, but the team finished with a disappointing 17–14 record, losing to eighth-seeded Western Kentucky in the first round of the NCAA tournament. At the draft combine, King raised his draft stock with a series of impressive performances, including a 38-point game in a scrimmage against a group of first-round prospects. An ankle injury cut his workouts short, but some scouts still believed the Michigan guard could be a mid-to-late-first-round pick.

On the night of the draft, King rented a hotel suite in Detroit and watched the broadcast with his parents, cousins, and girlfriend. Heading into the evening, King believed there was a chance the Phoenix Suns would draft him with the 21st pick. They decided to select Wisconsin small forward Michael Finley instead. The first round ended, and King was still sitting on his couch, waiting for his name to be called. "It was painful," he says. "No one in the room said a word to me because the look on my face said everything. They left me alone." With the 35th pick in the second round, the Raptors decided to take a flier on the fourth member of "the Fab Five" to join the NBA. (Jackson would go undrafted.) The excitement and energy had left the room as King hugged his family and tried his best to enjoy the moment.

After the lockout ended in September, King flew to Toronto and moved into a condo inside a gated community in Etobicoke, just outside the city's downtown core. He showed up to training camp in Hamilton ready to fight for a roster spot. "It was intense," King recalls. "We were all fighting for a spot. I welcomed that. It helped us get better. I was a second-rounder without a guaranteed contract, and being a rookie, I didn't want to piss anyone off. So I was there to soak up as much knowledge as possible."

King spent the first two weeks of camp feeling like he couldn't do anything to get on Brendan Malone's good side. "He was on me all day. He was singling me out, and sometimes I wasn't even the one making the mistakes," King says. "There was one time when we turned the ball over in practice, and he started yelling at me. I wasn't even the one with the ball. But I couldn't say anything. It is what it is. If he was going to make me his whipping boy, I would have to play better."

As opening night approached, King was on the roster bubble as the team decided on final cuts. In the last week of camp, he was asked questions about playing in the Continental Basketball Association or perhaps overseas in Europe. King would cut those questions short. "All I'm thinking about is the NBA and what I have to do to improve my game," he said. Malone had been annoyed at the rookie because he tended to pass up open jumpers during games. "He's got to take the 15-footer," the head coach told reporters. "He also has to learn to move without the ball better. He has to play hard, and he has to beat out somebody to make this team."

King would stay for an extra hour every day after practice to get more shots up. "Coach told me to work on a lot of things," he said. "I gotta stick it when I get the open shot. I gotta work on my defense. I gotta learn to fade when a guy's coming over the top of the screen."

A day before the team's home opener, King found out he would be sticking around. It was a relief, considering he was already growing to love the city. "It had the best food and the best entertainment. It was so diverse. I would tell my friends and family to come. I had a ball," King says. "I remember going to see *Phantom of the Opera* with my girlfriend. It was my first theater show. At first, I was like, 'So I gotta sit here, and I can't move? And if I'm late for the intermission, I get locked out?' I was like, 'What?' But after seeing the show, I was like, 'This is pretty cool.' I loved finding new restaurants. There was this one Chinese spot with the Szechuan shrimp. It was right off Yonge Street. I used to go after the clubs closed. There was this one deli down Lake Shore where they had these nice sandwiches. There were a whole bunch of these places around the city. I would always find new places."

On the court, the team's second-round pick would have to wait for his chance to make an impression. King came off the bench against the New Jersey Nets on opening night and went scoreless in seven minutes.

"Practices Were War"

There wasn't much time for the Raptors to celebrate their opening night win. After a few handshakes and hugs in the locker room, the players packed their bags and boarded a team flight the same evening for a game in Indiana the following night. It was time for the 82-game regular-season grind to begin.

In the second half of a back-to-back, the Raptors played a Pacers team coming off an Eastern Conference Finals appearance the year prior. Indiana built a 22-point lead against the Raptors at halftime in front of their home fans. The first half performance frustrated Brendan Malone, who ripped into every player in the locker room at halftime. The message was received. The Raptors came out for the third quarter and punched back. They were led by Damon Stoudamire, who scored 12 points in the period as Toronto went on a 25–5 run. They would take a four-point lead midway through the fourth quarter. The Pacers would land the final punch of the evening, though. Led by Reggie Miller's 23 points, Indiana pulled out a 97–89 win. Stoudamire finished with a game-high 26 points, adding 11 assists and six rebounds.

The rookie received a vote of confidence from Malone before their next game in Chicago. As Stoudamire sat in the visitor's locker room, watching his head coach diagram the team's offense on the whiteboard, Malone paused. "He erased everything on the board," Stoudamire recalls. There was a change of plans. The head coach looked at the rookie guard. "He said, 'First play, you guys flatten it out. Damon, you just go 1–4 low,'"

Stoudamire recalls. "At the time, Michael Jordan was the guy defending the point, so he was guarding me to start the game. I was like, 'Damn. This is my first game at the United Center and it's the first play of the game and Michael is guarding me.' I knocked down a shot against him to start, and it made me feel really comfortable."

The rookie finished with 22 points, 10 assists, and six rebounds in a 117–108 loss. Jordan complimented Stoudamire afterward. "I like his game," he told reporters. "He lit me up out there." The Raptors were heading home with two losses, but Stoudamire knew he belonged in the NBA.

"I heard those quotes from Michael," he recalls. "It made me feel good. My confidence started to go up. I felt like I would be in this league for a while." Malone had played Stoudamire for 43 minutes in back-to-back games. After the loss to Chicago, reporters asked if the head coach was worried about managing the rookie's workload.

"People usually hit the wall at 40 games," Malone told reporters. "I think he'll hit the wall at 25. It's not my problem. He's got to play."

The Raptors would land in Toronto at four in the morning and play the Sacramento Kings at the SkyDome in the evening. Malone warned his players not to use travel and jet lag as an excuse. They didn't seem to listen. In their second home game, only 16,793 fans showed up to watch Mitch Richmond score 32 points in a 109–90 blowout win for the Kings. Malone held a closed-door meeting after the game and expressed disappointment in his team's effort. "We played like an expansion team," he told reporters. "It's the first time I'd say that."

The Raptors played much harder two nights later when the Phoenix Suns came to town, nearly erasing a 17-point deficit in the second half. With the Suns clinging to a three-point lead in the final minute, Charles Barkley drew a controversial foul on Oliver Miller, his former teammate, and calmly made both free throws to put away the game. Even Tracy Murray's career-high 23 points wasn't enough in a 112–108 loss.

The following night, the team flew to Charlotte and put together another spirited effort. The Raptors were up by four in the fourth quarter, when the Hornets stormed back in the final two minutes to force over-time. Willie Anderson, who finished with a team-high 24 points, had two chances to tie the game in overtime but missed both attempts from beyond the arc. Charlotte escaped with a 123–117 win.

Two nights later, John Stockton threw a perfect in-bounds pass to Adam Keefe for a wide-open dunk with 7.5 seconds left as Utah escaped with a 103–100 win in Toronto. Murray could not get a clean look at the buzzer to tie the game. "We never quit and I'm happy about that," he said afterward. "But it seems like there's always something little at the end of the game that takes us down."

The trend would continue in the next game at home against the Houston Rockets. Žan Tabak got a bit of revenge against his former team, recording a career-high 20 points and 15 rebounds, outplaying his mentor Hakeem Olajuwon, who finished with 17 points, 11 rebounds, and seven blocks. The Raptors erased a 19-point lead in the second half, but after Tabak fouled out late in the fourth quarter, he watched from the bench as his former teammate, Robert Horry, hit a three at the buzzer to give the Rockets a 96–93 win.

"They say close losses build character," wrote Jim Byers of *The Toronto Star*. "If that's true, the Toronto Raptors have cornered the market on that particular commodity."

After their opening night win, the Raptors were now on a seven-game losing streak.

The loss to the Rockets also marked the NBA debut of Vincenzo Esposito, who grew up in Caserta, a town of 70,000 people located just outside Naples in Southern Italy, where he started playing basketball at age five. Growing up in Europe, Esposito didn't have a chance to watch the NBA on local television channels, so he read foreign newspapers and sports magazines to keep up to date. Esposito wore No. 6 after his favor-ite player, Julius Erving, and dreamed of one day being the first Italian player to appear in the NBA.

When Esposito turned pro and signed with JuveCaserta, he was 15 and did not have a driver's license. Every day, teammate Oscar Schmidt, a legendary scorer from Brazil, would pick him up from his house and drive him 30 minutes to practice. Schmidt played a massive role in Esposito's development. Before every practice, he would arrive at the gym an hour early to work on his jumper, getting 500 shots up before his teammates arrived. Esposito would join him, and for two years, he got to be around one of the best shooters in the world, picking his brain and mimicking his daily routine. Soon, Esposito was also a deadly shooter from beyond the arc and considered one of the best overseas prospects. When he turned 19, Esposito moved out of his parents' place and started traveling across Europe, competing in high-profile tournaments and becoming a member of the Italian national team. "This was all I wanted," he says. "I was living my dream, spending time in the gym, practicing with great players."

When JuveCaserta added two players, Charles Shackleford and Mike Davis, from the United States, Esposito started hanging out with them every day. He grew up idolizing the American lifestyle. Esposito listened to hip-hop and R&B, learned to breakdance, and rocked a flat-top. The first time he traveled stateside, Esposito visited Disney World in Orlando. He worked out with a celebrity trainer in the U.S. who also worked with Jon Bon Jovi and Bruce Springsteen. After meeting the two rock stars, his music taste started to expand.

At the start of the 1990s, signing a European player to an NBA roster remained a foreign concept. It was considered risky, an experiment, and there were still stereotypes around overseas players. They were deemed skilled but soft and not ready to make the NBA leap. Teams were starting to pay attention to the international talent pool, though, especially after Dražen Petrović, Dino Radja, and Toni Kukoč successfully made the jump from overseas to the pros. After leading JuveCaserta to their first-ever Italian League Serie A championship in 1991, the Milwaukee Bucks invited Esposito to summer league. It was his first experience with an NBA team. After spending two weeks with the Bucks, he didn't receive a contract, but Mike D'Antoni, their assistant coach, had been impressed.

He told Esposito it would only be a few years before an NBA team would sign him.

Back home in Caserta, Esposito became friends with Rich Dalatri, who had traveled from the United States to Italy after accepting a coaching job overseas. The two lived across the street from one another. Esposito's family welcomed Dalatri into their home and helped him overcome his overwhelming homesickness. Dalatri became close friends with Esposito and saw his potential up close. He would talk about the NBA lifestyle with the Italian star and warn him about adjusting from the relaxed schedule in Europe to the grind of an 82-game season. "Over there, you wake up and have a cup of double espresso with a croissant. You go to the gym. You go home, sleep for three hours, and practice again," Dalatri explains. "You have a meal that will knock your socks off every night. You drink wine. You meet girls that will break your neck because they're better looking than the next. And you only play twice a week."

In 1995, while playing for Fortitudo Bologna of the Italian League, Esposito decided he was ready to make the transition. He called Dalatri, who had moved back to the United States and was now an assistant coach with the Cleveland Cavaliers. After the two chatted, Dalatri met with head coach Mike Fratello and general manager Wayne Embry and convinced them to make a formal contract offer to Esposito. The following day, Embry called Dalatri into his office. The coach thought it was to finalize the details of the contract. When he walked in, Embry was beside himself. An agent who was repping Esposito decided to play hardball and made a counteroffer for an astronomical salary amount for a prospect from Italy. "Wayne starts 'motherfucking' me like you can't imagine," Dalatri recalls. "He said, 'What kind of people did you put me in touch with? We're bringing this kid over and giving him a spot, and now he's saying we're lowballing him?'"

The Cavaliers withdrew their offer.

Bob Zuffelato had scouted Esposito overseas and wanted the Raptors to sign the sharpshooter as well. Toronto offered him a three-year contract for $1.8 million. Esposito accepted the deal and flew to Toronto, where he was introduced in May 1995 at the Columbus Club in Little Italy as the first player signed in Raptors' history. He moved into a house in Oakville, outside of the downtown core, with his girlfriend, Adriana; and his two dogs, Ara, a black chow, and Elga, a rottweiler.

A horde of local Italian reporters arrived in Hamilton to cover training camp and to track Esposito's progress with his first NBA team. Every day, they asked Malone for an update on Esposito and whether he would make the roster. After repeatedly batting away the same questions, a clearly annoyed Malone finally told reporters Esposito was on a three-year guaranteed contract, making it likely he would make the cut. With over a decade of experience playing professionally overseas, Esposito did not consider himself a rookie at the age of 26, but the coaches did not care much about his résumé in the Italian league. He was starting all over again in North America, and the early returns were disappointing. Malone saw a player who was a step behind on the defensive end and someone who passed up too many open looks in practice. Esposito wasn't a player Malone believed could help the Raptors win games. He was officially placed on the injured list at the end of training camp with a groin injury, even though Esposito was healthy enough to have started the season on the roster.

As Esposito waited to make his NBA debut, he regularly confided in Dalatri and expressed his frustrations over the phone. Dalatri worked for the New Jersey Nets when the team traded for Dražen Petrović, a highly touted prospect from Croatia, and was familiar with the challenges high-profile European players faced once they joined the NBA. "They're idolized over there, then you come here, and they're like, 'You can't play,'" Dalatri says. "It's a pride thing. They worked their whole life to get here. They know they're better than the guys ahead of them, but they're not playing."

Away from the basketball floor, Esposito found a slice of home by visiting local Italian restaurants in the city. He had played against Tabak in Italy, and the familiarity brought the two closer. On the road, they would go to the local movie theater together and try to find an Italian restaurant in every city. Esposito found a couple of memorable spots in New York, Boston, and Chicago, but nothing compared to the cuisine in Toronto. In practice, Esposito and Tabak would speak in Italian whenever they wanted to talk trash about their teammates. "He always looked angry and serious, but he was actually really fun," Tabak says. "I loved the time I spent with him."

After being in street clothes for the season's first seven games, Esposito was activated from the injured list and made his debut against the Rockets. It was a special moment in his career. The journey from his hometown in Italy to put on an NBA uniform had been almost two decades in the making. Esposito was not in game shape and was out of rhythm after an extended period of sitting. He missed all three field goal attempts in eight minutes of play.

"I was really happy, but at the same time, I was disappointed," Esposito says. "I had not played in a real game for five months, which isn't easy when you're a shooter and you haven't shot in a game for that long."

The Raptors had lost seven in a row and Malone was losing patience with his players. Practice became the place for guys waiting to crack the rotation to audition for minutes. "That was a bonus for me," Malone says. "These guys knew they had a chance if they did well. Even if they didn't stick with Toronto, another NBA team would see them and sign them. It helped with how competitive our practices were."

Jimmy King started engaging in a friendly rivalry with Stoudamire in practice. "Damon hated coming into practice because I was always ready," he says. "I picked him up full court. I was fouling. I wanted to make sure he was so tired that I would get to play in the games."

"He practiced hard," Stoudamire says. "He had to work because that was his work."

Things would occasionally cross the line and become personal. "Practices were wars," Murray says. The sharpshooter landed in Toronto at the end of training camp and found himself in the middle of a heated scrimmage right away. His new teammates kept force-feeding him the ball and told Murray to go at Carlos Rogers. "I think the guys were getting tired of him in training camp," he laughs.

Rogers was one of five players acquired in the B.J. Armstrong trade. A 6'11" forward with a scrawny frame, he had the size and athleticism which made him an ideal fit for Isiah Thomas and his "Raptor Two" vision. After leading Tennessee State to two straight conference championships, the school's first-ever NCAA tournament appearance, and twice named Ohio Valley Conference Player of the Year, the Seattle SuperSonics selected Rogers with the 11th pick in the 1994 NBA draft before trading him to Golden State a few weeks later. His first NBA season was a disappointment. Rogers averaged 8.9 points and 5.7 rebounds in 49 games and butted heads with teammates in the locker room, including Tim Hardaway, the team's starting point guard. "It's to his benefit to keep his mouth closed but he can't," Hardaway told reporters. "He thinks he's a joker, but he's not."

When the Warriors landed the number one pick, Rogers was traded to the Raptors to make room for first overall pick Joe Smith. He arrived at training camp in Hamilton and didn't make the best first impression on his new teammates. Rogers was vocal and never bit his tongue. It would sometimes come across as disrespectful.

Rogers grew up in an inner-city neighborhood on the northwest side of Detroit. As one of 11 kids living in a two-bedroom flat, he watched his father battle heroin and alcohol addiction and regularly put his hands on Rogers' mom, who started suffering epileptic seizures. When his father accused him of stealing his gun in exchange for money, Rogers stood on the window ledge of his apartment and decided he needed a change. He jumped two stories, cutting his hand upon landing on the ground, and left his childhood home as an 11-year-old. Rogers spent the next four years living with his grandfather and did not return home until his father moved out. As a teen, Rogers followed his older brother Kevin around and started to hang out with the wrong crowd, selling drugs on the corner and stealing cars in the neighborhood. Every February, when Rogers celebrated his birthday, he would make the same wish: to stay alive for another year. Even his family watched from afar and told Rogers he would not make it to be a 20-year-old.

"I was a bad person," Rogers said. "I had an attitude problem. I was a knucklehead. I thought I knew everything, and I didn't listen to anybody. I knew nothing."

At Northwestern High School, Rogers became a coveted prospect and devoted himself to chasing a pro basketball career. After his senior year, he attended the University of Arkansas at Little Rock. A few days before the first day of his freshman year, Carlos was in the car, coming home from partying with his brother Kevin, when a vehicle pulled up behind them and started shooting. The bullets narrowly missed Carlos. His brother wasn't so lucky. He was pronounced dead on the scene at the age of 20. The tragic death of his brother was a wake-up call for Carlos. "I would have ended up in jail or in somebody's graveyard," he said. "If you run with gangs, it's just a matter of time before something goes down and somebody is eliminated."

After his freshman year, Rogers transferred to Tennessee State and joined the NBA in 1994. With his first pro contract, he was able to provide for his family and support his two kids, Carlos Jr. and Ariel. Rogers' life experiences hardened him and made him someone who wasn't always the easiest to be around. He never backed down from a confrontation, not even with his teammates. "Nothing in basketball will ever scare me. It's a game," Rogers said. "Life is what's scary."

Murray started to understand Rogers' confrontational ways a few weeks into the season. "Carlos didn't mean any harm," he says. "He spoke his mind whether you agreed with it or not, and you always knew where he was coming from. Sometimes you had to pull him aside and say, 'You don't want to do that,' but for the most part, he was cool. You have to accept someone for who they are. He came from the streets of Detroit, and that's what he knew."

On the court, Rogers found himself moving in and out of Malone's rotation during the season's first month. "Every time he came into the game, he made an impact for us," Stoudamire says. "He ran the floor and ignited us with his energy and effort. But it was hard to project what position he would play." NBA players in the 1990s who didn't fit one specific position on the floor were considered tweeners, which was a derogatory term. Where today's league might view their versatility as an advantage, it was difficult for teams to find minutes and a defined role for a tweener back then. Rogers fit the description. He didn't have the perimeter game to play the three and lacked the size to be a defensive presence as a four. On most nights, it left him sitting on the bench rooting for his teammates.

Rogers wasn't afraid to speak up in practice. One person who would talk back was Esposito, who was two years older. "It was hard for him to listen to me," Esposito says, "because I was this guy from overseas who sounded like I knew how everything worked." The rookie from Caserta didn't back down from any of his teammates in training camp, some of whom, perhaps buying into the stereotypes about European players being soft, wanted to test Esposito on the court. "They realized I was super confident and not scared of anything," he says. There would be plenty of trash talking, but Esposito let his game do the talking in practice. "Scoring has never been a problem for me," he laughs. "Ask some of my teammates. They'll tell you that too."

One day in practice, things started to get personal between Esposito and Rogers. The two started going at each other and jawing back and forth every time down the floor during a scrimmage. Teammates were amused. They started egging them on. "We were throwing gasoline at the fire," Murray laughs. The trash talking continued after practice was over. The two agreed to stay behind and play one-on-one to settle the score. Teammates were now hurrying to get dressed so they could take a seat on the bleachers to get a courtside view of this heavyweight match.

Esposito started hitting jumpers from every spot on the floor.

"You don't deserve to play," he yelled at Rogers. "You play 25 minutes a game, but I can score against you any fucking time I want.'"

Teammates on the sideline broke into laughter.

Esposito held the ball when it was game point and smiled at Rogers.

"The only thing you can do is dunk," he told him. "Watch. I can dunk too."

Esposito drove to the basket and won the game with a slam dunk.

When he looked to the sideline, even Malone had stayed behind. The head coach shook his hand, laughing at what had just happened.

Teammates would bring up the match in the locker room, on the bus to the airport, and on team flights, recounting every detail of the story for anyone who wasn't there.

"They joked about it for at least a week," Esposito laughs.

The foreign kid wasn't getting much playing time, but he was starting to earn the respect of his teammates.

The Big O

Since he was a young kid growing up in Fort Worth, Texas, people have been making fun of Oliver Miller for his weight. "You just get used to it, being the biggest kid at school," he says. "I was teased as a kid, but I never took anything personally."

Miller's love of basketball started when the Harlem Globetrotters came to town when he was a kid. He loved the razzle-dazzle entertainment on the court, and soon Magic Johnson and the "Showtime" Lakers became his favorite NBA team. After Lakers games, Miller would go to the playground and pretend to throw no-look passes to his imaginary teammates on the fast break. At Southwest High School, Miller made the basketball team but had to skip the state championship in his first year because he failed English. He became a starter in his second year and a star player by his junior season. After leading the school to a 31–5 record in his senior year, the 6'8", 250-pound center visited the University of Oklahoma campus.

The team had just appeared in the 1988 national championship game and was putting on a full-court press to recruit the big man. Miller got a chance to hang out with Mookie Blaylock, Harvey Grant, and Stacey King, and was close to committing to the school. Next was a visit to Arkansas, where head coach Nolan Richardson pulled up in a Mercedes SL-500 convertible and took him on a ride around town. The two chatted about Miller's role on the team. He was familiar with Richardson's hard-nosed and demanding coaching style. The coach had become known for the "40

Minutes of Hell" approach, where Richardson's teams would practice so much harder than their opponents that they would be in shape during games to wear them down over the 40 minutes on the court. After initially committing to Oklahoma, Miller had second thoughts about his playing time as a freshman there and announced in April 1988 he was going to Arkansas instead.

Richardson whipped the big man into the best shape of his life. After making the Final Four in his sophomore year, Miller averaged a career-high 15.7 points and 7.7 rebounds in his junior season, leading the nation with a 70.4 percent field goal percentage. His college experience took a turn during the summer after a local television station reported on an alleged rape in a dorm room on the Arkansas campus involving members of the school basketball team. Miller was the only player mentioned by name in the report. The story turned the locals who rooted for the basketball team against him. Miller would later sue the television network and receive a substantial out-of-court settlement, clearing his name. The hateful and racist remarks directed toward him destroyed his desire to continue playing basketball.

"As a young kid, you couldn't understand how people could cheer for you when you're doing good, but when something else comes along, instead of finding out the whole truth, you start calling me the n-word, a gorilla, a monkey, you want to hang me from a tree," Miller recalls. "These are the people that loved me? As a kid from the South, I had never really dealt with racism like that. I didn't want to deal with it. I didn't even care about basketball anymore."

Miller stopped working out altogether. He dropped out of summer school and flew home to be with his mom. When Miller was finally convinced to return to Arkansas for his senior season, he showed up on campus having ballooned to 330 pounds. The man they nicknamed "The Big O" became an easy target whenever Arkansas traveled to play at a rival school's gym. A Texas fan threw a Twinkie at Miller. Baylor fans attached hot dog wrappers to poles and dangled them at the Arkansas bench. When Miller looked up into the stands during a game at Kansas

State, he saw a fan holding a sign which read "Oliver's A Big Fat Hog." Miller rediscovered his workout routine, lost more than 30 pounds, and was getting himself back into game shape. After suffering a stress fracture injury midseason, which Miller played through during his senior year, the Arkansas center could not work out between games and saw his weight increase again.

Miller entered the 1992 NBA draft at nearly 300 pounds. When Phoenix Suns head coach Paul Westphal brought him in for a predraft evaluation, he sat down with Miller to speak about his weight. "We didn't even work him out," Westphal said. "We knew he could play if he was in shape." Miller spoke with the Suns' strength and conditioning coach and promised to work out three times a day during the summer. When a Suns official was tipped off who the team was picking in the first round, he texted local reporters, "Better start looking up background on Jenny Craig." In every newspaper nationwide, Miller's weight was the main topic whenever the Arkansas center was mentioned in a mock draft.

"Too much excess baggage."

"Talented player under all the weight."

"He may prove to be a hefty project."

Phoenix selected Miller with the 22nd pick in the first round on draft night. The front-page headline in *The Arizona Republic* read: SUNS MAKE WHALE OF A PICK.

"For his first NBA draft as the Suns' head coach, Paul Westphal wore a yellow tie with pictures of Bugs Bunny, Daffy Duck, and Sylvester the Cat," wrote columnist David Casstevens. "Then he drafted Porky Pig."

Miller showed up out of shape at his first NBA training camp. Phoenix saw little change in his weight despite mapping out a weight-reduction program with the rookie over the summer, and signed free-agent Tim Kempton to a two-year contract as a backup option. Reporters could not stop laughing when starting point guard Kevin Johnson strained his groin and abdomen trying to lift "The Big O" before a preseason game. Miller would make the opening day roster and get to an acceptable playing weight during the season, even if teammate Charles Barkley would occasionally make jokes, including referring to the center as the "UFO," an Unidentifiable Fat Object.

Led by Barkley and Johnson, the Suns would make the 1993 Finals, losing to the Chicago Bulls in six games. As a rookie, Miller appeared in all 24 postseason games off the bench. After the Bulls won Game 6 of the Finals and started celebrating at America West Arena in Phoenix, Miller saw two bottles of champagne in the hallway outside the visitor's locker room and grabbed it to go. Despite a promising first year in Phoenix, the weight problems never disappeared. In the summer of 1994, when Detroit signed Miller to a four-year, $10 million offer sheet, the Suns declined to match the offer. After two years, the franchise was happy to let Miller be someone else's headache.

Miller was in a cheerful mood at his introductory press conference in Detroit, ready to turn the page. He even joked about his weight when the topic came up. "I used to be a triple-burger," he said. "Now, I'm about a one-and-a-half." During games, Miller enjoyed talking back to fans sitting courtside who would give him a hard time. When a fan in Philadelphia asked if he wanted a cheeseburger, Miller looked over and responded, "Yeah, but hold the pickles." When a fan in Washington told Miller he was ordering pizza, the center replied, "Get me a meat lovers, man. Look at me. You think I want a vegetarian pizza?" His weight was no laughing matter to Pistons head coach Don Chaney, who expressed his frustration to reporters towards the end of the 1994–95 season, when Miller was at 330 pounds.

"You can't go out and bust your butt in practice, then go home and eat three chickens," Chaney said. "He's got to say, 'I'm going to work my butt off, but pull back from the table a little bit. So the next time I work my butt off, it's going to be a little bit easier.'"

After finishing 28–54, Chaney was fired and replaced by Doug Collins. The new head coach of the Pistons started telling reporters he had seen Miller tip the scale in the locker room to meet the weight requirement in his contract. It's something that still bothers Miller today. "He never even saw me work out, and he went and told people I cheated on the scale," he

says. "He's never even seen me weigh in. But once somebody says something about you, it just sticks with you." The Pistons found a loophole that
allowed them to make Miller the only available player in the expansion
draft and were happy to see him become a Toronto Raptor. Miller was
looking forward to a fresh start with an expansion team. "I was really
excited," he says. "It was something new."

When Miller's weight became an issue during his first season in
Detroit, he was going through a divorce with his wife, Christina. The
Pistons center was away from his son and started smoking weed every
day and averaging two hours of sleep a day. After games, he would drive
to Taco Bell and order a double-beef Mexican pizza. "Everyone always
thought they knew what was best for me. They didn't know what I was
going through," Miller says. "My friends knew what I was going through,
but I didn't share it with anybody else. Everybody is always judging
anyway, so what difference does it make what you're going through? A lot
of people said if I was in better shape, I could do this and that. But what
about the things I did when I wasn't in shape? What other overweight
person you know could do what I did?"

Tony Massenburg met Miller at training camp in Hamilton. After
spending time together as teammates, his perspective on the big man
changed. "I had played with guys who were bipolar. I had played with
guys who had drug problems. But I had never played with a guy with an
eating disorder," Massenburg says. "I never even believed it was a thing
until I met O."

Miller wasn't the only NBA player dealing with a weight problem.
Indiana Pacers center John Williams, who battled depression and stress,
weighed over 330 pounds. Stanley Roberts of the Los Angeles Clippers
weighed 353 pounds at one time. Thomas Hamilton, who the Raptors
had cut in training camp, struggled to keep his weight below 400 pounds.
NBA teams would enroll players in weight-loss programs, but people
who did not have to deal with the situation did not understand it was
a constant battle for the players. A professional athlete traveled at odd

hours, was on the road half the time, and ate meals late at night. Their lifestyle made it hard to maintain consistency in their daily eating habits. Chronic eating disorders were not viewed the same way as alcoholism or drug addiction, even though they required the same amount of discipline and the breaking of habits.

"I did not understand what an eating disorder was at the time. We didn't have the information back then the same way we do now," Massenburg continues. "I've been around guys who had weight problems because they were lazy and didn't work out. But that wasn't O. He loved to play basketball. After a while, I realized it was a mental thing. I had a different respect for O once I realized what he was dealing with and the toll it took on him because it held him back from being the player he wanted to be."

After serving a one-game suspension on opening night, Miller joined the rotation and was inserted into the starting lineup. He had reached a compromise with Brendan Malone, promised to get in shape, and was an early-season surprise on the court. With the Raptors on a seven-game losing streak, Miller held court with reporters at his locker before the expansion team played the Minnesota Timberwolves at the SkyDome. He guaranteed a win that evening.

Miller would back up his words with a season-high 18 points. Toronto shot 56.3 percent from the field, handed out 35 assists, and opened up a 29-point lead on the Timberwolves in the third quarter, en route to improving their record to 2–7 with a 114–96 win in front of 18,401 fans at the SkyDome. Stoudamire scored 20 points and had a career-high 13 assists in the win. He was developing excellent chemistry with Miller, a gifted passer and a defensive presence on the floor. "O could throw an outlet pass as good as anybody," Stoudamire recalls. "He was one of the best passing big men in the league. He was a great shot blocker. He could set a mean screen, and his basketball IQ was off the hook."

In Toronto, Miller's personal life also improved, and he could spend time with his family again. "My wife and I got back together around Mother's Day, and our second son was born shortly after that," he says. "My two kids lived with me in this big-ass house outside of downtown.

They would sit in the family section every home game and would be mad if they missed even one game." On the court, Miller transformed from an afterthought in training camp to an integral part of the team.

The following evening, the Raptors traveled to Washington looking for their second straight win. With the Bullets up one with 11 seconds remaining, John Salley drew a charge on Juwan Howard, forcing a turnover and giving the Raptors a chance to take the lead. Stoudamire, who scored 23 points and added 10 assists, would hit a go-ahead 16-foot jumper with 2.5 seconds left to seal a 103–102 victory. Miller scored 17 points in the franchise's first-ever road win.

The Raptors flew home having won two in a row and welcomed the Seattle SuperSonics, a championship contender led by point guard Gary Payton and high-flying power forward Shawn Kemp, to the SkyDome for the expansion franchise's only national television game in the United States. The Raptors put on a show in front of the largest televised audience of the year. Stoudamire put up his first triple-double with 20 points, 12 rebounds, and 11 assists. Willie Anderson scored 22 points, including a 19-foot jumper with 16 seconds left in the fourth quarter to put away a 102–97 victory for the home team. Malone was beaming with joy afterward. "We did a lot of wonderful things out there," he told reporters. "That was the best team effort we had all year."

The head coach also praised Miller, who kept the Raptors in the game with 13 first-quarter points, and finished with a season-high 23 points.

John Saunders

*L*eo. *Throw it to a commercial break. Leo. Leo? Can you hear me?*

The Raptors are in Cleveland to take on the Cavaliers, and Leo Rautins is standing courtside at Gund Arena with a mic in his hand, staring into the camera. No words are coming out of his mouth. A minute earlier, everything was fine. Rautins was going through his usual pregame routine, adjusting his suit and making sure his posture was picture-perfect as the producer in his ear counted him down to the broadcast's cold open.

Five. Four. Three. Two. One.

The graphics team has cued the opening shot of the Cleveland skyline, and now the camera zoomed in on Rautins.

"Hi, everyone," he said. "We are in Cleveland at the home of the Rock & Roll Hall of Fame."

And then, out of nowhere, all the lights inside the arena went out.

"What the hell is happening?" shouted Chris McCracken, the director of broadcasting.

In the production truck, Brian Sherriffe couldn't believe what was taking place. There had been a miscommunication with the in-arena crew. The national anthems were running a few minutes late and would take place at the same time Rautins was going on air. Sherriffe loved the adrenaline rush of live television. The downside was having to solve problems in real-time. He pressed the button inside the truck connected to Rautins' earpiece.

Leo. Throw it to a commercial break. Leo. Leo? Can you hear me?

The lights had gone down, and now a Jimi Hendrix impersonator had walked toward center court to perform the national anthem with his electric guitar. Rautins tried speaking into his mic to continue his monologue, but the anthem performance drowned him out.

Leo. Keep talking. Leo. Just throw it to commercials.

Rautins finally snapped out of it and shouted something incoherent into the mic.

"We're at the Rock & Roll Hall of Fame, and we'll be right back," he said.

The broadcast cut to a commercial break.

It was a disastrous start to that evening's Raptors' broadcast.

"I shit the bed," Rautins recalls. "I thought it was going to be my last day on the job."

While CTV broadcasted Raptors games to a national audience, the local television deal went to Citytv. The agreement, announced in November 1994, surprised many people. Industry insiders had expected CBC and TSN, networks that had experience broadcasting live sporting events, to push to own the rights to showcase a new NBA team in Toronto. But television executives were skeptical about the ratings a basketball team could draw and preferred to keep their primetime schedule intact.

The one person who stepped up was Citytv's president and chief executive officer, Moses Znaimer. Once described by *The Toronto Star* as someone with "a reputation for bullying his critics, bamboozling his competition, intimidating his staff, and creating what is probably the most eccentric TV fiefdom in the world," Znaimer was an innovator. In 1984, he created MuchMusic, Canada's first 24-hour music video station. On the channel's first day, they played Rush's "The Enemy Within" and interviewed singer Geddy Lee. The channel's playlist included Fixx,

Frankie Goes to Hollywood, Yes, and Slade. Launched three years after MTV in the United States, MuchMusic became staple viewing for an entire generation of music fans in Canada.

The channel also made a concerted effort to highlight talent from around the country, helping to push the music of The Tragically Hip, Jann Arden, Sloan, and many other Canadian artists. There was a creative energy to MuchMusic, which Znaimer brought to Citytv, where he set up an open-concept newsroom and recorded news segments live on-air with handheld cameras. John Bitove Jr. looked at Znaimer's approach and considered Citytv's lineup, which included *Xena: The Warrior Princess* and *Late Night with Conan O'Brien* and was geared towards a younger audience, and saw a perfect fit for where he wanted fans to watch Raptors games on television. Znaimer agreed. "Even though we never had a major sports property at our station, and it wasn't in our nature to do so, it resonated perfectly for me at that moment," he explains. "It aligned with our music. It aligned with our urban emphasis."

After an intense 24 hours of negotiations, Znaimer landed courtside tickets as an incentive to close the deal, Citytv landed the local broadcast, and Bitove landed the television partner he wanted. Raptor games would be broadcast on Citytv and The New VR, an independent television station in Barrie, Ontario, which had ended its partnership with CBC and was now under Znaimer's supervision. In a one-of-a-kind arrangement, the Raptors would pay $2 million for airtime, and in exchange, they would retain the right to sell ad space during the broadcast. Citytv would be allotted six minutes of commercial time every game. The network would also carry a regular *Raptors Report* news feature and a weekly *Coaches Show*.

As part of the agreement with Citytv, the Raptors were responsible for the production of every game. The person they would hire to oversee the broadcast was Chris McCracken, who grew up in Dundalk, Ontario, in a town of 1,500 people, where he worked at the family-owned grocery store, stocking shelves and helping cut the poultry. McCracken remains fond of the small-town life today. "We all had pickup trucks," he recalls. "So every Friday, we would find a back road somewhere off the beaten path and have these parties with lots of beer."

When McCracken got to high school, he started a disc jockey service with his friend Peter McKeown, organizing his record collection into milk crates, packing them into his truck, and driving to high school dances and weddings. In the summertime, McCracken would work at McKeown's family farm, where the two would dream about covering professional sports. McKeown would land a job at an Owen Sound radio station and later become a sports director at a television station in North Bay. McCracken would move to Toronto after high school and attend Ryerson University's radio and television arts program, where he interned at Maple Leafs games and stood in the locker room next to Paul Henderson and Lanny MacDonald, his childhood idols growing up. "That's when I knew I found the right thing," he says.

McCracken became the on-air television producer at CTV and worked on the Olympics and the CFL's Grey Cup. After he oversaw the broadcast of the 1994 FIBA World Championship, the Raptors hired him as the director of broadcasting. In the fall of 1995, McCracken started traveling around the United States, visiting broadcast teams around the league to prepare for opening night. Brian Sherriffe, the NBA's manager of broadcasting, would join him on the trips. "Brian was my mentor and teacher," McCracken says. "His charm and knowledge were infectious."

Sherriffe grew up in the Bay Area in California and studied television production at Laney College. After working as a television producer in Oakland, he printed a stack of résumés in 1975 and drove to Los Angeles, hoping to land a job with a major television network. Sherriffe got a ticket to sit in the audience of a taping of *The Tonight Show Starring Johnny Carson* on the trip. When he got to the studio, Sherriffe could not believe his eyes. One of the camera operators working the show was the same person Sherriffe had pulled cable for when he was in the Army in the Christmas of 1969 and comedian Bob Hope had flown to Korea and performed an NBC-televised taping.

"I waited for the taping to be over, and I asked the page if I could get on the floor," Sherriffe recalls. "I tapped the cameraman on the shoulder and said, 'Do you remember me? I was in Korea.' He looks at me and gives me the courtesy brush-off. I mean, it was six years ago. But then I asked him who I could talk to about getting a job, and he pointed towards the corner. 'That's the boss,' he said. It was this big, burly guy. So I walked over and handed him my résumé. He said, 'Meet me in my office in 15 minutes.' A week later, he hired me, and I moved to Los Angeles."

After working for a decade at NBC and helping to produce some of the network's most prominent live sports broadcasts, Sherriffe had moved into a different phase of his career when he met McCracken. The NBA job was a management role that took Sherriffe away from the production truck. He filed reports, sat in meetings, and helped to organize projects. The itch started returning as Sherriffe began to travel around the league with McCracken. He wanted to be part of the action again. "It was akin to the quarterback who had a pretty good career and left for whatever reason, but now he realizes he still wanted to be a quarterback," Sherriffe explains. "I felt like I hadn't accomplished everything I wanted to in my career."

McCracken was delighted when Sherriffe expressed interest in being his right-hand man, and the hiring was made. "We knew we didn't know enough about basketball in Canada. We needed someone with experience directing," he says. "We could produce hockey games because we knew where the puck was going. We weren't necessarily up on the fundamentals of basketball and even where the ball was going. We needed someone who understood basketball and could teach us."

In the months leading up to their first game, the broadcast team brainstormed ways to make the game's presentation more appealing to a younger audience and align with Znaimer's vision for his television network. The fonts on the on-air stat graphics would be fun and less traditional. The music would be hip and trendy. An animated dinosaur ran across the screen to start the game. (Znaimer was known to push outside-the-box ideas, one of which was replacing the scoreboard at the stadium with a reporter suspended in an open sphere above center court where he could update the score and play highlights during the game. The idea didn't make the final cut.)

The next step for the Raptors was to hire a play-by-play team for the local broadcast to be the voices who would help guide the new fan base along in the first year. Rautins would be the team's choice as the color commentator, a role he would have for both the local and national broadcast. To find a play-by-play person to pair with Rautins, the Raptors decided to track down the most recognizable Canadian broadcaster in the world.

John Saunders was born in Toronto in 1955 and grew up in Châteauguay, a Montreal suburb, where he dreamed of playing in the NHL one day. After dislocating his shoulder playing hockey at Western Michigan, Saunders moved back to his family home in Ajax, Ontario. He got a summer job working for the Government of Ontario's Public Transportation's GO Trains, hitting up every train station to paint shelters and cut the grass. When the school year started in September, Saunders moved to Toronto and attended Ryerson University. He became known as "Country John," spinning Willie Nelson tunes for $46 weekly while working six-hour shifts on Saturday mornings for CHOO-1400 AM, a local country music radio station. Saunders officially gave up on his NHL dreams after breaking his ankle playing at Ryerson. He received an offer to become a player-coach overseas in Belgium but decided to accept a news director position in Espanola, Ontario, and pursue a broadcasting career instead.

Saunders quickly grew impatient working in an industrial town of 5,000 people. He wanted to land a more prominent role in the industry and sent audition tapes to every television station in Toronto. When Saunders finally received a call from the sports director at Citytv, it wasn't exactly what he was looking for. He was offered to work as a news anchor at a sister station of the network in Moncton, New Brunswick, population 54,000. It wasn't the bright lights of Toronto, but Saunders made the move, covered local curling tournaments, and became a minor-league hockey reporter. In 1980, Saunders finally got the big-league call-up and moved back to Toronto to become a roving sports reporter for Citytv. When a Baltimore television station offered to triple his salary in 1982, Saunders jumped to the United States.

In the summer of 1986, his agent called. ESPN, a sports channel based in Bristol, Connecticut, was interested in interviewing him for a studio role. They branded themselves as the "Worldwide Leader in Sports." Saunders had heard of the network in passing. They had been on the air for only seven years and showed the America's Cup and Australian Rules Football in primetime. Saunders flew to Bristol for a tour and left underwhelmed by ESPN's antiquated single-studio set-up. But the network made a four-year offer which Saunders could not turn down.

After Saunders joined ESPN, the network went through a period of significant growth, acquiring rights to broadcast NFL games in 1987 and adding Major League Baseball to its lineup in 1990. The network's flagship show, *SportsCenter*, became the go-to television show for sports fans who wanted to catch up on the day's news and highlights. The sports anchors on *SportsCenter* became media stars. One of them was Saunders, who became one of the most recognizable faces at the network, providing play-by-play across various sports, hosting the NHL's Stanley Cup Finals, being a part of the network's World Series coverage, and working studio shows covering college football and basketball.

Bitove wanted to bring Saunders back home and make him the face of the Raptors' local broadcast. It would be a massive coup for the franchise. Saunders was living in New York and working for the biggest sports network in the world, and he didn't want to give up either of those things. The sides managed to find a middle ground. Saunders would keep his ESPN job and meet the broadcast crew at home and on the road during the season. When there was a scheduling conflict, Rautins would join Mike Inglis and Paul Jones on the radio broadcast and simulcast their commentary on television.

The first local broadcast took place in Chicago. It was the third game of the season. There was palpable excitement inside the production truck parked on a ramp inside the United Center as they counted down to the start of the broadcast. "The truck was located next to the dump trucks, so all bets were off in terms of what those places smelled like," Sherriffe recalls. The crew did not have a walkthrough during the preseason, so this was the first time everyone worked together. When Saunders and Rautins delivered a perfect opening monologue, Sherriffe's nerves started to calm. Maybe everything will be okay, he thought.

Sherriffe was wrong.

The rest of the evening was a series of cascading mistakes. "Audio cues were missed. Commercial breaks were not clean," Sherriffe recalls. "It had been a while for me, and the biggest thing was trying to get in sync with the announcers." It had been a forgettable debut. At one point, the cameras were whipping around in a violent fashion to catch up to the action on screen. McCracken's phone rang. It was Bitove. The Raptors owner was not only cheering on his team. He watched every game and made notes about how to improve the broadcast. Bitove had plenty of feedback to provide for the first game. "He was a sharp guy who picked up on everything we did," McCracken says. "He gave us constructive criticism but always encouraged us to push the envelope."

When the broadcast crew left the arena that evening, Sherriffe was dejected. "You always knew when you walked out of a truck whether you had a bad show," he says. "John and Leo were tremendous. They carried us that evening. So my first instinct was to say sorry to the guys. So I told them, 'You guys bailed us out. I promise we're going to get it together.'"

Saunders laughed. "Don't worry about it, man," he said. "Let's go out." The team went out for drinks afterward and laughed about all the mistakes.

"Everyone was a bit rattled," Rautins recalls. "John put everyone at ease."

Saunders was a calming influence, a quiet leader who made everyone feel like it would always be okay, and taught his play-by-play partner some valuable lessons.

"He always said, 'What's the worst that can happen? You fuck up. So what? Everybody fucks up,'" Rautins explains. "He also said, 'Don't plan what you're going to say. Just say it. If you've got a whole list of things you're going to say and you screw up the first line, it will be like dominoes. Just say it because you know what you're talking about.' And he also said, 'It's never as good as you think it is and never as bad as you think it is.'"

They were words to live by for the Raptors' broadcast during the first season.

The mistakes during the first game?

What's the worst that can happen? You fuck up. So what? Everybody fucks up.

The lights going out in Cleveland?

What's the worst that can happen? You fuck up. So what? Everybody fucks up.

"It could be total chaos, and I wouldn't have to worry about anything because John always made it okay," Rautins says. "He just had this cool about him."

He still remembers the times when Saunders would go missing minutes before a broadcast went on air and somehow always made it for the final countdown. "John was a diabetic, so a lot of times his blood sugar would be low," Rautins recalls. "It would be 20 minutes before we were going on air and we were all looking for John. He would text me, 'Blood sugar low, just need to get something.' John had this golden rule. He said, 'If I don't call, don't worry.' Now it's five minutes before we go on air and everyone is shitting their pants. Brian said, 'Get ready, you might have to go on air by yourself.' The camera guys are searching the arena for him and they see him all the way at the other end of the SkyDome. They see him walking toward our set. It's a minute to air. We're counting down. It's 30 seconds. Suddenly it's nine, eight, seven, six, John walks onto the court, grabs his microphone, plugs in. It's at zero and he goes, 'And here we are at the SkyDome,' and delivers a perfect open. Everybody would shake their heads. That was John. You never had to worry about him."

Saunders could have acted like a rock star and carried himself with an ego. Instead, the ESPN personality brought a sense of humor to the broadcast, which always relaxed Rautins. When Saunders found out his play-by-play partner grew up hating math, he started putting him on the spot during games whenever the Raptors took the lead. "We would be doing a game, and he would say, 'The Raptors gotta be careful here. The lead is shrinking. What's it down to, Leo?'" Rautins laughs. "I would look at him and say, 'It's shrinking fast, John.'"

Saunders' confidence allowed the rest of the broadcast crew to work out their early-season kinks and find their rhythm. "He always made sure I got what I needed on air," Sherriffe explains. "He was the best play-by-play guy you could have. If I cut to the wrong thing, he was always there to bail you out, then laugh about it after."

"He was smooth," McCracken adds. "You felt like the world was okay when John was around."

The mistakes became rare. The late-night phone calls from Bitove became less common. After some early-season blips, the broadcast team was getting into a groove. "We settled in after about a dozen games," McCracken recalls. "Every so often, you had a game where you came away saying, 'Oh my god. Everything worked.' It would make you feel really good. Brian and I rewatched every single game from start to finish. We would make notes on what worked and what didn't and how to improve on it for the next game."

During the first season, the crew would add one more on-air presence to the broadcast. Lori Belanger grew up in Wingham, Ontario, and studied sports broadcasting at Ryerson University. After graduating, she landed a role as a production assistant with *NBA Inside Stuff* and was hired by McCracken to be a producer on the Raptors' broadcast. "The entire broadcast crew was so welcoming," Belanger recalls. "There were no egos, there was room for everyone to grow, and you never felt like you were being judged. Those were all really important things." As a producer, she helped to produce the cold open for each broadcast and would travel around the city to film segments with players and coaches on off-days and spend hours in the studio editing the footage for the following day's broadcast. Belanger was 21 at the time. "It was a lot. But you're young, you're eager, you're keen, and you're having this incredible experience at your dream job," Belanger recalls. "It was exciting. There were new challenges and new opportunities every day."

She was offered an on-camera role during the first season, becoming the sideline reporter and conducting halftime interviews on the broadcast. Belanger laughs at all the challenges the broadcast faced in the season's early months. They always managed to find a way to move forward though. "The lights might have gone out," she says, "but they always came back on."

As Rautins stood courtside in Cleveland, sweat dripping from his forehead, wondering if it would be his last day on the job, the lights came back on. The broadcast came back from commercials. The Jimi Hendrix impersonator finished his national anthem performance. The show went on, and by the end of the night, everyone had forgotten about the disastrous start to the broadcast. As he left the arena, Rautins was reminded of what Saunders always said.

What's the worst that can happen? You fuck up. So what? Everybody fucks up.

Rautins still laughs today at how his friendship with Saunders started with a misunderstanding. The two had briefly crossed paths before working together with the Raptors. When ESPN covered Rautins' games at Syracuse, Saunders would sometimes be there. Rautins had watched Saunders grow into a nationally renowned media personality and was thrilled when he found out they would be working together. He also heard the ESPN broadcaster loved to have fun outside of work, which was perfect for Rautins, who was always up for a party. When they met for a production meeting before the start of the season, Saunders appeared to be distancing himself. Rautins got the cold shoulder. Over and over again, Saunders would always have an excuse for not hanging out. "A couple weeks later, we had to record these voiceovers before the start of the season. It was incredible. I was telling myself, 'I'm sitting in the studio with John Saunders. Are you shitting me? I shouldn't be in the room with this guy right now,'" Rautins says. "So we have an early dinner and I figure tonight's the night. But then John said, 'Yeah, I got an early flight out tomorrow morning.' I just replied, 'Yeah, me too.' At this point I'm smelling my armpits. I'm wondering what's wrong with me."

When the season started, Rautins confronted Saunders about the excuses. "It turns out he was thinking the same thing," Rautins laughs. "He was like, 'Man, I thought this guy was a lot of fun but he's always got an excuse.' The next thing you know, on our first West Coast road trip, we were like brothers from different mothers. It was insanity. I went from smelling my armpits to getting no sleep on the road every night. We laughed so hard every day and had so much fun. It was incredible."

The rest of the broadcast team struggled to keep up with the play-by-play tandem. "Brian and I called it a night way earlier than John and Leo," McCracken says. "It was a regular occurrence to hear clattering in the hallway in the wee hours of the early morning, and you go, 'Oh my god. Where have you guys been?'"

Rautins still laughs at all the moments he shared with Saunders on the road. "I used to get limo service when I couldn't drive from Syracuse to Toronto," he recalls. "There was one night when John and Bill Raftery were in Syracuse too for ESPN. We had to be in Toronto the following day. So I called my limo guy and said, 'We have to load up.' So we had beer. We had wine. We had pizza. We're toast by the time we get to the border, and the guy there knows who we are. He looks in the car, and it looks like a frat house. There are bottles everywhere. There are pizza boxes. The customs guy was laughing his ass off. We pulled into Toronto and just stumbled out of the limo."

Rautins also remembers how they would regularly go for drinks with players and coaches after games, including one memorable night with

Charles Barkley. "We were on the road, and Charles said, 'You guys are with me tonight,'" he recalls. "We got in his car after the game. I had a buddy from Toronto who worked in finance who happened to be at the game. So Charles said, 'You're coming with us too.' We get to the club. Charles calls the manager and says, 'I'm here, and I got John Saunders with me.' There's a huge lineup of people waiting to get in. We pulled up, and they cleared a spot right by the door for us. We go in, and there's a whole section cleared out upstairs. My buddy looked at me and said, 'Yeah. It's good to be king.'"

Over time, Rautins would learn that Saunders didn't care about fame. He just wanted to build genuine connections with the people around him. Their friendship became more than just late nights and partying. "We talked about everything," Rautins recalls. "John was so well-versed about everything. He was a proud Canadian and he was very proud of being Black. He was a wonderful human being. I remember one time he said, 'I hate what I do.' I was like, 'What are you talking about?' He said, 'All I do is talk about what other people do.' I said, 'Yeah, but John, you're the best at it.' He said, 'Yeah, but it's bullshit.' He was just a really humble dude."

Saunders would always make sure Rautins felt like an equal on the broadcast. When the two rehearsed a cold open for the broadcast early in the season, Saunders noticed the cameras panning to him to start the show, leaving Rautins out of the frame. It was a traditional television open. Saunders would come on camera, say a few words, then bring in Rautins. It was a one-shot, followed by a two-shot. Saunders didn't want his partner to feel left out. He didn't want the spotlight for himself. He wanted to share it. Saunders went to the producers and said he would only do the cold open if the camera opened with a shot of himself and Rautins.

"From that day on," Rautins says, "we always opened with a two-shot."

New Year's Party

I t's the end of training camp and Damon Stoudamire's car has been pulled over on Lake Shore Boulevard in downtown Toronto.

What you pull me over for?

The rookie did not want to make any bad headlines before the start of his first season with the Raptors, so he asked the police officer again.

What you pull me over for? I'm driving 80 miles.

The police officer laughed.

You were going over the speed limit. It's 80 kilometers.

Now, Stoudamire was laughing too.

My bad, man.

"That was my welcome to Toronto moment," he says.

For most of the Raptors players, the 1995–96 season was the first time they visited Canada. They were discovering new things every day. Bagged milk. Ketchup chips. The strange colors of Canadian money. The exchange rate. A grocery store named Loblaws.

For Jimmy King, it was the Canadian accent. "After every sentence, it was 'eh.' Everything just ended in 'eh,'" he laughs. "I noticed it in all my conversations."

For Stoudamire, it was the curling. Every time he turned on the television, it was curling. He would ask reporters to explain why curling was such a big deal in Canada. Tracy Murray would turn on TSN, the most popular sports network in the country, and wait for an hour before anyone would talk about the Raptors. It was the Maple Leafs. The Argonauts. The Blue Jays. And then curling. "A lot of us were pissed about that," Murray says. "We talked about it all the time. We weren't being seen here, and we weren't being seen back home because nobody cared about the two Canadian teams."

The team would help set up satellite dishes in the players' homes, so they had access to ESPN, but nothing could prepare them for their first Canadian winter. Murray grew up in California and had to buy his first winter coat. Žan Tabak made the mistake of packing summer clothes for a game in Miami and shuddered at the wind chill when he stepped off at Toronto Pearson International Airport on the return trip home. He had rented a house in North York, and it seemed like only Bon, his English sheepdog, adjusted to the weather. "We wanted to live in a place where the dog could run around and feel good," Tabak says. "He enjoyed the snow."

The winter road conditions became a hazard, both personally and professionally. One time, Murray was driving a date back home to Scarborough on Highway 401. There had been a snowstorm during the day, and the salt truck workers were on strike. Murray's black Jeep Cherokee fishtailed on the ice, spun out, and hit the side of the wall. "We just sat there for a second," he recalls. "I damn near shit my pants."

During his first Canadian winter, Oliver Miller opened his garage door in the morning and saw he had been snowed in. "It took me two-and-a-half hours to clear the driveway and get to practice," he recalls. "This is how crazy Brendan was. He held practice until I got there instead of just giving me the day off."

Crossing the border was another new experience. NBA players were traveling to Canada for the first time, and even visiting teams realized how time-consuming the process could be. After the Sacramento Kings played in Toronto in November, Mitch Richmond was detained at the border upon returning to the United States. He ended up signing a game program featuring himself on the cover for a customs officer, who allowed him back into his home country. Players on the Raptors had to go through the extra step of crossing the border every time they traveled. After a long flight home from a road game, the last thing they wanted was to have to wait to go home.

"Sometimes you just want to get off the plane and get home and sleep because you're dead tired," Murray says. "And now you're sitting in customs like, 'What are they holding me up for now?'"

It was especially difficult for Tabak and Vincenzo Esposito.

"There was a war going on in my country, so even though people knew who I was, the team would be at the hotel, and I would have to stay and go through certain procedures," Tabak recalls. "I had trouble every time we crossed the border."

"Carlos [Rogers] was always like, 'What the fuck, we gotta wait for these guys again?'" Esposito adds. "I would be like, 'Fuck you, Carlos. I got an Italian passport. So shut the fuck up.'"

In the locker room, players were adjusting to local reporters covering the NBA for the first time. "We just had to be patient and not take it as a dumb question," Murray says. "There were times when we would look at each other in the locker room and be like, 'Did he just say that?'"

Rick Kaplan, who worked in public relations, remembers some awkward moments at the start of the season. "There were a lot of silly questions in the very beginning," he laughs. "Someone would ask, 'What's it like being that tall?' A lot of reporters just marveled at how tall these guys were. I guess your typical hockey player wouldn't stand out like that. So they couldn't help but notice it. The players would come to me and say, 'How do I answer that question?' I would just say, 'Give them some leeway. This is all new to them.'"

It was also an adjustment for John Lashway, the public relations manager, who had worked with an experienced group of reporters in Portland for the past decade before being hired by Toronto. When Lashway read the local newspaper, he noticed the basketball writers using hockey jargon in their stories. The head coach was usually "standing behind the bench" instead of "standing courtside." A player's "sweater" could hang from the rafters one day instead of their "jersey." He decided to ask Malone to host a series of seminars during training camp. The head coach held two-a-day practices, then stayed at the gym and walked reporters through the basic principles of the game. "We needed the media," Lashway says. "The more we could help them learn the sport, the better media coverage we would get."

On the television broadcast, a segment called "Rautins on Roundball" was introduced to explain terminology Leo Rautins and John Saunders used during the game, including pick-and-roll offense, three in the key, and illegal defense, to the viewers at home. "It was tough," Rautins says. "You didn't want to talk down to people, but there were a lot of fans who didn't understand the basic rules like traveling. You'd be surprised what people didn't know. Even something as simple as calling the shooting guard a two. You had to tell people the one was a point guard. We'd try to explain things in a way that didn't piss people off so much."

The education process would sometimes come from the players themselves at practice, which took place inside an athletic club at Glendon College in North York. It was commonplace for Raptors players to show up and have to wait for the school volleyball team to clear the court. "We used to pull up to practice and students would be walking out," Stoudamire recalls. "We would be parking our cars with the general public. It got to a point where you had to pay somebody to watch your car." Malone had an open-door policy for media members to watch his team practice from beginning to end, which wasn't the norm in the NBA. It allowed reporters to try and pick up on more things and ask the head coach and players more basketball-related questions from what they had just seen.

After practice one day, Elliotte Friedman, who covered the team for the local sports radio station "The Fan," started chatting with Willie Anderson. The night prior, he had been in the locker room and witnessed an exchange between Stoudamire and Anderson. The team had just lost a close game to Utah, and Stoudamire was sulking in the locker room, being testy with reporters who wanted a quote. The rookie had the worst game of his career and had been outplayed by John Stockton. Anderson walked over and scolded the rookie when the media scrum was over.

"I took that one loss hard. It was an eye opener for me," Stoudamire recalls. "Willie pulled me aside to talk. He said, 'You're going to have some good nights and some bad nights in this league.' He was right. There were a lot of great point guards in the league at the time. You had to put your hard hat on every night."

The next day at practice, Anderson pulled Friedman aside and provided him with some wisdom too. He told Friedman that NBA players were going to have off nights, and sometimes it's best to keep that in perspective instead of writing something in the moment that might ruin a relationship with a player. "You have to understand, one game doesn't mean they deserve to be ripped," Anderson continued. "You'll go much further with people if you understand that, and treat players properly based on that."

Not everyone had time for the media. During the season, Oliver Miller would put the beat writers on three weeks' probation whenever he read something he didn't like. "But we still get paid, right?" one reporter joked.

The biggest adjustment for the players was all the losing on the court. Before the start of the season, the Las Vegas sportsbooks set Toronto's over/under betting line for total regular-season wins at 16. The line was fair. None of the recent expansion teams—Dallas, Miami, Charlotte, Minnesota, and Orlando—won more than 22 games in their first season. Two of them finished with 15 wins. The nationally televised victory over Seattle brought the team's record to 4–7. The Raptors were on a three-game win streak and on pace to win 30 games. They would lose seven of their next nine games, ending any early-season hopes of competing for a playoff spot.

At the start of December, the Raptors flew to Vancouver for the first regular-season matchup between the two expansion franchises. The Grizzlies had opened their season with a win, defeating the Portland Trail Blazers on the road thanks to 29 points from center Benoit Benjamin.

They would follow it up with a thrilling overtime win two nights later in front of a sold-out crowd of 19,193 at General Motors Place in downtown Vancouver against the Minnesota Timberwolves. Arthur Griffiths sat courtside and watched his team fight back from a 14-point deficit in the second half before Chris King, who was signed as a free agent back in training camp, tipped in the game-winning basket as the buzzer sounded in extra time. "The building was electric," Griffiths recalls. "It sounded like a rock concert the whole night. After we won that game, everyone walked away going, 'Oh, we're going to keep doing this, aren't we?'"

Almost a month later, Vancouver had yet to win another game since their home opener. There was a 36-point blowout loss in Seattle, a 49-point loss in San Antonio, and a fourth-quarter comeback by Michael Jordan and the Chicago Bulls in Vancouver. The Grizzlies led the game by double-digits with nine minutes left when point guard Darrick Martin decided to trash talk the Bulls guard. Jordan responded by scoring 19 points in the final six minutes for the win.

The matchup between Toronto and Vancouver was billed as "the Canadian basketball version of the Super Bowl," but the Grizzlies were just trying to snap a 17-game losing streak. They would fall to 2–18 after Stoudamire put up 24 points, seven rebounds, and eight assists in Toronto's 93–81 win. The Grizzlies, who were two losses from tying the all-time losing-streak record of 20 (shared by the 1973 Philadelphia 76ers and 1994 Dallas Mavericks), would snap their streak at 19 with an overtime win over Portland a few nights later.

The Raptors were the better of the two expansion franchises, but that did not make Malone feel much better about his team. He had grown increasingly frustrated with their effort, something which the head coach had wanted to be the central identity of his roster going into training camp. As the losses piled up, players started to build up bad habits. Their defense lacked intensity, and the Raptors couldn't stop turning the ball over on offense. Malone tried everything. He held closed-door meetings after games. He held one-on-one meetings with players during team flights. He put together 20-minute game tapes highlighting their mistakes and would play the videos at practice. He even benched his starters to start the second half of a game. "I told them if I'm not going to get the energy and the intensity from the people who are playing, I'm going to start using the bench more," Malone told reporters. "I'm not going to sit and watch people play soft or not give me an effort." Even with an impressive upset win at home over Shaquille O'Neal and the Orlando Magic, the Raptors went into the final game of the calendar year having won only four games in December. None of the head coach's motivational tactics was working. It was hard to close the talent gap between an expansion roster and the rest of the NBA.

Stoudamire had averaged 16.3 points and 8.3 assists in November, winning Rookie of the Month, but the losses were starting to wear on him. "I was a young player," he says, "and I wasn't used to losing."

The losses were starting to wear on everyone, so they were more than happy for a surprise from the organization during the holidays. John Bitove Jr. knew it was hard for the players to compete for an expansion team in a new country. For Christmas, he flew in friends and family members to join the Raptors for a holiday dinner in Toronto. "We wanted to show people this wasn't about what you do for us," Bitove says. "It was about what we can do for you. These guys were so young, and their families were still a huge part of their lives. We wanted to show them we cared."

Tony Massenburg was delighted to spend a few days with his parents. "It did guys a lot of good," he says. "Being outside the country can wear on you mentally."

Murray had a chance to catch up with his dad. "My brother was still in school so my mom stayed behind to make sure he was cool," he recalls. "That was special. They flew everyone in. I had never seen that before from a team. It was this big, giant, happy family gathering."

After the holiday dinner, everyone joined the team flight to Detroit, where the Raptors would try to end the month of December on a positive note. Even a career-high 27 points from Stoudamire could not stop the Pistons from running away with a 22-point win. "At times, it's frustrating playing for an expansion club," he told reporters afterward. "We dug our-selves too deep of a hole and you can't do that on the road. They were getting a lot of easy, open shots and we have to come out with a lot more intensity and sustain it."

The Raptors entered the new year with a 9–21 record.

The losing and the adjustment to living in a new country did not stop the locker room from being a happy place. The roster consisted of players who had been overlooked and passed on by other teams, and camaraderie was built through the common purpose of rebuilding their careers together on an expansion team. Once training camp ended and the opening day roster was set, players started to relax and open up a bit. For the late-arriving Murray, it was a welcomed change in atmosphere. "I've never been on a team where we worked extremely hard and had just as much fun off the court," he says. "We went out together. We ate together. We did everything together. We had a great time with each other."

The Raptors players enjoyed the nightlife in Toronto. It became part of the routine. After a game, everyone wanted to know where the party was. There became a rolodex of clubs that the players would frequent, including Pearl Lounge, G-Spot, Jaguar, Atlantis, Studio 69, and Fluid. "You always felt like you were gonna miss something if you didn't go out," Murray says. "I've been in the hot spots in Los Angeles since I was 19, so I knew what good nightlife looked like. I can tell you Toronto had a great nightlife scene." The 24-year-old sharpshooter remembers club-hopping with his teammates until the wee hours of the morning. Murray did not drink, so he spent nights sipping cranberry and orange juice and setting ground rules for the traveling party. "If you want to have a couple of drinks, don't have the whole bottle," he says. "Be social, go home, drink some water. If you're tipsy, don't drive. Get a cab. Be responsible."

The only players who didn't join the group were guys like Ed Pinckney, married and living with their family; Jimmy King, who preferred to spend his free time driving around exploring the city; and Vincenzo Esposito, who wasn't a huge fan of the partying. "It was not my lifestyle," he says. "But it was fun listening to all the stories on the bus the next day."

Stoudamire partied so much at the start of the season he had to learn to pace himself. "There wasn't a night I didn't close the party. I hung out, man," he laughs. "I went everywhere. I used to go to parties in Buffalo too. I had a good time." In the first year, the players were able to move around the city in relative anonymity, which led to some interesting exchanges with fans at the clubs. "We didn't have security back then. So we went out, and this guy came up to Alvin [Robertson] and said, 'Man, I'm better than you,'" Stoudamire recalls. "Alvin had a couple of drinks. He was feeling good about himself, so he said, 'Fuck that. You wanna bet? I bet I'll bust your ass one-on-one.' He always carried around a chunk of change in his pocket. He probably had like 10 Gs on him. They were about to go play, and I was like, 'Come on, man. We just played a game. You're not going to play this dude.' But Alvin was dead-ass serious."

At the center of every party was John Salley.

The 31-year-old center won two championships with Isiah Thomas in Detroit before signing with the Miami Heat. It was a disappointing three-year run in Miami, which ended with an ugly public feud after a team executive called out Salley for being lazy and lacking the work ethic to play on an NBA roster. Thomas called up his former teammate and asked if he wanted a chance to rebuild his value in Toronto. Salley was taken in the expansion draft, spent the summer filming on the set of *Eddie* (a sports-comedy film starring Whoopi Goldberg and Frank Langella), and landed in Toronto after the lockout ended. He rented a house in the posh neighborhood of Forest Hill with his wife, Natasha, and their seven-year-old daughter, Giovana. He immediately called Lashway to discuss promotional opportunities with the team's public relations manager. He wasn't just trying to rebuild himself on the court. Salley was thinking much bigger. He saw Toronto as a chance to expand his business portfolio. Early in the season, he was exploring launching several projects, including a men's underwear line ("I'll be dressing Americans and Canadians from the inside out," he boldly declared to reporters), becoming a music executive (he was in talks to rep local hip-hop artist k-os), and opening a downtown blues club called Salley's Alley.

Teammates who were around him say he was someone who was always networking and being in the same spaces with entrepreneurs, influencers, and celebrities. "Every city we went to, John would say, 'Come with me, I'm meeting somebody,'" Stoudamire says. "He was a relationship guy. If you needed something, you went to him. If you wanted to go to the best restaurant in any city, you went to him."

In the locker room, Salley was always in a cheerful mood. He was the team's social butterfly, and his larger-than-life personality rubbed off on other teammates. "You could talk to him about anything," Esposito laughs. "It could be women, music, or money. He loved Italian food. He loved Italian clothing." Salley set his teammates up with custom tailors around the city. He also set an example when it came to staying in shape. One time, Salley scolded Stoudamire after he saw the rookie eating a Filet-O-Fish and french fries from McDonald's at his locker before a game. "He used to call me 'young fella,'" Stoudamire recalls. "He said, 'Young fella, you can't eat that. Young fella, you need to get massages. Young fella, you need to try acupuncture.' Shit, back then I didn't even stretch."

Salley was also helpful to the rookie in another way. Because of his early-season success, everyone wanted to talk to Stoudamire. Local reporters tried to quote him in their columns every day. *Sports Illustrated*'s Phil Taylor flew to Toronto to write a profile on the rookie. TNT requested a one-on-one sit down with Stoudamire before their nationally televised game against Seattle. *NBA Inside Stuff*, a flagship show on NBC, booked him for an entire segment. Stoudamire was shy, especially compared to Salley, and reluctantly fulfilled all the media requests.

"Damon had the most responsibility out of anybody on and off the court," Murray says. "He used to fall asleep on the bus all the time. I would be like, 'Damn man, we just got on this bus.'"

As the season progressed, Lashway started leaning on Salley to talk to reporters whenever he needed a player to speak for the team. He was articulate and engaging and offered a unique perspective on what was taking place with the expansion franchise.

When the Raptors reconvened for the first practice of the new year, Salley held court in front of a group of local reporters and wasn't in his usual jovial mood.

After the team flew back from Detroit, they had a few days off before starting the new calendar year. Salley organized a New Year's party inside a large industrial building near the downtown Toronto Harbour to ring in the new year. It was the biggest party of the season. The evening started with high-quality hors d'oeuvres, champagne, and crab legs, and continued with a pyrotechnic show at midnight. A-listers including actor Samuel L. Jackson, R&B star Faith Evans, and singer Mary J. Blige were among the over 5,000 people invited to the venue. Tony Massenburg remembers arriving at the party and being blown away by the star power. "It was one of the wildest parties I've ever been to," he says.

As the evening went on, Acie Earl says things started to get a little sloppy inside the club. "I remember ladies coming out of the bathroom," he laughs, "and they would slip and fall because so many of them were throwing up on the floor."

When the party finally ended at three in the morning, most party-goers started to line up at the coat check counter, looking to redeem their ticket stub, grab their jackets, and head home after a memorable evening. There was one problem. The venue had been over-capacity, and throughout the night, the security at coat check ran out of tickets, so they just started taking people's jackets and hanging them up. There was no way for half the people inside the venue to find their coats in an orderly fashion at the end of the night. In the commotion, people just started jumping over the coat check counter and grabbing the first jacket they saw. When Massenburg walked past the crowd at the coat check and went outside, he saw a row of people passed out on the sidewalk. Then he heard a scream. He looked to Lake Ontario, right next to the venue, and saw a couple of guys driving their car into a frozen sheet of ice on the lake. "They were screaming, but they weren't screaming for help," Massenburg recalls. "They were just drunk out of their mind and yelling." The photo of the car on the lake appeared on the front page of *The Toronto Sun* the next day. The headline read: HOOPLA TURNS TO MELEE. The party was described as a near-riot, and there were even reports of gunshots outside of the venue at the end of the night.

The following morning, fans called the local radio station demanding an apology from the team and threatened to sue them. It was a public relations nightmare for the Raptors. For Salley, it was Groundhog Day. He had organized a New Year's party at a Miami Beach restaurant a year prior and gotten into a dispute with the promoter over the profit-sharing at the event. The two engaged in a war of words, and the promoter accused Salley of bringing security guards who carried weapons to the party. The story had become a distraction to the team. A year later, Salley was at the center of a controversy involving another party he organized. At the first practice after the new year, he addressed reporters, apologized for what took place, and denied reports of guns being fired at the party. "We had a lot of balloons going off. We had a show with a lot of firecrackers," he said. "I don't believe anybody got shot."

Salley told reporters he would spend next New Year's at home. "Next year," he smiled, "I plan on watching Dick Clark."

You picked me up like I was a toddler. Don't ever do that again.

Elaine Quan is standing inside the principal's office at a Mississauga high school, screaming at Tracy Murray, who is laughing hysterically.

After finishing outside the top five in sales for the season ticket drive, Quan, who had left her job at Gretzky's to take a three-month contract with the Raptors, had been hired to be part of the community relations department. "I had no idea what this role was," Quan laughs. "I was there for three weeks and didn't have a boss. I wasn't reporting to anyone. So I went through the NBA media guide, looked up every community relations manager, called them up individually, and asked them what they did. I gathered all the information and put together a community relations plan for the team."

For the Raptors, incidents like Salley's New Year's party and Robertson's arrest just days before opening night were public relations nightmares, as they ran counter to what the team was trying to accomplish in the community. The plan which Quan put together would include corporate partnerships with the team's sponsors. Nike would help to refurbish a number of basketball courts across the city. Sears would run a coat drive during home games. There would also be in-store player appearances at SportChek for autograph signings and school visits sponsored by Sprite.

When Quan started asking the players to make these appearances, they were not thrilled. "They were always grumpy and tired," she says.

There was one player who was always up for it. It was Tracy Murray.

"A lot of the guys didn't understand we needed to sell the game of basketball," he says. "We were being paid not just for our talent on the court. It could be overwhelming at times. You had to do autograph signings and public service announcements. Guys hated it. But that was your responsibility if you wanted to be a star."

At his first public appearance, Murray traveled in a minivan with the Raptor mascot and six members of the team's dance crew to Sears for a meet-and-greet session. "Six people showed up to our appearance. We signed a couple of autographs, took some photos, got back in the van, and just laughed about it," he says.

As the season progressed, the demand for players started to grow. So when Quan arrived at a high school in Mississauga with Murray, they walked into a packed gym. "The assembly was for the whole school. It was one of those gyms where you could pull out the bleachers on both sides. When we got there, I told the principal that after Tracy did his talk, to wait until we both left before he dismissed the kids," Quan recalls. "Of course, he did not do that."

"All of a sudden, these kids are jumping out of the bleachers and coming right for us," Murray says. "So I grabbed Elaine, picked her up, ran towards a room where they would put us after, and threw her in the room."

"He freaked out because he thought I was gonna get squished," Quan continues. "He picks me up like a child and puts me down in the office. That's when I lost my mind. I said, 'I'm a grown woman and you picked me up like a three-year-old.' It was so embarrassing. I got carried to the room in front of the entire student body. The teachers were all laughing at me."

The two managed to escape to Murray's car in the parking lot, with a bunch of kids running after them.

The player appearances would occasionally cause a stampede, but they were also critical for the younger fan base across the city to form a personal connection with the Raptors. Seeing players from the same backgrounds as them in the NBA was self-affirming for those who grew up dreaming of playing basketball. The organization wanted to provide more than just affirmation. They wanted to provide opportunities for kids to pursue those dreams. As part of their community initiative, an ambassador program was set up to provide outreach to ethnic neighborhoods across the city.

The idea had come from Al Quance, the head of the community relations department, who had spent a decade teaching at Oakwood Collegiate high school, beginning in 1969, and had helped take an already well-known hoops powerhouse to another level. After leading the school to seven championships, Quance became the head of physical education for the Toronto Board of Education. Canada Basketball approached him to help develop a coaching certification program, which helped certify thousands of basketball coaches across the country and allowed them to run clinics to train younger players. Quance recognized the enclave of multicultural communities in Toronto to tap into. Across the city, immigrants and second-generation kids came from around the world and needed a more organized setting to improve their basketball skills. There were community leaders in these different neighborhoods who could help the Raptors become involved.

"I set about identifying a well-known personality in each cultural community," Quance says, "and empowered them as a spokesperson for the team and helped give us a direct line to those communities."

An ambassador program was set up to include the Black, Jamaican, Spanish-speaking, Filipino, and the wheelchair basketball community, among others. Quance put together a training program for kids ages eight to 12, which was later adopted by Basketball Ontario and became the city's go-to introductory level hoops program, and encouraged the ambassadors to set up basketball clinics in their communities. It was sponsored by telecommunications company Bell Canada and called the Bell Raptor Ball program. A package with a manual accompanied by half-a-dozen Raptor-branded basketballs was sent to the ambassadors, allowing them to incorporate the instructions into their existing clinics or to start brand new ones altogether.

The Bell Raptor Ball program helped provide credibility to those trying to build a community around basketball in the city, including Clement Chu, who had grown up playing pick-up games where he was usually the only Chinese kid. "On the one hand, you feel like you have been let into an exclusive club, and you feel like you're good enough to be in this room," he says. "At the same time, I felt like an outsider." When he was invited to a Chinese run inside a Presbyterian church in the Chinatown neighborhood of downtown Toronto, Chu recognized there was a larger community who loved the game like him.

He signed up for a basketball tournament organized by the North American Chinese Basketball Association and started to meet more Chinese players in the city. They were immigrants from China, Taiwan, and Hong Kong and included Canadian-born Chinese hoopers. At the tournament, Chu met David Kuo, who was born in Taiwan, and moved to the United States to study as a visa student when he was 14. Kuo moved to Vancouver during high school, where he was a standout player. When he moved to Toronto during university, Kuo recognized many Chinese immigrants had trouble booking pick-up runs because of the language barrier. So he started to organize under-18 tournaments for Chinese players and invited Chu to help. It helped bring together Hong Kong immigrants living in Markham, the Toisan community in Scarborough, and Canadian-born Chinese living downtown.

In 1995, the two registered themselves as a non-profit organization and named it CCYAA, the Canadian Chinese Youth Athletic Association. They became involved with the team's ambassador program and were provided a manual from the Raptors. "That's when we started a youth development program," Chu says. "They gave us a curriculum where we would teach kids for an hour each week." The first CCYAA basketball clinic was held at A.Y. Jackson Secondary School in Scarborough. The cost of enrolling in the program was $80 per year. Chu asked Chinese players around the city to coach the program, so the kids who were participating could see it was possible to grow up and play the sport. "It was not something they saw on television," he says. "It helped open up their imagination." The partnership with the Raptors helped give CCYAA credibility and legitimacy, enabling them to grow their reach across the city.

CCYAA would eventually introduce a women's program, which helped provide greater access to the sport for everyone in the Chinese community. Jackelyn Lau remembers getting shots up at the local community center in ninth grade when her gym teacher informed her about CCYAA. She became a regular during the Saturday training programs and got the opportunity to travel to places like Boston and Arizona for tournaments. "It helped strengthen my love of basketball," Lau says. "The older women there were role models to me."

Darrick Tam joined CCYAA when he was 10 and still remembers the excitement of waking up on the weekend to play basketball on Saturday mornings. Tam says CCYAA helped shape him as a basketball player and a person. "It was a community where I felt a belonging because I didn't have that for so much of my upbringing. It became one of those places I loved going to every week," he says. "I was never a super confident kid. I had some basketball skills, and they helped me nurture it."

While there had been organizing of basketball communities in the years prior, from the local YMCA gyms to concentrated areas at schools including Oakwood, Eastern Commerce, Bathurst Heights, and Runnymede, the Raptors helped expand the interaction with the local community. They provided more visibility and better facilities for the next generation to interact with the sport. The impact was tangible in the exponential rise in sales of basketball hoops at local retailers, including The Canadian Tire and SportChek. The number of local basketball leagues and weekly pick-up runs also increased dramatically.

The new year would open with a 121–110 loss on the road to the Orlando Magic. Salley came off the bench and played six minutes. It would be his final appearance with the Raptors. After starting the season as part of the rotation, the big man slowly fell out of favor with Brendan Malone. Massenburg had returned from injury and was playing well alongside Oliver Miller. Ed Pinckney and Žan Tabak were the first options off the bench. Salley wanted more playing time. He met with Thomas and asked for a trade.

When Thomas met with reporters, he defended Malone's decision to bench the veteran big man. "Brendan is the type of coach that if he had the devil himself on his bench and thought the devil could help him win games, he'd play the devil," Thomas told reporters. "There are simply players ahead of Salley right now that Brendan thinks can help."

As Salley rode the bench, the team started to scour the league to see if they could find a trade partner. Thomas started preliminary talks with Charlotte about Robert Parish, an accomplished big man in the twilight of his career. Atlanta called and offered 31-year-old forward Ken Norman.

January would be another forgettable month for the Raptors. They lost eight of their first nine games to open the calendar year and would finish the month with just three wins. The blowout losses were starting to become more common. There was a 25-point loss against a New Jersey Nets team who had planned to hold a players-only meeting before the game but canceled it because the players couldn't agree on a start time, as well as a 27-point defeat in Sacramento where Stoudamire scored just four points, dropping the team to 2–18 on the road.

By the end of the month, Salley was still with the team, but he had mentally checked out. When none of the trade proposals fit what Thomas was looking for, the Raptors decided to waive the big man, allowing him to become a free agent. "I'm relieved," he told reporters. "I was waiting to exhale. I was smiling, but now I'm laughing."

Salley's brief run in Toronto was over.

He finished with 25 games played, averaging 6.0 points and 3.9 rebounds.

The Trade Deadline

The final game before the All-Star break would be another disappointing loss for the Raptors. The team missed all 12 of their three-point attempts and trailed the Milwaukee Bucks at home by double-digits in the second half. Toronto would show signs of life in the fourth quarter, battling back to cut the lead to two with less than two minutes left. The backbreaking play came with 29 seconds remaining, when the Bucks' frontcourt outworked the Raptors for three offensive rebounds on a single possession before Milwaukee guard Sherman Douglas hit a jumper to put the game away. The 93–88 loss would send the Raptors into the break with a 13–34 record. Brendan Malone had called a team meeting before the game to talk about the team's effort and execution, but they once again fell short in both categories. With 35 games remaining in the regular season, the expansion roster needed a shakeup.

The trade deadline was now two weeks away, and Isiah Thomas had started to engage other teams on potential deals. Through the expansion draft and in free agency, the Raptors had cobbled together a roster of promising young players with several experienced vets playing key roles on the team. It was time to start thinking long-term, which meant building around Damon Stoudamire and seeing if the deadline would allow Thomas to make the roster younger around his rookie point guard. Stoudamire had nearly made the All-Star team as a rookie, but the final reserve spots would go to Indiana's Reggie Miller and Cleveland's Terrell

Brandon. When he was invited to play in the Rookie-Sophomore game instead, Stoudamire had second thoughts. He was among the league leaders in minutes, averaging 41 minutes per night, and wanted to take the weekend off.

"I was tired, man," Stoudamire laughs.

It was Thomas who convinced him to go, telling the rookie he had earned the privilege to be in the spotlight. Thomas became Stoudamire's mentor in the first season. After a disappointing performance in an early-season loss, the general manager pulled his rookie aside in the locker room. He called Stoudamire out for being too passive on the court. Thomas set a high bar for his first-round pick, but it wasn't just about tough love. The two would talk about staying in shape, the importance of managing the mental health aspect of the game, and how to manage the 82-game regular-season grind. Thomas would pass on tips to Stoudamire throughout the season.

"He gave me everything," Stoudamire says. "He took me on as his project. He gave me the good and the bad. He was an open book. Our relationship was second to none."

The 1996 All-Star weekend took place in San Antonio, Texas, and Stoudamire was the star of the Rookie-Sophomore game. In the final minute, he hit a three-pointer, drove for a layup, then threw a perfect alley-oop pass to Sixers rookie Jerry Stackhouse. Stoudamire finished with 19 points and 11 assists and won the Most Valuable Player award. For many NBA fans in the United States, it was their first time seeing what the Raptors rookie was capable of on the court.

"It puts a capper on a great first half of the season for me," Stoudamire told reporters afterward.

Meanwhile, the veterans on the team went into the break wondering about their future with the Raptors. Willie Anderson also spent All-Star weekend in San Antonio, for different reasons than Stoudamire. He had flown back home to spend time with his family and believed his run in Toronto was over. While Anderson played a huge role with the Raptors, he was a free agent at the end of the season and the exact type of player

Thomas was looking to move at the deadline. The general manager was also talking to the Houston Rockets, who expressed interest in adding Alvin Robertson to bolster their depth. Reporters were surprised to see Anderson with the team when the regular season resumed the following week.

"I thought I was gone," Anderson told reporters. "I had my bags packed and everything."

The Raptors would get an inspiring win on the road against Miami to start the second half of the season, scoring a franchise-record 23 straight points in the second half in a 98–87 win. Stoudamire led the way with 29 points, seven assists, and four steals. As Thomas prepared to strip the roster of veteran players, he sat down with the rookie to give him a heads up. During Thomas' rookie year in Detroit, he had grown close to Greg Kelser, who the team had selected fourth overall in the 1979 draft. Kelser went to high school in Detroit and was a star at Michigan State. The hometown hero went out of his way to take Thomas under his wing, showing him around the city and teaching him how to be a pro in the NBA. The Pistons traded Kelser early in Thomas' rookie season, taking away an important piece in the locker room. The general manager knew how much Robertson and Anderson meant to Stoudamire's development and wanted to be sure the rookie would be okay if they were moved at the deadline.

The win over Miami was followed by a 19-point loss to Cleveland at home. After starting a seven-game road trip with another defeat in Detroit, a trade was announced. The Raptors were sending Anderson and center Victor Alexander, who spent the entire season on the injured list, to the New York Knicks in exchange for seldomly-used guard Doug Christie, who was buried at the end of the bench.

With just a few days remaining until the deadline, Thomas told reporters he didn't expect to make another deal, especially after the Rockets balked at the asking price of a first-rounder for Robertson. So when Ed Pinckney woke up in his hotel room on trade deadline day in Salt Lake City, the 32-year-old forward went through his usual game-day routine and jumped on the team bus for morning shootaround before that evening's game against Utah. He had no idea it would be his final day with the Raptors franchise. The Bronx, New York, native was a college star, leading Villanova to an upset of Patrick Ewing's Georgetown Hoyas in the 1985 national championship game and winning the Final Four Most Outstanding Player award. He was selected 10th overall by Phoenix in the draft the same year and had a productive NBA career that spanned four different teams over a decade. Pinckney was disappointed on the night of the expansion draft. He did not want to join a first-year team, especially not in Canada, which friends told him was a country that knew nothing about basketball. "I was being exiled," he says.

At training camp, Pinckney battled Žan Tabak in practice every day. The two became close friends. They explored the city of Toronto together, dining at restaurants in different neighborhoods while learning about each other's upbringing. Pinckney's perception of the city and the expansion team started to change. He also became a favorite of Malone's. Pinckney's blue-collar approach on the floor helped set an example for the rest of the roster. "We had to fight off the expansion label," he says. "It didn't matter if we were ahead or behind in a game. We had to compete and play hard."

Another player he had grown close to was Tony Massenburg. "I admired Ed before I ever met him," Massenburg admits. "He got it done in the same way I did. He was consistent. He didn't back down from anyone, especially seven-footers and guys with more hype around them. That earned a lot of people's respect. I talked to him a lot. I wanted to see what I could learn from him. He was the voice of reason on the team."

The second pick by the Raptors in the expansion draft after B.J. Armstrong, Massenburg faced his first bit of adversity after a successful four-year college career at Maryland when the San Antonio Spurs waived him a year after making him a second-round pick in the 1991 NBA draft. "It was the first time I had ever been cut in anything," he recalls. "I was always good at the sports I played, from football, basketball, and running track in high school. I was young and had never dealt with failure, so I struggled and started to question myself." Massenburg signed a 10-day contract with Charlotte. He then joined Boston, filling in for an injured Larry Bird, and was sent home after another 10-day. When the same thing happened in Golden State, the big man decided to play professionally in Malaga, Spain. He enjoyed his experience overseas and later signed with F.C. Barcelona, where Massenburg was named to the All-Star team.

At the start of the 1994–95 season, he signed with the Los Angeles Clippers and put up career-high numbers, averaging 9.3 points and 5.7 rebounds, starting 50 of the 80 games he appeared in. When the rebuilding Clippers decided to go in a different direction and left Massenburg off their protected list for the expansion draft, the Raptors were more than happy to pick up a player who was entering his prime. The idea of joining a first-year team in a new country was a familiar concept for the journeyman forward. "I was just happy to be still in North America and playing in the NBA," Massenburg says. He moved into a downtown condo by the lake with his dog Kane, a 150-pound rottweiler. When Massenburg discovered Vincenzo Esposito had a female rottweiler, the two decided to breed their dogs. Eight puppies were given away to friends, family, and even teammate Carlos Rogers.

At training camp, Massenburg battled for minutes alongside Pinckney and Tabak. He was the team's leading rebounder in the preseason and appeared to have a spot in the starting lineup locked up. Towards the end of the exhibition schedule, Massenburg felt a sharp pain in his foot while playing the Vancouver Grizzlies. At the next timeout, he asked the team trainer to loosen the tape on his ankle, hoping the pain would go away. On the next play, as Massenburg ran to chase down a loose ball, he planted his right foot, heard a pop, and dropped to the floor immediately, wincing in pain. Massenburg had suffered a broken foot which would keep him sidelined for several months.

"I was devastated," he says. "I had envisioned myself starting in the team's very first game and being part of history."

Pinckney was in the starting lineup instead on opening night. He scanned the SkyDome and took in what it meant to be part of the very beginning of an NBA franchise. It gave him goosebumps.

"I did not factor in the excitement attached to having a new team in a new place," Pinckney says.

Meanwhile, Massenburg spent the first six weeks of the season rehabbing from foot surgery, putting in two-a-day training sessions to speed up the recovery process. When he returned to the lineup towards the end of December, Massenburg made an impression right away and was in the starting lineup a week later. When Thomas approached him to discuss a contract extension during the season, Massenburg declined an offer from the team, choosing to take his chances in free agency instead at the end of the season. Because of the prorated salary cap, the Raptors could not match the big man's market value.

There didn't appear to be any significant offers for Pinckney and Massenburg, until Thomas received a call from Sixers head coach and general manager John Lucas just before the trade deadline. Philadelphia had a 10–41 record and just lost at home to Miami in a game where they scored 57 points. The team was looking to clear some cap space to rebuild their roster over the summer. The two sides reached a deal by the time the Raptors finished shootaround in Utah. Pinckney and Massenburg, whose contracts were coming off the books in the summer, were headed to Philadelphia. In exchange, the Raptors were acquiring 23-year-old center Sharone Wright, who had four years remaining on a six-year, $21 million contract.

Pinckney says Thomas had kept an ongoing dialogue with him in the weeks leading up to the deadline.

"He was very open and honest with me," Pinckney recalls. "If a trade didn't go through, he would tell me."

Meanwhile, Massenburg did not see the trade coming. He was now joining the seventh NBA team of his career.

"I'm totally surprised," he told reporters. "Nobody had said anything to me about this happening. It's very frustrating to be moving around."

As Pinckney took a cab back to the hotel in Salt Lake City to pack up his belongings, he was surprised at how difficult it was to say goodbye to the expansion franchise he had only spent four months with. Pinckney moved into a condo in the city's downtown core and was directly across from St. Lawrence Market, a two-floor public market he regularly visited with his wife, Rose, and their four kids. He had grown to enjoy Toronto and became a fan of the family environment which John Bitove Jr. and the organization fostered.

"We loved the area we lived in," Pinckney says. "We developed relationships there and made so many friends."

One of those friends was Paul Jones, who worked as vice principal at C.R. Marchant Middle School in the Jane and Lawrence area, while holding a second job as the team's radio analyst. Before he retired and joined the education system, Jones had been a high school star at Oakwood Collegiate, who later joined York University, winning three provincial titles, along with the Kitch McPherson Trophy in 1981 as MVP of the Ontario championship game. His résumé included two Ontario University Athletics All-Star selections and a silver medal with Team Canada at the Commonwealth Games. Jones grew up with immigrant parents from Jamaica, who brought him to Canada when he was four months old. His father, Hugh, worked an office job during the day and pumped gas in the evening to support the family. His mom, Marjorie, worked as a medical secretary and took on extra assignments at clinics around the city. They recognized Jones' athletic potential but warned him against pursuing it as a career. "Don't follow sports," they told him, "it will never put a dime in your pocket." Jones spent weeknights during his childhood at Winona Drive Senior Public School and visited New York City playgrounds in the summer. He had a Sunday pick-up run at George Brown College with the best hoopers in the city. Basketball fulfilled a part of his life, and Jones would explore every possibility to stay involved in the sport and prove his parents wrong.

After his playing career ended, he landed a full-time teaching position at Arlington Middle School in 1985 and coached the school's basketball team. It was in the same year when his brother Mark opened the door for him to work in sports. Mark was at TSN, a recently launched sports television network, and helped Paul land a job there. It was an intern-level role, but Jones was living the dream. After school, he would head to the TSN studio and watch the evening's slate of NBA games, scripting one-minute highlight packages for each game. Even on his nights off, Jones would come to the studio and watch the West Coast games while marking English assignments. Sometimes he would have no choice because the local pub Jones frequented refused to change the channel to basketball because a hockey game was also on. "It was frustrating," Jones says. "A hardcore group of people loved the game, but we didn't have a lot to eat."

As he moved up the ranks in the Toronto District School Board and became a well-known Ontario provincial basketball coach, Jones was offered an opportunity of a lifetime in 1992, when he lived in Barcelona, Spain, for a month while covering the Summer Olympics for CTV. The experience would land Jones the color commentator role for the 1994 FIBA World Championship's radio broadcast.

He would work alongside Mike Inglis, who grew up in Glasgow, Scotland, and immigrated to Canada as a kid. After studying broadcasting at Humber College, Inglis became a radio play-by-play man for the Toronto Blizzard, a North American Soccer League team, before moving to Winnipeg to call games for the Blue Bombers of the CFL. He received a call from a radio station in Indianapolis that offered him a job calling Pacers games alongside Clark Kellogg for a year. Jones says he developed an instant chemistry with Inglis. "Mike was an old-school radio guy," he says. "I grew up where there weren't a lot of games on television, so I listened to a lot of games on the radio. I understood what was going on. I knew he had to carry the play and be the main guy talking. I wouldn't fight him for air time."

"He knew more basketball than I knew," Inglis adds. "He was a junkie. As much as I taught him about doing radio, he also taught me a lot."

Jones came to appreciate calling a basketball game on the radio as an art form. "You had to be the person's eyes and ears and tell them everything from how much smoke was in the building to what a guy's shoes looked like," he explains. "I had to make sure Mike called the play, told listeners the score and the time, and when there was a break, I would explain what happened on the play."

There was the occasional on-air mix-up, like when Canada and China played at the tournament, and Weidong Hu, a two-time MVP in the Chinese Basketball Association, had the ball. "So Mike is describing the play," Jones recalls. "He goes, 'Hu has the ball.' I go, 'Mike, this is not Abbott and Costello. I know who has the ball.' He goes, 'No. That's his name. That's Weidong Hu. I'm not asking you a question, Paul. I'm telling you, Hu has the ball.'"

The two were providing a demo tape for Bitove to review. After the tournament, he reached out to the broadcast duo and asked them to be part of the Raptors' CFRB radio broadcast. Jones was now a vice-principal and didn't want to give up the job. "So the school board arranged for me to keep my job and travel with the team," he recalls. "It was difficult. There were times when the team left at three in the afternoon for a game the next day. I would do all my school work, fly in at nine in the evening, work the game the following day, travel back with the team, get back home at two in the morning, and be at school at eight in the morning to make the announcements. It was tough. I loved basketball but was dedicated to teaching and I wasn't going to give up either one. I ended up missing like 25 days of school that year."

It was an exhausting travel schedule, but Jones cherished every moment. He still remembers taking it all in on opening night at the SkyDome, where he got to sit courtside and call the first game in Raptors' history. When Stoudamire recorded the franchise's first triple-double, Jones handed him the official stat sheet on the bus afterward. On the team's first road trip, he sat and watched Michael Jordan warm up in an empty gym before the game.

The vice-principal was living the dream. "We would win a game, get on the plane, and the meal was ribs. There was a movie on. It was *Crimson Tide* with Gene Hackman and Denzel Washington," Jones recalls. "I'm sitting there. At one point, my hand was full of rib sauce, I'm watching the movie, and I thought, 'Man. I'm living. This is fun. I'm on a private plane. I've got NBA players around me. Come on, what could be better?' The city kid from Toronto whose mom and dad had to take extra jobs. These are the fruits that they gave me."

He also started to see a growing excitement about the expansion franchise at his school. "The kids, especially those in city schools, just jumped on it. For Black kids in the city, they saw people who looked like them. Suddenly, Damon Stoudamire, Oliver Miller, and people who looked like them were playing a sport they loved at a very high level," Jones says. "I was always taking little trinkets for the students. When there were game notes, I would say, 'Don't throw those out, give them to me.' I would keep them in my desk drawers and give them to the kids. I had some street cred with them."

Jones still remembers trade deadline day. "I woke up at seven in the morning," he recalls. "I'm traveling from Toronto to Detroit, then on a connecting flight to Dallas, and from Dallas to Salt Lake City. There was no internet. I didn't own a cell phone at the time. I walk into the hotel in Utah, and it's like four in the afternoon."

As he walked into the hotel lobby, Jones saw Pinckney with his bags packed.

"Eddie," he asked. "Are you going to the arena early?"

"Nah," Pinckney replied. "I got traded."

Jones flew on the team charter and quickly became friends with the players. In the back of the plane, Murray would hold court as the team's resident DJ, taking requests as he blasted music on his boombox. Jones would occasionally join in for a game of cards or play dominoes with the players. The area of the plane became affectionately known as "The Hood." It was where Jones and Pinckney became close friends, spending hours chatting about basketball.

The two hugged each other goodbye and promised to keep in touch. "It was a stark reminder that this was a business," Jones says. "I couldn't believe my guy got traded. It was devastating."

The Raptors would enter the season's final stretch with a revamped roster. Oliver Miller, Žan Tabak, and Acie Earl were the only players who remained from the expansion draft. The team wrapped up an eventful trade deadline day with a 16-point loss to the Utah Jazz. Doug Christie made his debut and had three steals in 14 minutes. The team had also acquired 38-year-old center Herb Williams in the trade with the Knicks. He played 31 minutes and scored six points, grabbing eight rebounds in the defeat. Williams had asked Thomas to see if he could be traded to a contending team. When the deadline passed without a deal, the Raptors waived Williams after his debut in Utah, allowing him to rejoin the Knicks for the remainder of the season. He would enter the exclusive club of Raptors players who appeared in only one game with the franchise.

The road trip continued in Phoenix the following night, when Wright played in his first game with the Raptors, coming off the bench to score 13 points and grab six rebounds. Wright grew up in Macon, Georgia, where he was a star at Southwest High School, becoming a top-10 high school player in the country with more than 50 NCAA Division I scholarship offers to choose from. At Clemson, Wright became the fourth-leading rebounder in school history, behind only Tree Rollins, Dale Davis, and Horace Grant, and was selected sixth overall by Philadelphia in 1994.

"As soon as they called my name, everything changed for my family," Wright says. "I was able to pull them out of the ghetto. I got my mother out of her apartment in Macon because it was run down. My grandmother didn't want a big house. She just wanted something better, so I took care of that." After being named to the All-Rookie Second Team in his first season, Wright became a whipping boy for the Sixers fan base that was growing frustrated with the team's lack of direction. In Wright's final eight games in Philadelphia, he averaged less than six points and six rebounds and shot 28 percent from the field. When the home crowd booed him, Wright fanned the flames, telling reporters, "The fans only come to the games to get drunk."

A few days later, he was a Toronto Raptor.

Thomas was excited to add a 23-year-old center to the roster and hoped Wright would pair well with Stoudamire. "He's a young talent who gives us a true center. I like our future a lot better now," he told reporters. "From what we've seen, Damon does have the ability to make other people around him significantly much better."

The two were USA Basketball teammates at the 1993 World University Games, where they won a gold medal together. "I always felt comfortable playing with Damon," Wright says. "He was such a dynamic player. He made everything easier on the floor. He wasn't a shoot-first point guard. He always made sure everyone was involved."

Stoudamire was excited too. "We were finally able to throw the ball to someone in the post who could make something happen," he says. "He was a perfect addition to our team."

The Raptors would lose by five points to Phoenix in Wright's debut, and proceed to drop the next three on the road to Dallas, Houston, and San Antonio, before salvaging a 1–6 road trip with a victory in Cleveland. It was the start of March when the team finally returned to Toronto. In his home debut as a Raptor, Wright gave the fans a glimpse at what the potential one-two punch of the team might look like for the next decade. Even though Toronto lost to Detroit in a 21-point blowout, the newly acquired big man joined the starting lineup and dominated in the paint, scoring a team-high 25 points and going to the free-throw line 17 times.

The loss dropped the Raptors to 15–42 on the season.

The SkyDome

On June 3, 1989, over 45,000 spectators attended the opening ceremony of the SkyDome. After a miserable experience sitting outdoors in the middle of the winter at Exhibition Stadium for the 1982 Grey Cup, the city commissioned a study on the benefits of an indoor stadium and predicted a dome would bring $370 million into the economy from tourism every year. Rod Robbie, a British-born Canadian architect, mortgaged his Moore Park home to obtain the cash needed to enter the stadium-design competition. He won the contest and was tasked with bringing the world's first fully retractable dome stadium to life with engineer Michael Allen.

Robbie described the SkyDome as a secular cathedral, a fun palace, and "a universal destination for all kinds of activities, just like the old Roman forum." It would be the home of the Toronto Blue Jays, and the CFL's Toronto Argonauts and host guided tours, convention dates, trade shows, and concerts. The stadium was going to be "a city within a city." There would be restaurants and lounges overlooking the field, including a Hard Rock Cafe, a 650-seat restaurant in centerfield called "Windows," a 400-seat bar in left field called "Sightlines," and the largest McDonald's restaurant in North America. The SkyDome would include a health club with squash courts, a 25-meter swimming pool, whirlpool, sauna, and a running track; the largest video display scoreboard in baseball at 115 feet long and 35 feet high; and a 350-room hotel attached to the stadium featuring 70 rooms overlooking the field. The stadium's main attraction was the retractable roof. It cost $80 million, was built to withstand a tornado, and could open with winds as high as 40 miles per hour.

The stadium's developers were anxious to show off the retractable roof at the opening ceremony, even if there was a downpour outside. When host Alan Thicke, a Canadian actor best known for his role as Dr. Jason Seaver on the ABC sitcom *Growing Pains*, urged the crowd to chant "Open up the dome!" with him, thousands in attendance shouted back: "Close it! Close it!" David Peterson, the premier of Ontario at the time, stepped up to the button and pressed it to open the roof. It left everyone inside scrambling for cover as rain poured down.

"It was the right call," Peterson laughs. "We're still talking about it, right?"

When the Liberal Party won the provincial election in 1985, Peterson took over as premier and needed to make a call on whether to proceed with the construction of the SkyDome. The development plan for the stadium had stalled, and the Metro government was considering pulling its funding for the project. After conducting his own research, Peterson gave the thumbs up for the city to move forward with the stadium. He saw potential in the location of the SkyDome, which would be built on vacant land adjacent to the CN Tower downtown, and be a seven-minute walk from Union Station. "The site was a genius of an idea," Peterson says. "In those days, stadiums were being built outside of the city. It was a leap of faith, but it was also smart to put it right in the hub of all public transportation. It symbolized us coming of age and becoming a world-class city."

The SkyDome became a tourist attraction and hosted several memorable events, including the 1989 Grey Cup and WrestleMania VI in 1990, where a record-breaking crowd of 67,678 people watched Hulk Hogan and The Ultimate Warrior in the main event. Rod Stewart, Elton John, Frank Sinatra, Alice Cooper, and The Rolling Stones held concerts at the venue. The Toronto Blue Jays clinched the 1993 World Series on a walk-off home run from Joe Carter at the stadium.

In 1995, the SkyDome became the home of the Toronto Raptors. The dome required some adjustment for players used to playing in a traditional basketball stadium. The team held morning shootarounds and practices at the SkyDome when Glendon College was fully booked. The empty, cavernous environment meant players had to adjust to practicing in the cold. Jimmy King says the team would show up with several layers of clothing. "We used to wear sweats in practice," he says. "We would have long sweatpants and hoodies on. It was that really thick heavy material. We would put our shorts and jerseys over top of that."

The dimensions of the dome created another problem for the players. They had to adjust to the depth perception of the stadium, which affected their shooting during games. "It's not a shooter's gym," Wille Anderson told reporters at the start of the season. "There's so much space, so much movement behind the baskets. It's like shooting outside in the wind. You can't focus."

Tony Massenburg compared it to a field in Iowa. "It felt like you were playing in a hundred-acre field," he explains, "and someone put a basketball court in the middle of it."

Tracy Murray was looking forward to draining threes at the dome but said the placement of the stadium lighting blinded him whenever he shot from the corners. "I tried to stay out of those corners with a passion," he says.

Damon Stoudamire says practice makes perfect. "I got a lot of shots up," he laughs, "so it didn't matter."

The SkyDome was also the *literal* home to some Raptor players. When Sharone Wright landed in Toronto after the trade deadline, the team got him a hotel suite inside the stadium, where he stayed for the rest of the season. Wright ordered food from the Hard Rock Cafe every day and would walk downstairs and find an empty seat at the stadium to watch the Blue Jays when they were in town. "If I were anywhere else, I would have gotten lost," Wright says. "It was a great experience."

Murray stayed in the SkyDome hotel during the first season and enjoyed the in-stadium catering. His go-to order was chicken fettuccine. "I would tear that fettuccine up," Murray says. "I would get it for room service. When we went on road trips, I would make sure to order it to the locker room so I could bring it with me on the bus."

Stoudamire also fell in love with the chicken fettuccine but a new chef hired midseason ruined the dish. "He started putting all kinds of shit on it," Stoudamire says. "I just wanted the chicken, the noodles, and the sauce."

Murray thinks it was the seasoning. "They took the garlic out of it," he says.

As the Raptors waited to move into a new proposed arena location for the start of the 1997–98 season, the SkyDome needed to be rearranged and reimagined into a basketball stadium. A court was set up with movable stands in the middle of the stadium, like a Lego piece sitting in a cavernous wasteland of nothingness. A work area was set up behind the bleacher seats down the first-base line for the media. Press meals were served in the baseball press box upstairs. One of the baseball clubhouses was transformed into the Raptors' locker room. A new clubhouse was built at the north end of the stadium for the visitors. After every game, the court and bleacher seats would be broken down to clear room for the venue to host other events.

The challenge facing the team was how they would turn the SkyDome into an attractive venue for first-year fans. It was a horrible place to watch a basketball game unless you had a courtside ticket. The seats extended to the 500-level of the baseball stadium, where you could rent binoculars for seven dollars at the concession stand because the court was so far away the players looked like thumbtacks. Initially priced at $26, the seats were discounted to five dollars during the first season. The team viewed the 500-level as a gateway for fans to experience an NBA game in person. They were able to bring in fans who couldn't afford the fancy courtside seats. It became a tool for the team to hand out rows of free tickets to community centers across the city, but the fans sitting in the upper decks were detached from the in-game experience.

In the first season, Brian Cooper, who ran the game operations and entertainment department, came up with the idea of having a mascot exclusive to the 500-level. He was named The Bleacher Creature and was played by Rob Pagetto, who was born in Port Colborne, Ontario, and had a lengthy résumé in the entertainment industry as a television host on YTV's *Video & Arcade Top 10* and an actor who appeared in Coca-Cola and NERF commercials. Pagetto would hang out in the 500-level wearing a backward baseball cap, ripped jeans, and basketball sneakers. The goal was for him to be a relatable regular joe average basketball fan who paid a small sum of money to hang out in the upper deck. Pagetto walked around with a megaphone, urging the crowd to cheer on the Raptors. Occasionally, he would upgrade a section of the 500-level fans to court-side seats for the second half. The Bleacher Creature had a brief run; during the first season, Pagetto was upgraded to courtside, becoming the team's in-arena emcee during timeouts.

The ideas flowed in the team's offices throughout the first season on making home games an immersive and fun experience for every fan at the SkyDome. "The question was always, 'How do you make this massive, intimidating space into one where you can create a shared experience?'" Cooper says. "We couldn't control the outcome of the game, but the thing we could control was the entertainment. We had to put on a show every night because the team wasn't winning. The audience wasn't as sophisticated as they are now, so we had to do something to entertain them every night."

Cooper grew up in Hollis, Queens, the birthplace of the iconic rap group Run-DMC, and was a benchwarmer on the Saint Mary's University basketball team in Halifax, Nova Scotia. After graduating with an accounting degree, he landed in Toronto and tried to start a Canadian pro basketball league in 1979. He had an entire business plan mapped out. Cooper would convince CFL owners to take on the new franchises. They would use the same employees in the cities the football teams were already playing in to run the operations. Each team would include a minimum of seven Canadian players, giving the basketball talent in the country a chance to play pro at home. He even chatted with the top players in Canada, including Paul Jones, and started discussions with several investors on bankrolling the project.

When the idea fell apart, Cooper started his own agency and called it Hollis Communications. The company landed Wayne Gretzky as a client, and Cooper helped broker a deal with Tom Bitove to bring Wayne Gretzky's Restaurant to life. He was hired to oversee game operations for the 1994 FIBA World Championship and then joined the Raptors in the same role after the tournament.

Today, Cooper credits Jamie Nishino, the senior manager of the game ops department, for making his vision come to life. "I might have sat there and creatively expounded on what we wanted to do," Cooper says. "She was the one who executed the plan."

Nishino was a theater show producer who worked for the Argonauts before joining the team. One of the things she noticed before the start of the season was the placement of the Jumbotron in the stadium, which would not be accessible to the fans. Cooper wanted a basketball scoreboard that would hang above center court instead. Nishino made some calls and found out the San Antonio Spurs were moving into The Alamodome and were trying to sell their old scoreboard for scrap. She flew to San Antonio with an engineer and confirmed the scoreboard was in working order. But there was another problem.

Nishino had no idea how to bring the scoreboard back to Toronto. She hired a group of engineers in San Antonio to take apart the scoreboard and ship it to the SkyDome, where the stadium's engineers reassembled the parts, delivering the scoreboard Cooper wanted. For every home game at the SkyDome, the scoreboard would be wheeled across the stadium floor and hauled to the ceiling, where it would be cabled and held together with chains. That was how the first year went for the game ops team. They could ask a question and try to problem solve and find an answer.

"It was terrifying and exciting," Nishino says, "and maybe those are the same things."

Sharon Edwards was the team's special event and game operations coordinator. On opening night, she had invited season ticket holders, corporate sponsors, politicians, industry leaders, and a *who's who* of Toronto to the SkyDome and successfully ushered them to their court-side seats just in time for tip-off.

"I remember getting off the elevator and just stopping to look up," she says. "I looked up at the bleachers. I looked up at the upper deck. I looked at people around the stadium and said, 'Oh my god. We've done it. The NBA is here.'"

Edwards grew up a basketball fan in the city's east end along the Danforth. She went to Central Tech and rooted for the school's basketball team. She watched the NBA on the weekend on television and grew to love the "Bad Boy" Pistons. Edwards was one of many people in the city waiting for a team to come to Toronto. After studying fashion and design at Sheridan College, Edwards worked at Holt Renfrew, a high-end retail company located on Bloor Street. When a volunteer position opened up at the 1994 FIBA World Championship, Edwards took the job, helping coordinate media access at the tournament, and decided she wanted to work for the Raptors. She wrote a heartfelt letter to Isiah Thomas, explaining how much the game of basketball meant to her, and was hired by the team.

Around 880,000 people watched the Raptors beat the New Jersey Nets on opening night on CTV's national broadcast. Along with the sold-out crowd at the stadium, it vindicated Edwards' belief that there was always enough interest in the sport for the city of Toronto to have its own team. "Every time someone said, 'This is a hockey town. Nobody knows anything about basketball,' I would say, 'Yeah, but that's the audience you're used to talking to,'" she says. "I would tell them, 'The audience you're not used to talking to, most of them understand the game. They're interested in the game. You never hear from them because you never focused on them.'"

As part of her role, Edwards was responsible for making sure famous people showed up at the SkyDome and made Raptors games feel like they were a special event, even if the expansion team was playing in a baseball stadium and losing every night. The national anthem was one way of drawing star power to the venue. When a singer like Alanis Morissette, the Ottawa native who sold 33 million copies of her 1995 album *Jagged Little Pill*, was in town, the team would reach out and ask her to perform at games. The halftime act was another way of bringing a celebrity element to the team. The team worked with Canadian theater producer David Mirvish to bring theater actors to perform a preview of their shows at halftime.

The Raptors also benefited from playing in a city known as "Hollywood North." In 1979, mayor John Sewell proudly announced Toronto had become the third-largest movie production center in the world after New York and Los Angeles. Major movie production companies in the United States took advantage of the Canadian federal government's subsidies and tax credits and started filming north of the border. The Toronto International Film Festival, founded in 1976 and held every September, became a rite of passage for any film looking to enter the conversation for Academy Awards consideration.

During the first season, the team would contact the Toronto Film Association and provide courtside seats to any television and movie stars in town. For any fans attending a Raptors game at SkyDome, they might have spotted Arnold Schwarzenegger, Gene Hackman, or John Cusack in their section. Will Smith and Denzel Washington were among the other Hollywood actors who would make a cameo at the game. When the team hosted the Los Angeles Lakers, Edwards organized a "Hollywood North" event, working with Spalding to create a custom ball that was sent to celebrities across the city. Similar to opening night, they were invited to a pregame reception and seated courtside for the game. On game nights, Edwards would be running around the stadium with the rest of the game ops team, making sure everything went according to script. When a celebrity arrived, Edwards would get a message on her headset to run to Gate 9 to escort the person into the stadium and to their seats. There was no bigger Hollywood presence at the SkyDome in the first season than Samuel L. Jackson.

When the 1995–96 season began, Jackson was living in the Forest Hill neighborhood of Toronto and filming *The Long Kiss Goodnight*, an action thriller co-starring Geena Davis. Isiah Thomas was friends with Jackson. When the actor was in town, the general manager extended an open invitation for him to attend any Raptor home game. "I went as often as I could. I was always there if I was off and I could make it to the stadium," Jackson says. "They were a fun team to watch."

The actor, who played chief engineer Ray Arnold in *Jurassic Park*, the film which influenced the Raptors' brand identity, would sit courtside, heckling the visiting players and occasionally asking Brendan Malone about his minutes distribution.

"I remember asking him why John Salley wasn't playing," Jackson recalls. "He would tell me, 'Sam, he's not in the rotation.'"

On most nights, the actor was the only person talking trash courtside. "The fans were so polite. They didn't understand you could yell at the players and the referees," Jackson says. "I would yell, 'He can't dribble left!' or tell one of the guys, 'He can't catch and shoot!' and the fans would look at me like I was going to get our team in trouble. I was having fun and teaching the fans how to be fans."

Aside from being the team's most vocal celebrity fan, Jackson enjoyed the city for its cuisine and would go golfing when the weather cooperated. "The club scene was banging, too," he adds. Jackson often found himself in the same nightclub as the Raptors players. "I would run into them at different places," he laughs. "I think it was interesting for them to find out that movie stars were way more popular than athletes."

In 1994, Jackson played Bible-quoting hitman Jules Winnfield in *Pulp Fiction*, one of the most iconic movie characters of all time. The film was written and directed by Quentin Tarantino, who had put himself on the map with his 1992 feature-length debut, *Reservoir Dogs*, described by Ella Taylor of *LA Weekly* as "a heist caper without a heist, an action movie that's hopelessly in love with talk, a poem to the sexiness of storytelling, and a slice of precocious wisdom about life." Critics and moviegoers fell in love with the pop-culture-driven dialogue, non-linear storytelling, and black humor of *Reservoir Dogs*, which would become Tarantino's stylistic trademarks.

The director ran into Jackson at the Cannes Film Festival after the release of the movie and told the actor he was writing a character specifically for him for his next film. The movie would feature a series of intertwined caper stories, drawing inspiration from crime novelists Raymond Chandler and Dashiell Hammett, who wrote similar tales in the 1920s and 1930s pulp magazines. It would be called *Pulp Fiction*. Jackson read for the role of Winnfield and expected to land the part. When his manager told him Tarantino wanted the actor to fly out to Los Angeles for another audition with actor Paul Calderón, who had impressed the director in a separate audition, Jackson was pissed.

When he arrived at the studio, he only grew angrier when a line producer mistook him for actor Lawrence Fishburne. Jackson had landed at the airport and stopped by a fast food restaurant. He walked into the audition with a burger in hand and a drink in the other and channeled his anger into a readthrough that blew everyone away. *Pulp Fiction* began shooting in California on September 20, 1993. Jackson had arrived on set having created an entire backstory for his character. He also grew muttonchop sideburns to give Winnfield a distinct look. The character's iconic look was complete when a production assistant was sent to buy an Afro wig but returned with a Jheri-curl wig.

On a budget of just over $8 million, *Pulp Fiction* became the first independent film to gross over $200 million. The movie won the Palme d'Or at the Cannes Film Festival and received seven Oscar nominations. Movie critic Roger Ebert called it the most influential movie of the 1990s.

Adam Nayman, a film critic, was 13 when he tried to sneak into a local screening of *Pulp Fiction* in Toronto. The film received an R rating in Canada, meaning you had to be over 18 to watch the movie. Nayman would succeed in seeing the film and later rewatched it several times when it became available on home video. As a kid, he fell in love with the characters in the film and the references to classic movies, including Brian De Palma's *Dressed To Kill*, Walter Hill's cult classic *The Warriors*, and Jean-Luc Godard's *Band of Outsiders*. There was also the film's soundtrack, which featured Kool & The Gang's "Jungle Boogie," Dusty Springfield's "Son of a Preacher Man," and Al Green's "Let's Stay Together."

"*Pulp Fiction* was immersed in the ideas of cool, which has to do with knowledge and frame of reference," Nayman says. "As a 13-year-old, I wanted to see it because I felt like I'd be smarter. I felt like participating in this movie's release was a way to show that I *got* it. This was the biggest thing that ever happened in terms of what was taste-making in the teenage cinephile circle."

After *Pulp Fiction*, Nayman eagerly anticipated Tarantino's next film, *Jackie Brown*, an adaptation of the Elmore Leonard 1992 novel "Rum Punch." The film's emotional core would be centered around two characters, Jackie, played by Pam Grier, and Max, whose role went to Robert Forster. After the success of *Pulp Fiction*, Tarantino decided to partner with Jackson again, casting him as a dangerous Los Angeles–based black-market drugs and guns dealer named Ordell Robbie, who would be the main antagonist in the film. In one of the scenes, Jackson's character has to hand over $10,000 in cash. He reaches into the chair next to him to show the money and holds up a Raptors-branded black duffel bag. The team had provided Jackson with plenty of merchandise during his stay in Toronto, from hats to jerseys to a leather jacket he often wore sitting courtside. He was also given a duffel bag, which Jackson brought to the set of *Jackie Brown*, asking the prop manager if it would be okay to use in the scene. "He said yes, and Quentin didn't mind either," he recalls. "So I got to say, 'Got it right here in my Raptor bag.'"

Nayman went to a *Jackie Brown* screening at the Hollywood Theater on the east side of Yonge Street, north of St. Clair Avenue, within walking distance of his house, and remembers the entire theater applauding the reference to the Raptors.

"It brought the house down," Nayman says. "I remember laughing and just being like, 'Where did that come from?'"

Celebrity sightings would become a part of the appeal of going to a Raptors game at the SkyDome, but the team relied on a core group to provide in-game entertainment at the stadium every night. It included Kenny Solway, who managed the game-day script; Ryan Bonne, the team mascot; and Herbie Kuhn, the public address announcer. "We worked really hard for every piece of entertainment to have its own brand," Nishino says. "The mascot and all his little bits of humor, from being self-deprecating to being a bit saucy, was Ryan's brand. Even Herbie was his own brand. He engaged with the fans and helped bring things on the Jumbotron like the kiss cam to life." (When fans were asked to participate in an exit survey rating the overall entertainment quality at the game as they left the stadium, the Raptor mascot placed number one in terms of what fans thought was the most entertaining.)

The Raptors also assembled a dance team, which Tamara Mose managed. Before the start of the 1995–96 season, Mose was a 21-year-old working retail at Gentlemen's Court at Eaton Centre and as a go-go dancer at Phoenix nightclub. The Guelph, Ontario, native took ballet lessons growing up, discovered jazz dance and hip-hop as a teenager, and had flown to Los Angeles and auditioned to be part of The Fly Girls dancing troupe on the popular Fox sketch-comedy show *In Living Color*. After beating over 500 dancers for the role, Mose started rehearsing with the dance crew and even taped a few episodes on set when she received news her visa application had been rejected. Mose moved back to Toronto.

"I was dating someone. He was a designer and had submitted a bunch of logo ideas to the Raptors," she recalls. "The team sent him a letter and told him they weren't accepting unsolicited designs. I started thinking, 'Wait a second. They're gonna need some kind of a dance team, and this is something I can do.' So I put together a reel of my *In Living Color* clips and a résumé and mailed it to them." Mose landed an interview with Cooper, who hired her to be the coordinator and choreographer of the dance team.

When it came time to brainstorm a name for the squad, Mose wanted something hip and related to the team's nickname. She kept coming back to how raptors traveled in packs. The "Dance Pack" sounded perfect. But something wasn't right. After thinking about it for a few more days, Mose realized the name needed more of an urban feel. So the Dance Pak was born.

Over 400 applicants arrived at the Westin Harbour Castle Hotel in downtown Toronto for an audition to be part of the Dance Pak. Mose wanted the team to reflect the diversity of the city. She also wanted to hire both men and women. The Dance Pak wasn't going to be a bunch of cheerleaders who wore skimpy clothing and waved pom poms during timeouts, an idea that had become in vogue in the NBA in the late 1970s when Los Angeles Lakers Jerry Buss introduced the Laker Girls. They were going to be live-event entertainers with expertise in dance.

Vanessa Cobham, an 18-year-old with jazz and hip-hop dance experience, remembers walking into the Westin Harbour listening to Blackstreet on her Walkman. She lived in Ajax, Ontario, and had begged her mother to drive her to the audition. "I had never seen anything like it," Cobham recalls. "I grew up in a small town, and now I get there, and there are hundreds and hundreds of girls." As one of the 50 dancers who made the first cut, she was invited to the Randolph Academy for the Performing Arts for a second tryout. After another impressive audition, Cobham was one of 20 people hired to be part of the Dance Pak.

As a high schooler, Cobham rode the GO Train three times a week to rehearsals. She would tell her classmates about being part of a pro basketball team's dance team, but no one believed her until one of her teachers saw Cobham on television during a Raptors game. The SkyDome also became a place for the Dance Pak to finish their schoolwork. "In between our performances," Cobham recalls, "I would be doing my calculus homework."

One of three men on the team, Chris Medina, was studying at the University of Toronto at the time and would do his schoolwork on the subway to the game. In between in-game performances, he would take 15-minute power naps. "I would go to the closet and sleep," Medina recalls. "They would knock on the door and say, 'It's time to go perform,' and I would wake up and perform."

Mose helped liven up the atmosphere at the SkyDome in the first year with various dance routines. The team would dance to Michael Jackson one night, salsa dance another, and occasionally entertain the home fans with a disco set. Mose worked with music composer Orin Isaacs to create several original dance numbers. Popular dances, including the Tootsee Roll, the Robocop, and the Roger Rabbit, became part of the routine. Mose says it took time for the audience to learn the rhythms of the in-game entertainment. "We had to teach fans how to react at certain points of the game," she says. "We would have to get them hyped up in the fourth quarter. We'd stand and clap. We used to call it 'the 20-minute workout.' It was cardio for us."

The team didn't have a substantial wardrobe budget, so Mose took a do-it-yourself approach. She worked with her designer boyfriend to create daring costumes for the Dance Pak, including an outfit that featured a white dress shirt, and purple unitards, with a fedora to match. Mose helped pick out colorful wigs for the dancers and landed a sponsorship deal to get everyone Indian Motorcycle leather jackets to wear during games. The most memorable costume remains a set of red mechanic suits that the Dance Pak wore regularly. "That's going to go down in history," Mose says. "It was the easiest to put on because it was loose. It didn't matter what body shape you had. We could do any dance move without worrying about anything showing."

The Dance Pak was a transformative experience for many of the members professionally. They would go on to land other gigs in the entertainment industry. Mose made it a point to hire a diverse group of dancers. "It was something I wanted to put forward in terms of a legacy for the dance team," she explains. "I've always thought about diversity and inclusion, including how much the dancers were paid. I did a lot of research and made sure the pay was comparable to the top end of what other NBA teams were paying. I also wanted to make sure we had gender equality and that the team was representative of Toronto. That was important to me."

One of several Filipino dancers hired by Mose was Alma de Jesus, who was born in the Philippines and immigrated to Canada in 1975. Growing up in a predominantly White neighborhood in Hamilton, Ontario, de Jesus was bullied at school and called racial slurs by the other kids. When her father demanded that the principal punish her daughter's classmates, the school decided against any discipline. It made de Jesus grow up thinking what made her different was something she shouldn't be proud of. De Jesus would find joy in dancing, paying for her own classes in high school, and traveling downtown for jazz classes while she studied psychology at McMaster University. After landing a role with the Dance Pak, de Jesus discovered a new Filipino-Canadian community within the dance crew. It included Madonna Gimotea, a Scarborough, Ontario, native who had competed in rhythmic gymnastics at the 1992 Summer Olympics. The two became close friends, and salsa danced through every Latin club in the city. They were joined by another Dance Pak member, Theresa Runstedtler, who grew up with her Filipino mother and German-Canadian father in Kitchener, Ontario. "They were people I didn't have to explain my experience to," Runstedtler says of her friendship with de Jesus and Gimotea. "We just understood certain things about each other."

The Dance Pak was personally rewarding for dancers around the city to come together with a group of like-minded people. "Tamara gave people from different cultural backgrounds an opportunity to share their love for dance and showcase their talent," Medina says. "The color of your skin didn't matter. What mattered was your heart, spirit, and ambition for dancing."

"Where would young Canadians go and practice dancing hip-hop back in those days? Where would you go to get paid to do that and be able to perform with the best dancers in the city? You went to the Dance Pak," Runstedtler adds. "Where did somebody who did not fit the ideal, White, typical blond, skinny girl type go to find community? This was one of those places. You didn't have to be this rigid ideal of this skinny, White body. You could be a different body shape. You could be muscular. You could be curvy. And you would still be considered a good dancer."

The in-arena experience would evolve during the first season. One of the main adjustments was finding the right music for Raptors games. At the start of the season, the SkyDome disc jockey would play Top-40 pop-rock songs and "Jock Jams" tracks. John Bitove Jr. recognized it wasn't the right vibe for an NBA team, so he asked his older brother Jordan to fix the situation. Jordan spent the next week browsing the hip-hop and R&B section at "Sam The Record Man" and returned with a much more appropriate playlist. "I got fined several times by the NBA for going over their 85 decibels rule," Cooper laughs. "The sound system in there sucked, so the only way you could hear it was by cranking it up."

The players approved the in-game music adjustment, but one song would get cut. It was Coolio's "Gangsta's Paradise." A member of the team's front office saw the song title and complained about having any gangster imagery associated with the team.

When it came time to come up with tunes to play when the Raptors shot free throws, The Beatles' "Come Together" became a favorite. Another one was Eddie Money's "Two Tickets To Paradise," which would only play after someone made both free throws. One time, the song was played after Oliver Miller hit his first free throw. When he missed the second shot, a voice came over the speakers to apologize to the Raptors center.

The game ops team brainstormed a series of video clips and sound-bites to use during games. The most popular one involved a character named Sister D, a nun dressed up as a boxer, who would appear on the

Jumbotron regularly during Raptors games, encouraging fans to chant "defense." The team also encouraged fans to stand up and cheer during stoppages in play and would feature the most enthusiastic people from the crowd on the Jumbotron.

During the first season, the game ops team noticed an East Indian man in a turban who showed up to every game, waved his rally towel during every timeout, and cheered on the Raptors more passionately than anyone in the SkyDome. "We couldn't keep him down," Cooper recalls. "I kept telling our camera operator, 'Keep going back to this guy.'" The person's name was Nav Bhatia.

"I met him at one of our first games," Nishino recalls. "He was a wonderful guy. He had a huge heart and a huge personality."

Bhatia moved to Toronto in 1984 with his wife, Arvinder, during the anti-Sikh riots in India and worked odd jobs to pay the bills in a new country until he became a car salesman at a Hyundai dealership. After selling 127 cars in a three-month span, Bhatia, who had trained as a mechanical engineer back home but could not find a job in that field after immigrating to Toronto, had found a new passion. He would eventually become a dealership owner with 145 people reporting to him. When Bhatia bought a pair of Raptors season tickets at the SkyDome, he quickly fell in love with the game and became the most recognizable fan in the stadium. The Raptors decided to name him the team's official "superfan."

"It was a two-way thing," Bitove says. "He loved it because it made him feel like a big shot. We loved it because it represented what we believed was part of the fan base's DNA."

Throughout the season, Cooper and Nishino pushed for more in-game entertainment ideas. "I would listen to anybody," Nishino recalls. "Whenever we looked at each other and wondered if we could do something, the answer was usually, 'Sure, why not.'" Some ideas would turn out much better in the brainstorming process than in execution. When the team tried throwing CDs into the crowd during one game, they realized the sharp edges of the compact disc jewel case could injure someone and result in a lawsuit. A parachute drop prize giveaway was also shelved after a member of the crowd got hurt.

The team did not stop with their giveaways because they always brought the crowd to their feet.

"When we needed to get people riled up when there were two minutes left, they were down four, and we needed people out of the seats, we gave them free shit," Cooper explains. "We had a gun that would shoot t-shirts into the stand. People went crazy."

A segment called "60 Seconds of Madness" was introduced, where the game ops team spent a whole minute during a stoppage in play tossing t-shirts into the stands.

"Everyone loves free stuff," Solway says. "You had all these people sitting courtside spending tens of thousands of dollars, and clearly they could afford them and many other things. The level of enthusiasm court-side was just as high as those people sitting up in the nosebleeds in terms of 'Hey, give me a free t-shirt!' I was like, 'Really? You want this free t-shirt?'"

With a more modern approach to in-game entertainment than the other pro sports teams in the city, the game ops team was helping to turn the SkyDome into an acceptable place to watch a basketball game, even though the views were often terrible, and the on-court product left much to be desired for.

"We set a tone for sport and entertainment in Toronto," Cooper says. "We woke Toronto up to what hip was. We set a bar and gave everyone else permission to try new things. This was a town stuck in tradition and liked to say, 'We don't do it that way. We don't do those things.' We gave all the other teams permission to say, 'Okay, this is who we are, and we're proud of who we are.'"

The game ops team accomplished a lot during the first season. So is there anything Cooper would have changed?

"Be in an actual basketball arena instead of a baseball stadium," he says.

Part Three
Wins and Lessons

"They Should Have Been 73—9"

On March 18, 1995, Michael Jordan returned to the NBA with a two-word fax from his agent David Falk, which read: "I'm Back."

The best player in the game had surprised the entire sports world when he announced his retirement in October 1993, just several months after averaging 41.0 points, 8.5 rebounds, and 6.3 assists in the 1993 NBA Finals and leading the Chicago Bulls to a third straight championship. "The desire isn't there," Jordan said at his retirement press conference. "When I lose the sense of motivation and the sense to prove something as a basketball player, it's time for me to move away from the game. It's not because I don't love the game. I always will. I just feel that I have reached the pinnacle of my career."

At the age of 30, he was walking away from the game.

The following year and a half would see Jordan transition to professional baseball, a sport he had played growing up. The Chicago White Sox signed him to a minor-league contract and invited him to spring training. Reporters saw the entire thing as a publicity stunt, and after Jordan hit .152 in spring training, they believed the ill-advised pursuit was over. The White Sox demoted Jordan to their Double-A team, the Birmingham Barons.

Was the most famous athlete in the world going to ride the bus as a minor-league baseball player?

To everyone's surprise, Jordan flew to Birmingham, struck out twice, and went 0-for-3 as the starting right fielder against the Chattanooga Lookouts in his minor-league debut. Over 130 media members were credentialed for the game. The Barons set an attendance record that season, drawing 467,867 fans. After a 13-game hit streak sparked whispers of a potential promotion to the majors, Jordan went into a midseason slump and finished with a .202 batting average in 127 games. He never received a call-up to join the White Sox.

In March 1995, Jordan was prepared to begin his second year as a pro baseball player. There was a player strike in Major League Baseball. Instead of crossing the picket line and joining a group of replacement players at spring training with the White Sox, Jordan issued a statement announcing his retirement from baseball. The 1994–95 NBA regular season was wrapping up and everyone wondered if Jordan would return to the Bulls.

In their first season without Jordan, the team had won 55 games. They were led by Scottie Pippen, who finished third in MVP voting, but the team fell short in their bid for a fourth consecutive championship, losing to the rival New York Knicks in the second round. The Bulls had taken a step back in their second season without Jordan. With a month left in the regular season, they were a middle-of-the-pack team in the East, hovering around .500. Jordan started to make regular appearances at the team's practice facility in Deerfield, Illinois, participating in informal workouts and playing one-on-one with his former teammates. In late March 1995, he finally issued that famous two-word fax via his agent and returned to the NBA.

The next day, he was in the starting lineup at Market Square Arena in Indiana against the Pacers. Wearing the number 45 (his original number 23 was considered retired), Jordan shot 7-for-28 from the field and scored 19 points in an overtime loss. It was the highest-rated NBA regular-season game in 20 years. Jordan would shake off his slow start and hit a game-winning jumper at the buzzer in his fourth game back. Three days later, he went into Madison Square Garden and scored 55 points against the Knicks. In 17 regular-season games, Jordan averaged 26.9 points, 6.9 rebounds, and 5.3 assists. The Bulls went 13–4 to finish the season and beat the Charlotte Hornets in the first round, setting up a matchup against the Orlando Magic.

Led by Shaquille O'Neal and Anfernee Hardaway, the Magic were the up-and-coming team in the league, and they would cement their claim as the best team in the East by beating the Bulls in six games. At the end of Game 1, Magic guard Nick Anderson forced a turnover on Jordan in the final seconds to steal the game for Orlando. "Number 45 is not number 23," Anderson said after the win. "I couldn't have done that to number 23." Those comments would linger with Jordan for the entire summer.

Ron Harper, who started in the backcourt next to Jordan, still remembers walking into the locker room after the Magic's series-clinching win at the United Center in Chicago in Game 6. "We're going to start working out tomorrow," Jordan told him. "They want to see number 23? I'm going to give them number 23."

Even though he was going to spend most of the summer filming the live-action sports animated comedy *Space Jam*, Jordan wasn't going to allow his schedule to prevent him from preparing for the 1995–96 season. He asked Warner Bros. Studios to build a full-length basketball court on their studio lot and worked with personal trainer Tim Grover on a training program to get him back into basketball shape. Every morning on set, Jordan would work out for 30 minutes, shoot his scenes, then go to the weight room for an hour and a half during lunch break. In the evening, he invited college and NBA players to scrimmage.

Nathaniel Bellamy Jr., the movie's basketball coordinator, helped organize the runs. "You needed special passes to get in," he says. "There was an entertainment center with a big-screen TV, a sound system, a locker room with showers, weight machines specifically for Michael, a card table, and a putting green. It cost about $10,000 a week to air condition the place." The place was named "the Jordan Dome."

Charles O'Bannon of the UCLA Bruins remembers being in awe when he got the invite. "We tried to act like we were supposed to be there, but we were college kids," he says. "Between games, we would sit around, hang out, and guys would just stare at Michael."

The games were intense and competitive, and Jordan set the tone. Kris Johnson, another member of the UCLA team, remembers one evening when Jordan got into a back-and-forth with Lakers forward Cedric Ceballos, who also wore 23. "So Michael is isolated against Cedric. He's palming the ball and gives him a bunch of jab fakes," Johnson recalls. "At the same time, he's telling him, 'Why are you wearing that number? Why you wear my number, man? You make my number look bad. Take that off.' Then boom, he dunks on him and says, 'Take my number off. Don't ever wear my number again.'"

The Jordan Dome became a spot for A-list celebrities to hang out and watch the best hoopers in the world. The Hollywood stars who dropped by included George Clooney, Halle Berry, Angela Bassett, Will Smith, Mark Hamill, Clint Eastwood, and Kevin Costner. The other NBA players who had a cameo role in *Space Jam*, including Charles Barkley and Patrick Ewing, were regulars at the runs and the late-night card game table. It was Ewing's teammate Charles Oakley, a former teammate of Jordan's, who became the star of the scrimmages. "Charles played like there was money on the line," Bellamy says. "He was hitting people and giving hard fouls."

After a summer of filming, working out, and trash talking his friends, Jordan returned to Chicago for training camp, ready to reclaim his spot as the best player in the world and prepared to lead his team to a fourth NBA championship. The front office had spent the off-season upgrading the roster. They had shed B.J. Armstrong's salary in the expansion draft and traded for power forward Dennis Rodman, landing the best rebounder in the league and upgrading their defense. Jordan switched back to the number 23 jersey, and Chicago entered the season hoping to reclaim their status as a contender in the Eastern Conference. Phil Taylor, *Sports Illustrated*'s lead NBA writer, remembers walking into the

Bulls locker room before a preseason game in Peoria, Illinois, and having a one-on-one conversation with Jordan.

"This is how little fanfare there was around them," he says.

After starting the season with a 23–2 record, the Bulls had everyone's attention. Jordan was again the best player in the world, averaging over 30 points per night. Pippen was the best number two option in the league, and the team was managing Rodman's personality in the locker room and getting significant contributions from him on the floor. The Bulls were not just winning games. They were destroying opponents on a nightly basis. During a stretch of the season when Chicago went 31–1 over a four-month span, they won by an average of 14.5 points. Jim Cleamons, who passed on an opportunity to become Toronto's head coach and remained an assistant in Chicago, remembers the historic year. "The winning just became infectious," he recalls. "The guys realized they were having a phenomenal run and wanted to win as many games as they could."

By the All-Star break, the Bulls were 42–5 and a national attraction everywhere they went. The team drew sold-out crowds in every arena they visited. Ahmad Rashad was a close friend of Jordan's and worked for NBC, which covered a significant number of Bulls games for the national audience. "Their season was like a tour," he says. "Every night, it was the biggest game in town. There was nothing quite like it."

After a six-game win streak at the start of March, the Bulls were 54–7. They were championship favorites and threatening to accomplish something historic. The Los Angeles Lakers had set the record for regular-season wins during the 1971–72 season. The team had put together a record 33-game win streak during the season and went 69–13. Over two decades later, the Bulls were on pace to break the record. Following a 21-point win over the Knicks at home, Chicago brought their 60–7 record to Toronto for the season's final matchup with the expansion team.

On March 24, 1996, a record-setting crowd of 36,131, the largest ever for a basketball game in Canada, packed the SkyDome on a Sunday afternoon to watch the Raptors take on Jordan and the Bulls.

With Sharone Wright on the injured list with back spasms, the spot start at power forward went to Carlos Rogers, who opened the scoring with a thunderous one-handed dunk. Jordan would draw "Oohs" and "Ahhs" from the home crowd a minute later as he responded with an up-and-under layup at the basket to get the visitors on the board. The Raptors would push the pace and open up an early seven-point lead. Just as it looked like they would run away with the first quarter, Jordan hit a patented fadeaway jumper to stop the run. On the next trip up the floor, he drove to the basket and missed a layup. A familiar face was in the paint to grab the offensive rebound and clean up the possession with a put-back. It was John Salley, who signed with Chicago in early March after the Raptors waived him. With Dennis Rodman serving a six-game suspension after head-butting referee Ted Bernhardt and Luc Longley sitting out with knee tendinitis, the Bulls would patch together a frontline of Salley, Dickey Simpkins, and Bill Wennington, a Montreal, Quebec, native who had been taken 16th overall by the Dallas Mavericks in 1985. After hitting another midrange jumper, Jordan was already at nine points. He smiled at Alvin Robertson. The two were Team USA teammates at the 1984 Summer Olympics in Los Angeles, where they won a gold medal together. The two had become friends but remained rivals on the court.

The Raptors had gone toe-to-toe with the Bulls in their previous three matchups. Chicago had barely escaped with a 92–89 win in a January visit to the SkyDome, exhaling at the buzzer when Oliver Miller's game-tying three-point attempt went wide. The Raptors had a seven-point lead at halftime, but Jordan scored 38 points, including 15 in the fourth quarter, to narrowly avoid an upset. In the fourth and final meeting, Toronto was once again pushing the best team in the league. After the end of a back-and-forth first quarter, the Raptors held a 28–23 lead. Back-to-back threes from Steve Kerr would tie the game a few minutes into the second quarter. Another fadeaway jumper from Jordan over Robertson would give Chicago the lead. On the next possession, he drove toward the basket and drew contact with Robertson, who picked up his third personal foul. As Jordan hit both free throws to put the Bulls ahead by four, Robertson headed to the bench. Midway through the second quarter, it was Doug Christie's turn to be Jordan's primary defender.

Growing up in Seattle, Washington, Christie learned the game of basketball in the streets, spending many afternoons and late evenings on the playground, even when there was a downpour outside. He was raised by his mother, Norma, a single mom who worked as a grocery clerk at the neighborhood store and supported him in chasing his hoop dreams. But the inner-city neighborhood drew Doug toward the wrong crowd. In middle school, Norma sent her son to Longview, Washington, to spend time with his dad, John. It was the first time the two met. Doug and John played softball, went on fishing and hunting trips, and talked about growing up and learning to be an adult. It was the perfect time for Doug to have a father figure come into his life. He decided to become more than just a streetballer. Basketball would be Doug's ticket to do something meaningful with his life. He met Mark Morris High School head coach Dave Denny, who molded Doug into a player with the athleticism and fundamentals to be one of the best players in the state.

After nearly two years with his father, Christie moved back home to live with his mom in Seattle. In his senior season at Rainier Beach High School, he led the school to its first-ever state championship and accepted an offer to play at Pepperdine University. After averaging 19.5 points, 5.9 rebounds, and 4.8 assists in his junior year at Pepperdine, Christie entered the 1992 NBA draft and was selected 17th overall. It was a dream come true. He was a member of the Seattle SuperSonics. It was his hometown team, and Christie still had memories as a nine-year-old watching the Sonics, led by Dennis Johnson and Gus Williams, win the 1979 NBA championship.

But the dream scenario turned into a nightmare. Before his rookie season, Christie became mired in a public contract dispute with the team. The Sonics offered him a $500,000 annual salary, but Christie wanted $1.5 million, the same amount given to Victor Alexander, the previous year's 17th pick. The two sides started going back and forth in the local newspapers, and the verbal jabs became personal. "There were things that were said about my mom that just weren't right," Christie says. "They came at it wrong." After missing training camp and the first half of the season, Christie was traded to the Los Angeles Lakers in February 1993. At his introductory press conference, reporters compared him to Magic Johnson. In his two seasons in Los Angeles, Christie's play did not exactly evoke memories of the "Showtime" Lakers. He was traded to New York before the start of the 1994–95 season.

Christie walked into Knicks head coach Pat Riley's office for a pre-season meeting and sat down for a conversation that would change the trajectory of his NBA career. "He pulled no punches," Christie recalls. "He said, 'Look. You're not going to play. I got my guys, and that's who we're going with. What I suggest to you is that you find something that you can do that'll keep you in this league for a long time.'" The Knicks had taken the baton from the "Bad Boy" Pistons and become the most physical team in the NBA. Heading into his third year in the league and already joining his third team, Christie needed to be honest with himself. If he wanted to stick around and have a long career, Christie would have to heed Riley's advice and earn his minutes by being a defensive stopper.

Even though he only appeared in 12 games during his first season in New York, Christie spent every off-day working to become a better all-around pro. "I would get to the gym at eight in the morning. I'd lift, run a couple of miles, go shoot, practice, cool down, then stay in the gym until eight at night," Christie says. "Guys like Derek Harper, Charles Oakley, Anthony Mason, and Patrick Ewing taught me so much about toughness, competitiveness, and this other side of the floor that I usually ignored. Defensive skills became something I wanted to possess. Not everybody wanted to play defense, but also not everybody could do it. I would watch tapes of players and try to figure out how I could take things away from them. I would figure out what they liked to do, what they didn't like, and how many dribbles they took to score. I was trying to figure out how to take things away from them when we played." While he studied every player around the league, Christie waited for his opportunity. After the 1994–95 season, the Knicks parted ways with Riley. His replacement would be Don Nelson, a more offensive-minded coach. Christie was pinned to the bench during the 1995–96 season, unable to crack Nelson's rotation. He was moved to Toronto at the trade deadline.

In his first practice with the Raptors, Christie showed up at Glendon College and found Isiah Thomas on the court. The general manager had ditched his usual suit-and-tie look and was in sweats, getting shots up with the rest of the team. He challenged Christie to a game of one-on-one. "I knocked him down," Christie recalls. "We kept playing and had a great conversation after. My wife was there watching. When we got to our car, she said, 'Ain't that your boss? You knocked him down. Are you crazy?' I said, 'That's what he wanted to see. He wanted to see who I was and what I was willing to do.'"

When the two finished scrimmaging, the general manager sat with Christie to chat about his long-term role with the team. "He said, 'Look. I watched you in college. I watched you in the NBA. I know you can play,'" Christie recalls. "He told me, 'You're gonna play, so don't worry about messing up. Basketball is about mistakes. Just try not to make the same mistake twice. Don't look over at the bench when you make a mistake. Just go play. So be in shape because you're going to play a lot.' I said, 'I won't let you down, bro. Let's go.'"

It was the first of many sit-downs between the two. When Christie found out he was living in the same Queens Quay condo as Thomas, he started visiting his general manager weekly and continuing his journey of becoming a better defender. "He opened my eyes to mastering the game of basketball. They were incredible conversations. I took so many gems from them," Christie says. "He had me keep a journal. There were these workbooks, so whenever we played a player, there was a page where you would put the player's name, their averages, and what you would hold that player to that night. There was this next column where you would write down what actually happened, and at the bottom, you could put in your notes. Some nights I was guarding six guys, sticking everyone from point guards to small forwards. Suddenly, I was like, 'Okay, he likes to go left. This guy likes to go right. Are they strong? Are they weak? Are they in shape?' There was so much information."

Teammates started to see Christie's new-found approach to defense in practice. "He was a tough motherfucker," says Vincenzo Esposito. "He would guard every position. I loved practicing against him even though it was so hard. He was probably the best defender I've ever played against."

Christie was also the perfect backcourt mate for Stoudamire, who was initially upset at seeing Willie Anderson get traded. "Then Isiah said we were getting Doug, and I said, 'Shit. Okay.' That made it easier," Stoudamire says. "He could play point and allow me to play off the ball. He guarded the best perimeter player. He took so much pressure off me."

Christie remembers Stoudamire being his biggest supporter. "I would be in someone's jersey, and we would go to the huddle, and Damon would be like, 'Hold up. Wait, wait. Is nobody going to say it? D was in his shit,'" Christie recalls. "Damon was a scorer. I always told him, 'Do your thing. I'm here. I will guard your guy some nights because their point guard might be their best player. I'm not tripping. I got you.' He respected that. We had a great vibe."

As Robertson walked to the bench in the middle of the second quarter, Malone signaled for Christie to switch defensive assignments and become Jordan's primary defender. "I was hitting him, holding him, pushing him," Christie says. "It was like streetball at the highest level."

The home crowd was getting an up-close look at the Raptors' backcourt of the future. Stoudamire had averaged 22.7 points and 11.7 assists in his first three games against the Bulls. After their first game, Jordan told reporters he needed head coach Phil Jackson to switch up the defensive assignments in the second half so he didn't have to spend all game chasing the rookie around. Chicago was the best defensive team in the league but had no answers for stopping the rookie guard all season.

"Damon could score on the Monstars," Murray says. "He was a natural-born scorer. He could shoot it. He could create his own space to get his shot off. He was fast enough to get by you. He could score at all three levels. That was a nightmare matchup for anyone."

Stoudamire's team-high 14 points in the first half gave Toronto a two-point lead over the Bulls at halftime. The rookie was once again leading the way on the court. In his first season, Stoudamire had established himself as the leader of the team.

A classic was unfolding at the SkyDome between an expansion franchise and a team chasing history, and Eddie Williams was in the stadium to witness it in person. The evening before, he hosted a party and invited players from both teams to attend. Williams moved to Toronto from London, England, when he was 11. He grew up in the Little Italy neighborhood of the city and paid six dollars to watch an NBA exhibition game at Maple Leaf Gardens. Williams traveled to Niagara Falls to watch NCAA hoops and even pooled together enough gas money once with friends and drove to Syracuse to watch Leo Rautins. After studying recreation and leisure services at Humber College and working for an event-planning services company, he organized an event on his own for the first time at 18. Inside a Portuguese banquet hall, Williams served Jamaican beef patties and Sarasoda, a go-to drink in the 1980s advertised as a non-alcoholic beverage but widely known to contain 0.9% alcohol, which was perfect for the young adults in attendance who wanted to feel a slight buzz. He started to promote and organize parties across the city and soon made enough money to pay his bills. Williams created a company called Party People Productions. The small production crew of seven people started to work with the local nightclub scene and were now planning parties on a much bigger scale.

Williams had met Thomas at a guest-speaking event before the start of the season. "He told me the players were going to be looking to do endorsements and appearances," he recalls. Williams connected several players with the Don Valley Lexus-Toyota car dealership and helped them secure four-runner trucks when they arrived in Toronto for training camp. He started hanging out with the players, introducing them to the club scene. One evening, Williams threw out the idea of throwing a weekend party towards the end of the season. Robertson liked the idea, and the two started looking at a date that made sense. They landed on a Saturday in late March. The Bulls would be in town on an off-day. Robertson convinced Jordan to endorse the party officially and agree to put his name on the flyer. It became the biggest party of Williams' career. "I remember having meeting after meeting about it," he says. "I had never planned an event with more than 200 people. The closest thing was probably a wedding reception. So this was a big deal."

Williams had worked with the event staff at the Holiday Inn on King Street West in downtown Toronto, and decided to host the party there. Three banquet halls inside the venue were transformed into a proper-looking dance floor with custom lights and wall decorations. A local DJ was hired. The live entertainment included a comedy set. The in-house catering would provide Caribbean dishes for the guests. An indoor area was set up for smoking cigars. Security guards were hired and would be assigned to every NBA player who entered the venue. Over 800 people, featuring the city's most well-known entrepreneurs, influencers, and athletes, attended the event. The most important person of the evening would show up at one in the morning.

"As soon as Michael walked in the room," Williams says, "the girls started getting prim and proper to get a better vantage point."

Murray remembers leaving the party at around two and looking across the room to see most of the Bulls starters enjoying themselves. "They were smoking cigars and having a great time," he recalls. "They were still there when we started to trickle out." When the party officially ended at four in the morning, Williams says Jordan and his teammates were among the last to leave.

The following afternoon, Murray walked onto the court an hour before tip-off and noticed something strange. No one was warming up on the Bulls' end of the floor. Murray finished his warm-up routine, walked back to the locker room, and ran into Harper.

"He said, 'Man, we're all still hungover in the locker room,'" Murray recalls. "He told me they didn't get back to their hotel until eight in the morning."

The Bulls might have looked a step slow to start the game, but they woke up after halftime. "They were out of it in the first half," Murray says, "and then suddenly they flipped the switch." Led by Jordan, the Bulls came out of the locker room and erased the halftime deficit, taking a six-point lead in the third quarter.

Standing courtside by the players' tunnel entrance, Thomas watched as his expansion team appeared to be letting the game slip away. The first season had involved a lot of growing pains on the court, but the general manager kept reminding himself to take a longer view of the roster building. The Raptors were 17–49, but Stoudamire and Christie had the potential to become a formidable backcourt. Wright, Žan Tabak, and Oliver Miller gave the team a solid big-man rotation. Rogers remained a project but had room to grow. Murray had been a godsend after joining the team at the end of training camp. Thomas' inner circle of trust included Stoudamire, Miller, and Murray. He would regularly update the three players on the team's roster construction. "We were like a mom-and-pop organization," Stoudamire explains. "He would pull us aside and tell us what he was thinking and what direction he wanted to go. He would talk to us about the shaping of the roster."

Murray remembers running into Thomas after one of his first practices with the Raptors. "He was watching us. Afterward, he came up to me and nodded his head. I was like, 'What?' He said, 'I see you. I see that gangster in you. I see it coming out,'" Murray laughs. "He made me feel tougher. He made me more fearless. He saw me in a different light than anyone else. It gave me so much confidence as a young player. He was always there for you. He was a big brother. He was available to us."

After the trade deadline, Murray replaced Anderson in the starting lineup and started playing the best stretch of basketball of his career. At the beginning of the homestand, he made six three-pointers and scored a career-high 40 points against Denver, besting the 31 points he had scored a week earlier. He had signed with Toronto looking to prove himself, and now Murray was the number-two option on offense behind Stoudamire.

"I remember having a conversation with Damon at the start of the season. I asked him what he wanted out of his first year," Murray recalls. "We were candid with each other. He said, 'I want to be Rookie of the Year and average 20 and 10.' I said, 'You can get 20 in your sleep. I can help you get the 10 assists. Find me on the catch and shoot. I'm not going to miss. I'm locked in.'"

Trailing by six in the third quarter, Murray calmly hit a three-pointer to cut the lead in half. On the next possession, he rose up for another shot from beyond the arc, tying the game.

The Bulls would take a four-point lead into the fourth quarter when the one-on-one matchup between Jordan and Christie intensified. Jordan drove to the basket for a layup on one end, drawing a foul on Christie in the process. The three-point play put Chicago back ahead by two. Christie would respond with a three-pointer to put the Raptors back ahead on the next possession. After Jordan missed a midrange jumper, Miller would sprint the length of the floor, spinning to the basket on a post-up for a layup that put Toronto ahead by three. Out of a timeout, Jordan responded with another fadeaway jumper over the outstretched arms of two Raptors defenders.

On the next trip down, he dribbled inside the three-point arc, pulling up for a midrange jumper, which swished through the net. The home crowd gasped in unison as Jordan walked back upcourt with his tongue hanging out, staring at the Raptors bench. On the sideline, Malone could only grin and shake his head.

"Are you ever gonna miss?" Malone yelled at Jordan.

"Brendan," he responded, "you know better than that."

The "Bad Boy" Pistons developed a rivalry with an up-and-coming Bulls team in the 1980s, and Malone was widely credited with coming up with a scheme to slow down the best scorer in the league during the playoffs. The Pistons deployed "the Jordan Rules," a set of defensive principles devised by Malone. "We didn't want him going baseline, so we pushed him toward the elbow," he explains. "That's when we would double-team him. If he had the ball up top, we would make him go left. We would double him from the top if we got the ball in the low post." In consecutive years, the Pistons executed the game plan flawlessly and defeated the Bulls in the Eastern Conference Finals on their way to back-to-back championships. Malone had implored the Raptors to follow "the Jordan Rules" before the game but also recognized it was not a foolproof plan. "You don't stop Michael," Malone says. "You just hope to contain him."

With just over two minutes left, Jordan hit another midrange jumper to put the Bulls ahead.

104–103.

Robertson could only give his friend a playful shove as the two jogged back upcourt. Jordan would finish with 36 points on 14-of-22 shooting in 39 minutes. Moments later, he would hit two free throws to extend the lead.

106–103.

With a minute left in the game, Stoudamire would respond, driving to the basket, drawing a foul from Jordan, and sinking his first free throw to set a career-high with 30 points. The second free throw would bounce off the rim, but there was Christie, jumping over two players for the offensive rebound and getting a foul call. He would miss both free throws, but Stoudamire chased down the rebound along the baseline, finding Miller for a two-handed slam. The wild sequence had tied the game with 50 seconds left.

106–106.

The crowd was on their feet and cheering on their expansion team to pull off the upset. A hush would fall over the stadium on the ensuing possession. Jordan caught the ball at the top of the key, took a dribble to get inside the arc, and hit another fadeaway jumper to put the visitors back ahead. Timeout, Toronto.

108–106.

On the inbounds play, Miller would throw a perfect pass to Murray as he curled to the basket for an open layup. It was delirium again.

108–108.

On the next possession, it appeared Jordan was going to put the Bulls ahead. He drove to the basket and saw an open lane for a layup. Christie was there to chase down the attempt and swat the ball right into Miller's lap. The Raptors bench roared in approval. The decibel level at the SkyDome was at a record high. Jordan committed a loose-ball foul in the process. Miller stepped to the line and hit one of two to give the Raptors the lead. Timeout, Chicago.

109–108.

The game would come down to the final play.

On the sideline, Malone huddled up with his players. He grabbed his whiteboard and started diagramming their defensive strategy. Every player sitting on the bench knew where the ball was going. Malone decided to play man-to-man and told each player to stay on their assignment.

We're not double-teaming Michael. We're going to make him take a tough shot.

The challenge of guarding Jordan had been shared by Robertson and Christie throughout the game.

"Those two guys did the best job they could," Murray says. "Whether he's hungover or not, that's the baddest man on the planet you're guarding. This is what people don't understand. The hardest part about guarding Michael Jordan is the 35 shots he's going to shoot. You know that every time he touches the ball, there's a possibility of the ball going up. You have to keep him from shooting the ball, and if he does shoot it, you just gotta make sure it's not a good look."

Malone wanted Robertson to take the assignment on the final possession.

"Coach said, 'Alvin, I want you to stick Mike,'" Christie recalls. "The huddle got quiet, and Alvin goes, 'Coach. I think the young fella's been doing a good job on him. Let him go ahead and guard him.' For me, that was a defining moment in my career. That was your sensei telling you, 'You're ready.' That's everything you want as a player, for your coach to say, 'We're gonna do this,' and then for the player you're learning from to say, 'No, we're gonna do this.' So I said, 'I got him.' I mean, it was Michael, and nobody's got Michael like that, but I said it anyways."

The game has resumed and the seconds are ticking down on the game clock. Christie is following Jordan's every step as he calmly dribbles the ball past the Raptors logo at center court.

14.9 seconds.

Bill Wennington runs to the top of the key to set a screen. Miller switches on Jordan. The Bulls guard loses his dribble as he tries to drive past the Raptors' big man.

8.3 seconds.

The loose ball ends up in the hands of Steve Kerr. Christie has switched over and is right up on him.

6.9 seconds.

The ball swings to Scottie Pippen on the perimeter. He passes it back to Kerr.

4.7 seconds.

As Kerr rises to attempt a go-ahead shot, Christie runs over and contests the three-pointer as it's in the air.

2.9 seconds.

The shot is short.

It takes a bounce off the side of the rim, landing right to Jordan, standing wide-open on the baseline. He catches the ball and, in a single motion, rises and banks in the go-ahead shot.

0.0 seconds.

No one in the stadium knows how to react.

Did the Bulls escape with a buzzer-beater?

The referees quickly step in and wave off Jordan's shot. It had left his hand just after the buzzer sounded.

The Raptors had pulled off the season's biggest upset by a fraction of a millisecond. Malone pumped his fist and acknowledged the home crowd. As teammates embraced one another, Stoudamire stood on the court and took in the enormity of the moment. "That was our championship," he says. Murray hugged his teammates as the fans gave their home team a standing ovation. "There was a different type of energy in the building that afternoon," he recalls. "Everybody was fired up. It was a different atmosphere. Even Herbie Kuhn lost his voice by the end of the game."

"It was pandemonium," Christie adds. "I remember just thinking, 'Did we really do it?' The city was alive that evening. Think about how many fans left that night saying, 'I'm going to buy a Damon Stoudamire jersey.' So many kids probably watched that game at home and started playing basketball the next day."

A year earlier, when Jordan returned to the Bulls and scored 55 points at Madison Square Garden in his fifth game back in the NBA, Christie had watched from the Knicks' bench. After the game, his teammate Monty Williams had asked for Jordan's game-worn sneakers and received them. Christie wasn't going to make the same mistake again. After the victory, he walked into the visitors' locker room and spotted a horde of reporters surrounding Jordan at his locker. The two exchanged eye contact. Jordan asked the media to clear a path for Christie. He explained the reason for the postgame visit. Jordan smiled. He was keeping the sneakers but agreed to sign a game program for Christie's four-year-old daughter. The two exchanged handshakes before Christie joined his teammates in their celebration.

"There was champagne waiting for us when I got back to the locker room," he recalls.

After losing at the SkyDome to the Raptors, the Bulls resumed their march towards the all-time regular-season wins record by winning 11 of their next 12 games. They would set the record in April at Milwaukee, winning their 70th game of the season. The Bulls finished the season with an astonishing 72–10 record. Before the start of the playoffs, Ron Harper went out to lunch with Scottie Pippen. The two were bouncing around ideas for a team slogan for the postseason.

"We were just throwing out ideas. 72–10 this, 72–10 that," Harper recalls. "I said to Scottie, 'I got one. 72–10 don't mean a thing without the ring.' He's like, 'That's kinda hot.' We were just playing around when we said it, but Scottie had a good friend who made t-shirts. So we called him up and told him about our t-shirt idea. We wore them throughout the playoffs."

The Bulls swept the Miami Heat in the first round, eliminated the New York Knicks in five games, and swept Orlando in the Eastern Conference Finals to avenge the previous year's defeat. Jordan scored 45 points in the clincher. The Bulls won the first three games of the NBA Finals and secured their fourth championship of the decade with an 87–75 win over Seattle in Game 6 at the United Center in Chicago.

They would become known as the greatest team ever, but when the 1995–96 Bulls are mentioned in Toronto today, the first thing anyone remembers is how the expansion Raptors made history at the SkyDome on that fateful Sunday afternoon in March.

"That game was special. We made the city so proud. It made us feel good to represent the city of Toronto and the whole country of Canada. We represented them that night with that win. It's still a trademark win in the organization's history. It's part of NBA history," Murray says. "They were 72–10, but they should have been 73–9."

Isiah vs. Brendan

As Doug Smith watched a record-setting crowd at the SkyDome celebrate the biggest win of the Raptors' season, he smiled from his media row seat. The arrival of an expansion franchise in Toronto opened up an opportunity for local sportswriters to find their niche in the basketball space. Smith was eager to jump at the chance to establish himself as the city's best. He started playing basketball at age 15 and followed the NBA closely by consuming a daily diet of newspapers and watching the marquee games on television on the weekends. After playing at Niagara College, Smith graduated from the school's journalism program and landed his first job as a 21-year-old working for *The Tillsonburg News*, covering the local high school sports scene. He would then move to a local newspaper in Woodstock, Ontario, where Smith made the 90-minute drive into Toronto several times a week to cover the Blue Jays at Exhibition Stadium. After working at *The Orangeville Banner* as an assistant managing editor, followed by a brief stint in Newfoundland, he landed a job with *The Toronto Sun* and moved to the city for the first time, living with his brother Paul, who was pursuing a stand-up comedy career.

The *Sun* experience transformed Smith's career. He worked alongside the most prominent sports voices in the country, including Bob Elliott, Wayne Parrish, Lance Hornby, and Scott Morrison, and after starting as a copy editor, he got to pitch his own stories. Smith's first byline in the paper came in 1988. It was the year the romantic comedy *Bull Durham*, starring Kevin Costner and Susan Sarandon, arrived in theaters. Smith loved Costner's character, Crash Davis, who was on a decade-long chase for the minor-league home run record, and decided to find a real-life version of the fictional character. His first long-form feature was on a 32-year-old pitcher in Rochester who had played professionally in the International League for over a decade.

From there, Smith became one of the up-and-coming writers in the city, and learned to develop sources and form relationships with players and front offices. The local sports section was competitive. The *Sun* was fighting with *The Toronto Star* and *The Globe and Mail* to break the news daily. "If you had a quote for your story that they didn't have, you felt great because you beat them. It could be an innocuous quote from a third-line left winger. You won the story if you had it," Smith explains. "We were the underdogs. We were the little paper. We had some bulldog reporters and worked really hard."

In 1991, there was a job opening at *The Canadian Press*. Smith jumped at the opportunity and worked with Steve McAllister on the Blue Jays beat. He still remembers being at the SkyDome to witness Joe Carter's iconic three-run, walk-off home run to clinch the 1993 World Series. "I was in the press box," Smith says. "Steve wrote the main story, and I wrote the sidebar. You couldn't appreciate what you just saw because you had to write. The next day, I was like, 'Holy crap. That was amazing. I was there. I saw this.' Then I was like, 'What's next?'"

John Bitove Jr. won the ownership bid in the same year, and *The Canadian Press* decided they needed someone to start covering the Raptors regularly in 1994. Smith put his hand up. "I thought getting in on the ground floor would be a lot of fun. You don't get a whole lot of startups in this business. You don't get a lot of firsts. I thought it would be neat," he explains. "I also wanted to cover basketball because I knew the sport well."

When Smith returned to the SkyDome in 1995 for the first regular-season game in Raptors' history, the place looked much different than it did when Carter hit his homer. It was now the home of an NBA team.

"It was bizarre," Smith recalls. "When they first said they would play in the SkyDome, we were like, 'How? Where are they going to put the court?' It was the worst basketball venue ever. We sat courtside between the players' benches. The work area was behind the south bleachers down the first-base line. They would tear the building down minutes after the game. There would be tractor trailers moving the bleachers as we were trying to write our stories."

Smith became one of the team's regular beat reporters, joining Craig Daniels of *The Toronto Sun*, Chris Young of *The Toronto Star*, and Neil Campbell of *The Globe and Mail*. Isiah Thomas was the first person to welcome them to their new jobs. "The day he ripped through the logo at the press conference, he pulled us aside and said, 'If you need anything, call me. I won't lie to you. I won't mislead you. If I can't answer your question, I'll tell you,'" Smith recalls. "He would always be available on the phone. I would call his assistant, Jessica Guyor, and say, 'I need to talk to Isiah.' She would ask me when my deadline was. If it was at five, he would always call you at four."

Another person who helped the media find their early-season footing was John Lashway, who would explain concepts including the salary cap and the mechanisms of placing a player on the injured list to the novice reporters. "You put a guy on the injured list back then, and he would lose his roster spot for five games. He went to great lengths to explain those things so we could put them in our story for people to understand," Smith says. "He knew what was important to writers. He also knew that information was currency, and if he gave it to everybody, it would be better for the organization. He never played favorites."

The first season wasn't very competitive among the reporters as everyone tried to figure out how to cover an NBA team throughout an 82-game regular season. "We wanted to get a better story than the other guy, but there wasn't always news every day," Smith explains. "We also weren't sure what the readers wanted. Did they want game stories? Did they want personality-driven stories? It was a balancing act. I moved towards the people-driven stories because not all the games mattered.

They just weren't very good. When they lost five in a row, you couldn't just write, 'Hey, they lost again.'"

Damon Stoudamire received the most coverage from the beat reporters in the first season, but he wasn't always accommodating. "People were tugging at him all the time, and he didn't want to do any of that stuff," Smith says. "That was just his personality. He was a very intense competitor. He hated losing. He could be short with you if you bugged him after a loss."

There are many great memories from the first season. The win over Michael Jordan and the Chicago Bulls was the season's high point, but Smith also remembers a game that took place at the SkyDome five days after the historic upset. It was a 40-point loss at home to the Orlando Magic and the beginning of the end for head coach Brendan Malone.

It started when the front office decided to waive Chris Whitney at the end of training camp. It might have been an innocuous footnote, a player at the end of the roster of an expansion team being released after the preseason. For Malone, it was the start of a season-long struggle to find enough players he could trust. Whitney had impressed in training camp and earned a second-unit role on the team. But the Raptors needed to preserve cap space, and after all, Thomas saw second-round pick Jimmy King as the team's best option to run the offense off the bench. Malone vehemently disagreed.

"Jimmy wasn't a point guard," he says. "When we put him in, we'd lose. When we took him out, we'd start winning."

Malone wanted to win every game possible, even if it came at the expense of developing the younger players on the team. While Stoudamire played 40 minutes every night, a group of players kept waiting for an opportunity that never came. "I always asked Brendan what I needed to do. He would say, 'You're a rookie,'" King recalls. "I would talk to Isiah about it. I told him, 'Just give me an opportunity.' I would play a few games, and then I would sit. We had the conversations, and there was nothing more I could say. All I could do was remain professional."

Another player who never earned Malone's trust was Vincenzo Esposito. "He would say, 'You gotta wait. The way you guys play over there isn't how we play over here,'" he recalls. "I told him to give me an opportunity to play a few minutes, and if I didn't deserve it, he could sit me. He would tell me to get ready a few times and then wouldn't play me. I would play for 40 seconds, and he would kill me as if I was responsible for losing. He would be like, 'What the fuck happened? You're not playing defense. Why'd you take that shot?' I mean, we were down by 28 points. I never understood what he wanted from me. I didn't feel respected as a person. I didn't like how he treated me in front of my teammates. I'm not saying he's a bad man. But in the end, it is what it is. He was an old-fashioned American coach."

Other players, like Tracy Murray, would take Malone's straightforward approach in stride. "Brendan never sugar-coated anything. When we made mistakes, he would light us up. He made guys feel a certain way," he says. "Brendan would say some stuff that would make you mad. I didn't take it personally. We would end up laughing about the things he said to us."

Tony Massenburg says there was a generational gap between the head coach and the players. "The new guys didn't take too well to his old-school-type mentality," he says. "A lot of times, the message can get lost in translation because of how the message is relayed."

The player Malone was toughest on was the one he relied on the most. Throughout the season, the head coach pushed Stoudamire to find a better balance between scoring and sharing the ball with his teammates as the starting point guard. Malone wasn't afraid to check the box score and criticize Stoudamire for hogging the ball too much. He wouldn't be scared to call him out in front of the entire team.

"There's one game that stands out in my mind when it comes to Brendan," Stoudamire recalls. "We were playing Atlanta and they had Mookie Blaylock. We were right there in the fourth quarter. They made a little run. So I'm dribbling to the side and Brendan wanted a timeout. I'm dribbling and I see the Hawks walking to the bench. I said, 'Fuck it.

I'm going to sneak me a layup here.' So I drive to the basket but Mookie sees me and he taps the ball from me from behind and they go back the other way and score. We called the timeout, I walked back to the bench, and Brendan was furious. He was like, 'You motherfucker' and was just yelling at me. Sometimes all you could do was sit there and take it."

During the first season, Malone stayed at the Westin Harbour Castle Hotel, his stay arranged in exchange for season tickets provided by the team to the hotel manager. "I loved Toronto," he says. "I could walk up Yonge Street all the way to St. Michael's hospital and check out all the different neighborhoods in the city." Malone would run into Raptors fans on his long walks during the season, who would compliment him on how hard the team was trying. It would lift the head coach's spirit during the losing streaks, even if it were just for a brief moment.

After every win, Malone usually got a call from Glen Grunwald. He was passing on a message from Thomas, who wanted the head coach to manage Stoudamire's minutes and give the other young players some more rope. The Raptors wanted to see what they had on the roster. "The strategy was not to win as many games as possible," Grunwald says. "Brendan was a very good coach, but he was single-minded and focused on winning games. Isiah didn't want to do too well because he wanted to get a good draft pick. We had to make sure we weren't too good too soon so we could build through the draft."

The idea of not trying to win every game was blasphemous to Malone. *How could you build a team's identity of hard work and defense and ask the players to compete for 48 minutes without trying to win?* "Coaches coach to win. We don't coach to lose," Malone says. "I remember driving to the SkyDome for a game and seeing a man holding his son's hand. They were going to the game. I sat there and thought, 'We're cheating these people by not trying to win a game. We're cheating the players on the team.'"

The phone calls would keep coming after games, but Malone kept coaching to win. He kept Stoudamire on the court for entire games. He relied on his veterans and kept the players he didn't trust on the bench.

He was going to try and win every game. Malone was upset when the team dealt Willie Anderson, Ed Pinckney, and Massenburg at the trade deadline. "Isiah got rid of every good player we had," he says. "He was always trying to strip the roster of quality players."

The front office was hoping for more opportunities to see what players like King, Esposito, and Carlos Rogers could do on the court, but Malone didn't expand his rotation. A week after the deadline, a media luncheon was held in San Antonio. It was when reporters first became aware of friction between the head coach and the front office. Malone and Thomas had a face-to-face conversation at the event. The head coach was honest with his general manager. He couldn't coach to lose.

"I can't do what you want me to do," Malone told Thomas.

The day before the Raptors took down Michael Jordan and the Bulls at the SkyDome, the head coach finished practice at Glendon College when a reporter on the beat pulled him aside. He told Malone the team was going to fire him at the end of the season. The news wasn't surprising to the head coach, but Malone was upset he didn't hear it directly from his general manager. He found Thomas after practice. "Listen," Malone told his general manager. "I'm a grown man. You can talk to me to my face." Thomas did not deny the reporter's claim. The Raptors only played seven players in the win over Chicago the following afternoon. Stoudamire played 46 minutes.

When the buzzer sounded on the most memorable win of the season, Malone rejoiced on the sideline and waved to the sold-out crowd. He looked into the stands and spotted his family. His son, Michael, had made the nine-hour drive from Providence, Rhode Island, to support his father. The joyous day would end with a family dinner in Etobicoke at Grappa, Malone's favorite Italian restaurant in the city.

The head coach also recalls running into Thomas on the court after the win and exchanging a terse handshake. "He shook my hand and congratulated me," Malone says. "But I could tell he wasn't happy."

He was right. After the game, Thomas sat down with John Bitove Jr. at the owner's home and asked for permission to fire Malone the following day. "He was pissed," Bitove recalls. "I had to calm him down all night. I said, 'This might be one of the greatest moments in Toronto sports history. Sit down, have a drink, and relax.' That was not a fun night. The trust had ended between them. When the trust deteriorates, it's like a divorce. There's only so much you can do. I would try to talk to each of them, but I don't think they would even get in the same room at that point. It was really bad. From then on, every game, I was like, 'Can we just get through the season?'"

Two nights after their historic upset win, the Raptors played at the SkyDome to much less fanfare against Atlanta. Stoudamire scored a career-high 30 points for a second straight game in a loss. Thomas was not thrilled to see his head coach play the franchise's most important player for the entire 48 minutes in the defeat. Stoudamire sat out the following night's defeat in Philadelphia with knee tendinitis. The Raptors would return home for a Friday night matchup against the Orlando Magic.

On the morning of the game, the headline on the front page of *The Toronto Star* sports section read: RAPTOR BRASS FEUD HEATING UP. "Damon Stoudamire's knee injury has heated up a brewing battle of wills in the Raptors' front office and may shorten Brendan Malone's coaching career in Toronto," wrote Mary Ormsby. "The prized point guard, a leading contender for the NBA's Rookie of the Year award, is the central figure in a philosophical dispute that has simmered all season between general manager Isiah Thomas and Malone regarding floor time for younger Raptors." The feud between Thomas and Malone was now public. "Going into this expansion year, Thomas prioritized evaluating potential long-term talent above winning games in the club's inaugural season," Ormsby continued. "However, Malone has been committed to winning and competing. He shortens his bench, uses last-gasp veterans ahead of young players and keeps the go-for-broke Stoudamire on the floor as long as possible."

The storyline reached a climax that evening when Malone surprised everyone by emptying the Raptors' bench in the second quarter. Dwyane Whitfield, a rarely used power forward who played in just eight games all season, spent 26 minutes on the court. Martin Lewis, who appeared in 16 games, played 12 minutes. King came off the bench and got 22 minutes. Esposito got 19 minutes of run. The second unit got extended run together in the first half as Orlando's lead grew to 20 points at half-time. Malone did not bring back his starters until the game had gotten out of hand. The head coach seemed to be proving a point. *This is what happens when the starters don't play.* The Raptors would lose 126–86 on their home floor to the Magic. Stoudamire only played 29 minutes, his second-lowest total of the season. (Today, Malone says he doesn't recall what happened during the Magic game, before adding, "Maybe I don't want to remember.")

Sitting courtside, Smith could not believe what he was watching. "It was a big fuck you to Isiah," he says. The general manager gathered the reporters and called a media scrum at halftime, expressing his disappointment at Malone's first-half strategy. "To play them all at the same time and play them together," Thomas said, "I don't think anybody wanted to see that."

In case anyone had missed the point, Malone openly criticized the roster after the game. "We shouldn't have five two-guards on our team," he said. "I understand what he wants, but when you have an overload situation, it's hard to satisfy that need."

After the Magic game, it was clear the two sides would be parting ways at the end of the season. Malone started heading into the team's offices to pack up his belongings, preparing for the next move in his career, while still trying to win a few more games before he moved on.

Two nights after the embarrassing defeat, Malone went with a six-man rotation as Stoudamire logged 45 minutes in a loss to the Los Angeles Lakers at home. "Every game is a different game," Malone explained afterward. "This was a different game than the one we played against Orlando. I coach by feel." Perhaps he was coaching the only way he knew how, the only way he would be satisfied with himself. He was coaching to win. Malone pumped his fist at the buzzer when the Raptors snapped their four-game losing streak a few nights later with an overtime win at home over the Los Angeles Clippers. "It was very satisfying to win this game," he said. "This was one of the most fun games of the season. I liked our defensive intensity and it was good because everyone contributed. The team had completely divorced itself from the publicity in the papers. They were completely focused on the game."

Stoudamire played 44 minutes in the victory.

Dan and Acie

The overtime win over the Clippers was followed by two blowout losses to Cleveland and New York to close out a five-game homestand. The team's record stood at 19–55 as they headed out for their final road trip of the season, which would span six games in nine days. With Žan Tabak, Sharone Wright, and Carlos Rogers on the injured list, the Raptors needed to sign a big man to a 10-day contract for the trip. They reached out to Dan O'Sullivan, who had just finished the season with the Shreveport Storm of the Continental Basketball Association.

O'Sullivan grew up in The Bronx, New York, and played stickball, baseball, and basketball on the playground and tackle football on the field with his three siblings. After moving to New Jersey, O'Sullivan made the basketball team at Bayonne High School and rode the bench for four seasons. "I might have scored 100 points in high school," he laughs. O'Sullivan's size and athleticism was enough for Fordham University to offer him a scholarship, where the big man worked with assistant coach Buddy Maher to improve his low-post game. After averaging just 6.2 minutes in his freshman year, O'Sullivan blossomed into the team's starting center. After a 22-point performance against Marquette as a sophomore, scouts began to consider him an NBA prospect.

"I was just getting better by the day, and the game became so much more fun," he recalls. "It was fun to show up to the gym. I went from riding the bench in high school to thinking I had a chance to play in the NBA."

O'Sullivan finished his four-year career at Fordham averaging 12.5 points. He started 31 games his senior season, was invited to the pre-draft combine in Chicago, and was projected to be a second-round pick. He was back on campus at Fordham running a basketball camp on the night of the 1990 NBA draft and watched it at a friend's house. O'Sullivan ended up going undrafted.

"I wasn't exactly sitting on the edge of my seat," he explains. "The next day, everybody wanted to know if I was okay. I was totally fine because I had no expectations of being drafted."

Before the start of the season, O'Sullivan was invited to training camp with the New Jersey Nets. The team had often-injured Sam Bowie as their starting center and was looking for backup options. Even though O'Sullivan played well at camp, New Jersey decided to carry four point guards on the team, so he was waived. While he was waiting for overseas options, the CBA's Omaha Racers drafted O'Sullivan. A week after he joined the minor-league pro team, O'Sullivan received a call from Utah Jazz general manager Scott Layden. He was offered a 10-day contract and made his NBA debut on December 29, 1990.

"I was on cloud nine," O'Sullivan recalls. "You just run around like a chicken with your head cut off. You're so full of energy just running around, and the ball bounced my way a couple of times."

He played eight minutes and scored six points in a win over the Los Angeles Clippers. After the game, the Jazz television broadcast celebrated O'Sullivan's debut by naming him the Player of the Game and giving him a $100 gift certificate to the local mall.

Utah signed O'Sullivan for the rest of the season, but as an end-of-the-bench option, he did not make the postseason roster. The Jazz moved on in the summer. After no other NBA team expressed interest in signing him, O'Sullivan ended up on the Louisville Shooters of the CBA. For the next five years, he would bounce around the minor leagues, playing for the New Jersey Jammers, Jackson Jackals, and Jersey Turnpikes, and earn a few extra paychecks overseas in Puerto Rico and Spain. O'Sullivan would get several more cracks at the NBA with New Jersey, Milwaukee, and Detroit. They were all brief stops. He didn't play more than 13 games with any of those teams.

O'Sullivan enjoyed the lifestyle of being a journeyman player. He was able to travel the world and eventually got used to learning a new package of plays every few months. "It wasn't like I was the focus of the offense, so it wasn't that hard," O'Sullivan says. "You catch the ball, you pass it, you cut, and you set picks." The only regret he has is how few teammates he still keeps in touch with. "You just don't have enough time to make connections with people in a meaningful way," he adds.

Being around the best players in the world and competing against them on the court made O'Sullivan appreciate just how hard it was to be in the NBA. "When you look at the all-time great players, it's a marvel to think about the amount of punishment guys like Michael Jordan endured every night," he says. "I don't think I could have done it. I'm pretty competitive, but there's a difference when the lights are on, and the whole world is watching. I remember playing against Hakeem Olajuwon and David Robinson. I was like, 'I'm on the wrong planet. I can't compete against these guys.'"

O'Sullivan recognized his limitations on the floor, but in 1996 he was hoping for one more chance to stick with an NBA team. "Once you're there, you don't want to leave," he says. "But there's a whole new crop of college seniors coming in every year, and you're constantly fighting a numbers game."

When his agent called and told him the Raptors were offering him a 10-day contract, O'Sullivan was hanging out in his New Jersey home listening to the local sports radio station. The journeyman was used to packing up his bags on a moment's notice at this point, having lived the life of a basketball nomad for over half a decade. O'Sullivan hopped on the next available flight and joined the team in Milwaukee.

"It was gratifying to walk into that locker room," he says. "I knew I was pretty much done, but I just wanted one more taste of the NBA."

O'Sullivan made his debut with the Raptors in Milwaukee, where he went scoreless in 19 minutes. He was soaking in every moment of being part of an NBA locker room again and enjoyed the camaraderie of an expansion franchise.

"They were a group of happy-go-lucky guys," O'Sullivan recalls.

The team's spiritual leader was Acie Earl, the 6'10" big man who sported a hi-top fade and always walked into the locker room with a coffee and a sheepish grin on his face. "I was the guy who kept everyone in line emotionally," he explains. "I was all about never being too high and never being too low."

Earl grew up in Moline, Illinois, population 45,000. He idolized Kareem Abdul-Jabbar and wanted to become the first player from the Quad Cities since 1969 to make it to the NBA. "I was a tall, gangly kid who wasn't very coordinated," Earl says. "In the beginning, all I could do was block shots. My dad started coaching me in third grade. He taught me how to shoot, how to dribble, and how to be a smart player. It was a process because it wasn't always easy to be coached by your dad."

Terel McIntosh met Earl in fifth grade, and the two quickly became close friends. "He was never in a bad mood," McIntosh recalls. "He was a prankster and a jokester. He was always cracking on somebody. You had to give him the business because he was sure to give it to you." Earl loved to crack jokes and interrupt coaches during practice, which earned him a reputation for not taking the game seriously enough. "Unfortunately, he got criticized for having a great personality," McIntosh says.

Earl became a star at Moline High School, but when he arrived at the University of Iowa to continue his basketball career, the school decided to redshirt him for his first season. He would be ruled ineligible to play and was relegated to practicing with his teammates in between games. "It was hard to be told you're not good enough to play," Earl says. He spent an entire summer in the gym and returned the following season determined to prove everyone wrong. Earl led the Big Ten Conference in blocked shots despite averaging only 16 minutes. In four seasons at Iowa, he finished seventh all-time in blocks in NCAA history and entered the 1993 NBA draft as the second-leading scorer in school history.

Earl was a disappointment in his rookie year after the Boston Celtics selected him with the 19th overall pick. Head coach Chris Ford called him out for being lazy. The home fans started to turn on him. Earl was a foul-prone center who couldn't stay on the floor and averaged only 5.5 points and 3.3 rebounds in his first NBA season. The Celtics used their first-round pick the following year to draft North Carolina center Eric Montross. When Celtics icon and team president Red Auerbach was asked about the selection, he didn't hesitate to throw Earl under the bus. "We need a center," Auerbach told reporters. "What would you have us do? Go with Acie Earl?"

In his second year in Boston, Earl fell out of the rotation and only played 30 games. After the final game of the season against Miami, the Celtics' big man was walking off the court when John Salley approached him. "I'll see you in Toronto," he said. The prediction would come true several months later. Earl was traveling in the Swiss Alps when his agent called. The Raptors had selected him in the expansion draft. The big man walked into training camp and gave himself only a 50-50 shot at making the opening day roster, but Earl was excited at getting a fresh start with an expansion franchise.

"It was a land of misfit toys," he says. "We were all in a situation to rebuild ourselves, and now we had a pen to write our own book."

A series of impressive performances towards the end of preseason helped Earl lock down a roster spot on the team, but he found himself riding the bench for most of the season. "Brendan wasn't always fair as far as giving minutes to guys, but I understood where he came from," Earl says. "I didn't agree with it, but I understood."

He didn't let the lack of minutes discourage him. Earl bonded with his teammates and found a locker room where he could open up again and showcase his larger-than-life personality. Soon, every player on the Raptors had a nickname. "It's something I've been doing since high school," Earl says. "Everyone from my friends to classmates to teachers had a nickname." Damon Stoudamire was "Little B," but Earl started calling him "Biggie Smalls," which John Salley had coined as a reference to the point guard's small stature and big heart. Tracy Murray was "Sharp Hay" because there were always wrinkles on his forehead whenever he got angry. Willie Anderson was "Willie D," named after a member of the Houston-based rap group the Geto Boys because the swingman had played in San Antonio. Žan Tabak was "Tobacco." Vincenzo Esposito was "Don Corleone" because he showed up to games in a suit. Doug Christie was "Hadji" because Earl thought he resembled the character from the animated series *Jonny Quest*.

Earl was also the most supportive teammate. During games, if a Raptor player scored in bunches, they would inevitably start hearing a familiar voice from their bench. Earl was always up for some trash talk to hype up his guys. "He was your biggest fan," Stoudamire recalls. "He would be on that bench just screaming, 'Man. Y'all can't stop Biggie. He's giving it to you right now.'" During the season, Earl started a running limo joke. "If you were busting somebody's ass and got a couple of buckets on somebody, Acie would be on the bench saying, 'Damn, we're going to send a limo for you because Biggie's busting your ass,'" Stoudamire explains. "It became a running joke. We would play the same team again, and he would tell them in warm-ups, 'You ready for that limo to come again?'"

Earl was an equal-opportunity wise-cracker and wasn't above getting on his teammates as well. Jimmy King remembers Earl walking into the locker room one time and giving a long stare at his pregame meal. "I don't know if you need that double cheeseburger right now the way you're playing," he joked. Earl was once called to Carlos Rogers' hotel room on a road trip to help him fix the coffee maker. He then hid in his closet for 10 minutes and waited for his teammate to finish a call before jumping out and scaring him.

Teammates still remember getting on the team bus after a blowout loss in San Antonio in February when a suspicious smell started to spread from the back of the bus to the front. Earl, with a grin on his face, decided to let one rip to lighten the mood. "Whatever he ate or drank that day, he should never do that again," King says. "He dropped a serious bomb. I've never smelled anything like that since. Something crawled up in him and died that day."

Stoudamire shakes his head at the mention of the bus. "That motherfucker stank, man," he says. "That motherfucker's farts were the worst."

When Earl was asked to comment on the bus incident, he laughed and said, "I'm denying it. Some of these stories have been regurgitated over the years and put on other people."

Ed Pinckney had been teammates with the big man in Boston and got to know Earl much better in Toronto, where they often sat next to each other on team flights. "He was the most eclectic person I've ever met in the NBA," Pinckney says. "He was so well-read and well-versed in a lot of things. We would get on the plane and talk about all kinds of things that was happening in the world. We could be talking about the stock market, then he would get off the plane, hop in a red Ferrari, and head to a music recording session."

Earl loved reading about religion, Black history, and hip-hop, and started going through a catalog of biographies about the best basketball players in the history of the NBA. He founded his own music production company and owned a recording studio. "He was one of the smartest brothers I knew," Stoudamire says. "When you look at him, you wouldn't know that. But he was always kicking knowledge from some book he was reading. Or he would talk to you about music. He was a Wu-Tang guy. He would talk to you about Wu-Tang and start teaching you about Shaolin."

Earl had plenty of connections in the music industry. When Raekwon, Method Man, and Ol' Dirty Bastard—members of the New York rap group Wu-Tang Clan—were looking to put on a show in Toronto during the team's first season, Earl helped the trio secure a venue in Scarborough and invited all his teammates to attend the show.

On the final road trip, Earl found himself in the starting lineup for the first time all season. On the same evening O'Sullivan made his debut with the Raptors, he scored a season-high 16 points and received a call from his dad afterward. Earl had expected a congratulatory message, but instead, his father wanted his son to know he had only shot 5-of-17 from the field. "He said, 'You missed a couple layups, you missed a couple free throws, which means you're due for a big game,'" Earl recalls.

Those words would prove prophetic the following game when the Raptors traveled to Boston to take on the Celtics. Earl was in the starting lineup again and wanted to prove a point against the franchise that had given up on him.

"He was giving them the shimmy and then the turnaround jumper," King recalls. "He was giving them the business."

When he looked up at the scoreboard midway through the second quarter, Earl saw he was at 23 points. After every basket, he would look towards the Raptors' bench and see how excited everyone was. Teammates were jumping up and down, cheering him on.

"The refs had to calm down our entire bench," Esposito recalls.

Midway through the game, Earl started to realize it might be a career night. After another easy basket down low, he looked at former teammates Pervis Ellison and Rick Fox, who shook their heads in disbelief at what was happening. "I knew those guys. They could never hold me in practice," Earl laughs. "They put Fox on me. I told him, 'Come on now. You don't want any of this.'"

The Raptors were getting blown out in the second half, but nobody on the bench cared. When Earl reached 38 points in the fourth quarter, even the home fans in Boston started to cheer for the team's former first-round pick.

"I was dead tired and ready to pass out," Earl admits.

At one point, teammates started telling him to stay on offense to conserve energy.

"He was huffing and puffing," Christie laughs. "We just kept telling him to get in the post. We were coming back to the big fella every time."

Finally, one of the referees walked over to Earl.

"I had 38 with like six minutes to go, and the crowd was cheering me on to get 40," Earl recalls. "He said, 'Listen, next trip, just go to the basket, and I'll get you two free throws.'"

The big man would reach the milestone a few possessions later without help from the officials as he grabbed an offensive rebound and gently laid the ball into the basket.

"We were all super geeked for him," Christie says. "You would've thought we won the championship."

When the buzzer sounded, the Celtics walked off with a 136–108 win. But the Raptors' locker room was in a cheerful mood because Earl had finished with 40 points and 12 rebounds in 44 minutes, going 13-for-23 from the field and 14-for-19 from the free-throw line.

"Everybody had a perception of Acie. His hair was wild. He had these long gallops when he ran. You looked at him and thought he was a character," Murray says. "But he could score the ball. He was extremely talented. He had a soft touch, a great turnaround jumper, a little jump hook in the paint. Boston saw it that night. He was cooking them. He ran out of gas. He could have had 50. Maybe even 60. It was a clinic."

Earl got a few texts from friends and family, but the career night went largely unnoticed. The game was not on the local television broadcast schedule in Toronto, which meant most Raptors fans found out about his performance by scanning the box score in the newspaper the following morning. It also took place toward the end of the season with the Raptors near the bottom of the league's standings.

"It was an afterthought. People didn't realize it until much later," Earl says. "It was still so rewarding. I was sore as heck after that. That whole week I was playing major minutes. I was ready to pass out."

After the blowout loss in Boston, the Raptors traveled to New York for the second-to-last game of the trip. It was a special moment for O'Sullivan to play in an NBA game at Madison Square Garden. "I was always a Knicks fan," he says. "I was too young for the Willis Reed days but I always loved hearing about the history of the team. Ray Williams. Micheal Ray Richardson. Those were my guys growing up."

At the start of the 1991–92 season, the Knicks had invited O'Sullivan to training camp. "It was Pat Riley's first year and we were getting set to play a preseason game at the Garden," he recalls. "I knew I was probably not going to make the team, but I wanted to wear that Knicks jersey at the Garden. They cut me the night before the game."

Five years later, O'Sullivan walked into the visitor's locker room at the Garden and found his name in the starting lineup on the team's whiteboard. In his 44th career NBA game with his fifth team in four seasons, O'Sullivan got his first career start. He played 47 minutes, scoring eight points and grabbing 10 rebounds and was interviewed after the game by fellow Fordham alum John Andariese, who was now a color commentator with the Knicks. The Raptors lost 125–79.

"I knew we didn't win but I definitely don't remember us losing that badly," O'Sullivan laughs. "I didn't care."

Two nights later, he was once again in the starting lineup, scoring 15 points in 46 minutes in a 107–95 loss to the Nets. The Raptors finished 1–5 on their final road trip of the season.

O'Sullivan was a cab ride away from his New Jersey home, and his 10-day contract was set to expire. The Raptors still hadn't made a decision on whether to extend his deal through the rest of the season by the end of the trip, so O'Sullivan boarded a team flight back to Toronto with his teammates. With two home games remaining on the schedule, he landed, checked into a downtown hotel near the SkyDome, and started to unpack. That's when the phone rang. The Raptors had decided to let him go.

"I was bummed," O'Sullivan says. "I was having fun. I wanted to play two more games."

He repacked his bags and took the first flight home to New Jersey the following morning.

Caribana

While the Raptors embarked on their final road trip, Stoudamire flew back home to Portland. The team had shut him down for the trip, and the rookie was home receiving treatment for his tendinitis, while also tending to his mom, Liz, who had fallen down the stairs and fractured both of her shoulders. When the team returned home to Toronto to finish the regular season, Stoudamire rejoined his teammates with hopes of taking the court one more time. The front office sat him down and told Stoudamire they were shutting him down for the year. There was nothing to play for, and it wasn't worth risking further injury. "I wanted to play, but it wasn't my decision. The team decided for me," Stoudamire says. "They said, 'D, we're shutting you down. You're good. You've done everything.' The tendinitis would get bad, but I knew I could play. I wasn't thinking long term." He would finish his first NBA season playing in 70 games, averaging 19.0 points, 9.3 assists, and 4.0 rebounds.

The Raptors would open the final homestand with a win over Washington. Now there was just one game remaining. On April 21, 1996, a crowd of 27,118 packed the SkyDome to watch the season's final game. The Raptors hosted the Philadelphia 76ers, the only team in the Eastern Conference with a worse record than the expansion franchise. Sixers beat reporter Phil Jasner walked into the home team's locker room before the game and found Malone drawing up plays on the whiteboard. On the season's final day, the head coach was still trying to get one more victory. Jasner didn't want to bother Malone and told him they could catch up after the game instead. "I'm getting fired after the game," Malone responded. "So let's talk now."

It was the head coach's 54th birthday.

The Raptors would provide one last bit of excitement for the home crowd on the season's final day. Trailing by three on the final play, Doug Christie hit a game-tying shot from beyond the arc with 1.4 seconds remaining in the fourth quarter to send the game into overtime. Despite the thrilling finish, the Raptors would fall short in their bid to end the season on a winning note. The Sixers would pull out a 109–105 victory, overcoming Oliver Miller's career-high 35 points. The final pick of the expansion draft finished his first season with Toronto averaging 12.9 points, 7.4 rebounds, and 2.9 assists in 76 games. In the first preseason game, Miller had stood up for his teammates, coming off the bench and challenging Sixers center Shawn Bradley to a fight, drawing a one-game suspension. At season's end, the big man would stand up for the locker room again, but this time it was with a parting shot toward Malone.

"He had plenty of opportunities, but he dug his own grave," Miller told reporters afterward. "He didn't respect us enough as people, and he didn't give everybody a chance to show what they've got."

The season was over, and Malone was no longer in the mood to exchange barbs publicly.

"At the beginning of the year, I told Oliver I was not looking forward to coaching him because of my experience with him in Detroit," the head coach responded. "But this year he played great, he played hard."

Malone returned to the Westin Harbour Castle Hotel after the game and found some legal paperwork waiting for him under his door. The following day, Malone would officially resign as the head coach of the Raptors.

"I never even had an exit meeting with Brendan," Stoudamire recalls. "He was just gone the next day."

By the end of the season, the rookie was barely talking to his head coach.

"I didn't have anything against Brendan. I was put in the middle of it. It was something I didn't want to be in the middle of," Stoudamire says. "I don't think Brendan and I had a relationship by the end. It was fucked up. All of it was fucked up."

The Raptors finished the season with a 21–61 record.

Isiah Thomas addressed Malone's resignation at his season-ending press conference. "I feel bad we just couldn't have had a resolution," he told reporters. "I wish we could've seen eye to eye. His competitive nature made him short-sighted in terms of seeing the big picture."

The general manager promoted assistant coach Darrell Walker to replace Malone.

"We're on the same page," Thomas told reporters about his new head coach.

Stoudamire was named Rookie of the Year, winning the vote in a landslide, receiving 76 of a possible 113 votes from a panel of writers and broadcasters. "It meant everything," he says. "That was for the city and the organization. If I could have given a piece of that trophy to everybody in the organization, I would have."

Thomas would get to add another lottery pick in the 1996 NBA draft to complement his rookie. Per the expansion agreement, the Raptors and Grizzlies were not eligible for the first overall pick. So when Toronto won the lottery, a redraw was required. Philadelphia would land the number one pick. Toronto would draft second. Thomas and the team's scouting department were already honing in on several players, including UMass forward Marcus Camby, who won College Player of the Year and led his school to the Final Four; Ray Allen, the University of Connecticut guard and first-team All-American who set a single-season school record with 115 three-pointers in his senior season; and Shareef Abdur-Rahim, a freshman from California.

A few weeks after the season ended, Malone was back in his posh suburban home in Birmingham, Michigan, when his phone rang. It was

Thomas. The general manager wanted to thank him for the first season. The conversation was brief.

Soon after, Malone sat down with Michael Clarkson of *The Toronto Star* to chat about his one year with the Raptors and expressed his disappointment at the organization. "In New York, we had an expression: 'stand-up guy,' a guy who stands up for what he thinks is right," he said. "In situations like this, you find out about the character of people. There aren't too many people who'll stand up for what's right anymore. None of them stood up for me. I guess it was their insecurity. They just wanted to survive." Malone also stood firm on how he coached the team. "They say I didn't use the younger players enough, but when you look at it, Tracy Murray was really a rookie. He'd never played that much before in the NBA," he continued. "And the same goes for Žan Tabak, Sharone Wright and Doug Christie. We gave them all a chance."

The Seattle SuperSonics hired Malone as a consultant during the 1995–96 playoffs. After the season, he interviewed for an open head coaching spot in Milwaukee and finished as a runner-up to Chris Ford. He would spend the following two decades back in a familiar role as an assistant coach. Outside of an 18-game interim coaching stint with Cleveland at the end of the 2004–05 season, Malone retired without getting another permanent head coaching job in the NBA. He admits it is still hard to move on from how things ended in Toronto.

"It hurt me from getting another job," he says. "In retrospect, I can understand where Isiah was coming from, but I still have bad feelings about how I was treated there."

After a career year where he appeared in all 82 games, averaged 16.2 points, and made 42.2 percent of his threes, Tracy Murray had established himself as an NBA starter. He was heading to free agency, looking for a considerable pay raise.

Thomas wanted to bring Murray back, but based on the salary cap rules, the Raptors could only offer him a 20-percent raise on his league-minimum annual salary of $250,000. Thomas knew Murray would receive much more lucrative offers on the open market and petitioned the league for a one-time exception to allow the Raptors to sign him to a higher salary.

Murray did not want to sign anywhere else. After three seasons in the NBA, he had found a home. "It was a happy marriage between us," Murray says. "They took care of me." Because he was on a minimum contract, the Raptors arranged a free stay at the SkyDome hotel during the season. They helped Murray land several paid appearances and advertising deals across the city. When Murray told the team his parents couldn't watch Raptors games at home because of the lack of television coverage in the United States, the organization compiled highlight tapes and mailed them to his house.

The first year in Toronto was also a one-of-a-kind experience on the court. "We were a bunch of guys nobody wanted, and we banded together to show people we could still play," Murray says. "We enjoyed each other and genuinely loved being around each other. I don't care if it was practice, on a bus, on a plane, on a road trip, after the game, going to eat, or going out. We had a bond. It was different. It doesn't happen in every locker room. You usually get close to one or two guys but never the whole team. Vincenzo and Žan were my brothers, just like Jimmy and Sharone were my brothers. Willie. Alvin. Doug. Tony. Oliver. Carlos. Damon. We were all brothers. One of us would say, 'Yo, we're gonna be over here,' and everyone would show up."

By the end of the season, Murray had grown to love Toronto. "I went everywhere from Scarborough to Rexdale to Barrie to Richmond Hill. I was everywhere. I would be up on Yonge and Eglinton," he says. "I remember the fans too. They started to chase me down whenever I was out. After a while, I got tired of running from them. So one day, I just decided to stop running to see what they were all about. I started talking to the fans, and that's when you see the love. I didn't want to go anywhere. The fans embraced me. I had my second chance here. The team was special. We were extremely close. I felt like we were building something."

Murray flew back to Toronto in July for Caribana, North America's largest annual street festival, which drew millions of people to the city to celebrate Caribbean culture and traditions. Free agency had started, and his agent, Arn Tellem, was fielding offers from other teams. Murray was still trying to find a way to return to the Raptors. Thomas' petition to the league had been rejected. The only way for Murray to come back to Toronto would be to sign another one-year deal for near the minimum. He would have to risk passing on securing a long-term contract if he wanted to remain a Raptor.

At his 25th birthday party in downtown Toronto during Caribana weekend, Murray was partying with Jamie Foxx, Vivica A. Fox, Tommy Davidson, and Tamala Jones, who were in town filming the buddy comedy movie *Booty Call*, when he got a message on his pager. It was Tellem. The Washington Bullets and Los Angeles Lakers had submitted their offers. They were both six-year deals. Murray asked Tellem to ask the Bullets to add an extra year. They agreed. The contract would be worth $17 million. It was a deal Murray could not pass up. He told Tellem to finalize the agreement and stepped outside to give Thomas a call. The general manager had rescued his career at the end of training camp, and Murray wanted to have one final word with Thomas before moving on.

"Isiah told me to go ahead and take the deal," he recalls. "He said, 'I know you want to be here. I know you love the fellas. I know you love me, but you gotta take the deal and secure the future of your family.'"

Murray hung up the phone and started crying.

"Nothing else in my career compared to the experience I had in my first year in Toronto. The organization cared about you. They got to know you as a person. I felt like I was leaving a family," he says. "It was a door closing on a season. It was a door closing on a team I wanted to be with. The city, the organization, and my teammates embraced me. It was all those emotions."

After sitting outside for 20 minutes reminiscing about the season, Murray stood up, gathered himself, and walked back inside to celebrate his birthday.

Significant changes were coming to the roster over the summer. After Murray left in free agency, Thomas acquired Hubert Davis in a trade with the Knicks and signed Walt Williams to the league minimum to replace his shooting.

Miller surprised everyone by opting out of the two years and $5.4 million remaining on his contract and becoming a free agent in the summer. He says the decision was made to help open up cap space to re-sign Murray. Miller ended up signing a one-year deal with Dallas for the league minimum.

"I really thought it was going to help us bring him back," he says. "It turned out to be one of the worst decisions I made in my career."

Stoudamire could not believe he was losing Murray and Miller, two players the organization had considered part of the long-term core moving forward. "It fucked me up, man," he says. "That's the business. A part of me was happy for Tracy, but I hated to see him go. When you have someone who could shoot like that, it was like, damn, those automatic assists are gone. I was mad at Oliver. I didn't want him to put himself out there like that. He was giving money back, and he was making good money at that time. I was like, 'Sheesh, man. Don't give no money back.' I missed their friendship. You only have each other when you're not winning, and I hated watching them leave."

Alvin Robertson, who started 69 games, and averaged 9.3 points and 2.2 steals per game in 32.2 minutes, retired after the season. Jimmy King, who appeared in 62 games and averaged only 4.5 points on 43.1 percent shooting, playing 14 minutes a game, was traded to Dallas in exchange for power forward Popeye Jones.

Meanwhile, Thomas was trying to convince Vincenzo Esposito, who played in 30 games and averaged 3.9 points in 9.4 minutes, to come back for a second season, promising him more of an opportunity with Malone having moved on. "I had received an offer to go back to Italy," Esposito explains. "Isiah was disappointed when I told him. He said, 'I brought you over there. The coach isn't here anymore. You're going to challenge for a starting spot. I want to show everyone I made the right choice because I know you can play.' He told me the truth, but I had gotten bit too many times in the first season. Isiah had gotten a trade offer from Philadelphia but didn't want to send me there. He said, 'I want you here. You're going to get minutes.' But I decided to go back to Italy. It wasn't a hard decision. Sometimes there are things more important than how much money you make."

When he returned home and signed with Scavolini Pesaro of the Italian League in the summer, Esposito became teammates again with Dan O'Sullivan. The 10-day contract with the Raptors would be the journeyman's final NBA stint.

"It was so fun," O'Sullivan says. "I was honest with myself. I wasn't a great player, and that's okay. I am what I am, but that doesn't mean I can't be happy about my NBA career."

He would continue his pro basketball career overseas.

"The people in Italy were wonderful," O'Sullivan recalls. "We all know about the food, but it was the people. After a game, whether we won or lost, we'd all go out to eat. We would all go to this one restaurant, and they had a table waiting for us. The wives would come. The game would end at 10:00. You would be at the restaurant at 11:00 and be there until one in the morning."

The ownership group of the Raptors would also change by the start of the 1996–97 season.

On October 18, 1996, two weeks before the franchise's second opening night, Allan Slaight announced he was invoking a shotgun clause in his ownership agreement with John Bitove Jr., signifying the end of their partnership. Doug Smith was among the many sports reporters in the city who had to scramble and become a business writer overnight. He discovered that the shotgun clause was a mechanism of last resort, providing two options: a partner could sell their stake or buy out the offering partner. In this scenario, Bitove would have a month to decide whether he wanted to pay $47 million to buy Slaight's ownership stake. If not, Slaight would purchase Bitove's stake.

The team's new proposed arena at the Canada Post Office location near Union Station in downtown Toronto was at the center of the ownership split. After significant delays, the arena's construction was finally ready to begin at the end of 1996. Bitove wanted the Raptors to be the only primary tenant at the arena. Slaight wanted to partner with the Leafs. Steve Stavro, the owner of Maple Leaf Gardens, had reportedly told Slaight he would not proceed with an arena partnership if Bitove remained part of the ownership group, and the shotgun clause was triggered.

Bitove spent the next month exploring his options. He talked to investors. He consulted with advisors. He huddled up with his family. Bitove tried his best to hide the emotional toll the process took on him. "I would go in the office and be smiling and talking to everyone," he recalls. "It was painful, but I knew the people took cues from me."

Justina Klein, who became a full-time employee with the Raptors after finishing as a top-five salesperson during the season ticket drive, remembers the mood around the office changing as the shotgun clause deadline approached. "We were freaking out in the two weeks leading up to it," she recalls. "You could see the sadness on John's face whenever he came into the office. He was stressed out."

While reporters focused on whether Bitove could come up with the money to buy Slaight's ownership stake, David Peterson says that was not the main issue. "It's funny because the public reading is that John was scrambling to come up with the money," he says. "He could have made it happen. He could have afforded to buy Allan out, but John and his family had to decide whether they wanted all of their money tied to a basketball team, which was still a very speculative asset in the city. There was still a lot of money that needed to be spent to make the team successful."

Bitove agrees. "It was too risky at that point in my life," he says of the financial commitment.

On November 1, 1996, the Raptors opened the 1996–97 season at home against the New York Knicks. Wearing throwback blue-and-white Toronto Huskies jerseys to celebrate the 50th anniversary of the NBA's first game at Maple Leaf Gardens, Stoudamire scored 28 points and handed out 10 assists in a 107–99 loss. In the days leading up to the 1996 NBA draft, Thomas debated between Abdur-Rahim and Camby, a defensive stalwart from UMass. After Philadelphia selected Georgetown guard Allen Iverson with the first overall pick, Thomas went with Camby, pairing the big man with Stoudamire. Abdur-Rahim would go third to Vancouver. Camby came off the bench in his NBA debut and fouled out in 15 minutes, scoring five points and grabbing four rebounds.

Two weeks after the opening night loss, Bitove let the shotgun clause deadline expire and allowed Slaight to purchase his ownership stake. He addressed his employees at the start of his final day at the office. "It was very emotional because this was my dream," Bitove recalls. "I just told everyone, 'Keep being different.'" He held a press conference on the same day to officially announce his decision.

"You can't get that emotional," Bitove told reporters while barely holding back tears. "I said to the staff this morning that we'll all get over it. There's been no lives lost, no blood shed. Since the time I was seven years old, when I picked up my first basketball in my grandmother's driveway in Indiana, I loved this sport. I played it all through school, went to a university where I could watch it, and I always dreamed one day and never understood what took so long for Canadians to embrace this sport.

"Winning 21 games our first year, Damon as Rookie of the Year, beating the top two teams in the NBA, being fifth in the league in merchandise sold, some people can't experience that in a lifetime. I'm only 36 years old. There are lots of other opportunities in my life."

The Raptors were never going to win a lot of games in their first year, but if they could win over a fan base and convince them there was a product worth investing in long-term, it would be the only win the organization would need in their ledger for the first season. In those terms, the first year of the Raptors was a success, and there was a long list of people who deserved credit for playing a part. From the salespeople on three-month contracts making cold calls to help meet the league's season ticket goal to the game ops and entertainment department helping to turn a desolate baseball stadium into a half-decent venue for an NBA game to the television broadcast crew working their way through their mistakes to help an audience at home fall in love with the product to the community relations team making sure the Raptors laid the groundwork in the city to make personal connections with the fan base to the players who established a presence in the city, they had all helped to start rewriting the city's forgettable history with professional basketball.

But many of them would not be around to see where the franchise would go from here, including the team's owner, who grew up dreaming of bringing an NBA franchise to Toronto.

After one season, Bitove's run with the Raptors was over.

Part Four
Postscript

Historic

Two weeks before the official release of *Prehistoric*, Brendan Malone passed away at the age of 81. When I interviewed him for this project a few years ago, he spoke at length about how frequently he watched the Denver Nuggets. They are coached by his son Michael, who remembers hanging out at Power Memorial Academy as a kid with his dad. He would tag along on recruiting trips with his father, where Michael met Kenny Smith and Mark Jackson, players who would end up in the NBA. Brendan would drive his son to his basketball camp in Maine every summer. They would spend hours in the car talking hoops. When Brendan became the assistant coach at Syracuse, Michael was at the Carrier Dome working as a ball boy. When Brendan joined the Knicks, Michael got shots up at Madison Square Garden before games. When Brendan was with the Pistons, Michael hung out in the locker room after games cracking jokes with Dennis Rodman and John Salley.

At Seton Hall Prep, his father would sit in the stands and take notes. After Michael scored 20 points and grabbed 10 rebounds in a game, Brendan would show him the list of things he did wrong. "He was hard on me because he wanted to see me do well," Michael says. "I feel fortunate to have that." After his junior year at Loyola University in Maryland, Michael realized he wasn't on the path to making the NBA and decided to become a coach like his father. Michael wrote letters to over 75 NCAA Division I schools and was hired as an assistant at Oakland University. He eventually landed a job at Providence. "I thought I had made it. I was making $6,000, and it was the best thing ever," Michael recalls. "They paid for my housing, and I couldn't have been happier."

Even though his son was following in his footsteps, Brendan didn't always encourage Michael to get into coaching. He missed significant time with his six kids growing up and didn't want Michael to make the same sacrifices.

"He understood the pitfalls of being a coach," Michael says. "He told me, 'You're too smart. You can do whatever you want. Get a real job.' But I think he saw me working my ass off, and I had a real passion for the game."

When Brendan realized his son wasn't going to chase another career, he started to provide advice to Michael to make him a better coach. "Coaching is one thing, but teaching is what great coaches do," Brendan told Michael. "You teach the why, and that will allow players to understand what you're trying to say that much better."

In 2001, Michael got his first NBA coaching job as an assistant with the New York Knicks. After working in the same role for Cleveland, the New Orleans Hornets, and Golden State, he landed his first NBA head coaching job in 2013 with the Sacramento Kings. In 2023, Michael won his first NBA championship as head coach of the Denver Nuggets.

Tracy Murray spent four seasons in Washington and scored a career-high 50 points against Golden State in 1998. He was traded to Denver at the start of the 2000–01 season. In January 2001, the Raptors traded for Murray. He appeared in 78 games across two seasons, and retired from the NBA in 2004, playing three more years overseas in Greece and France.

Oliver Miller's run in Dallas lasted only 42 games before he was waived in February 1997. He rejoined the Raptors and spent another year and a half with the franchise. His weight continued to be a problem for the remainder of his career, which ended in 2004 with the Minnesota Timberwolves. The 1995–96 season with the Raptors was the high point of his career.

Jimmy King was waived by the Mavericks before the start of the 1996–97 season and signed with the Quad City Thunder of the Continental Basketball Association. He signed a 10-day contract with the Denver Nuggets during the season, appearing in two games. King ended up playing overseas in Venezuela and Poland before retiring in 2005.

Vincenzo Esposito would lead the Italian League in scoring for three straight seasons from 1999 to 2001 and was named the Italian League MVP twice during that span. He became a coach in 2009.

Dan O'Sullivan played overseas until his retirement in 2000.

After winning the championship with the Bulls in 1996, John Salley signed a one-year deal to play for Panathinaikos in Greece. He played seven games for the club before reuniting with Phil Jackson, who was now coaching Shaquille O'Neal and Kobe Bryant in Los Angeles in 1999. Salley won his fourth championship with the Lakers that season and retired.

The Knicks did not offer Willie Anderson a new contract in the summer of 1996 after trading for him at the deadline. He joined Olympiacos in Greece before signing with the Miami Heat during the 1996–97 season. Anderson appeared in 28 games with the team, returned to Greece, and then ended his pro career after a season with Israel's Maccabi Tel Aviv in 1999.

After he was traded to Philadelphia, Tony Massenburg became a free agent in the off-season and signed a one-year, league-minimum deal with New Jersey. He would end up setting an NBA record, playing for 12 teams over 13 seasons. (Ish Smith has since broken the record.)

Ed Pinckney signed with the Miami Heat and retired after the 1996–97 season.

Acie Earl was traded to the Milwaukee Bucks during the 1996–97 season before spending the next seven years playing overseas in Australia, Turkey, Russia, Poland, Austria, Montenegro, and Kosovo. He retired in 2004.

In the summer of 1997, Sharone Wright was driving to a basketball clinic at a Boys and Girls club in his hometown of Macon, Georgia, when his car skidded off the road. The car accident left Wright with a broken arm, a fractured collarbone, bruised ribs, and minor knee damage. He underwent surgery and had two metal plates inserted into the humerus bone in his left arm. Wright returned in March 1998, but, after playing 44 minutes in seven games, he reaggravated his damaged left shoulder and was placed on the injured list by the Raptors. It would mark the end of his NBA career. He spent the next decade playing overseas before retiring in 2008.

The Raptors would finish with a 30–52 record in their second season, a nine-game improvement from year one. Damon Stoudamire improved on his rookie year as a scorer, averaging 20.2 points and adding 8.8 assists. He played 40.9 minutes per game. Doug Christie started 81 games and averaged 14.5 points and 2.5 steals. Walt Williams, who replaced Murray, averaged 16.4 points per game and shot 40 percent from three. Marcus Camby finished his rookie season averaging 14.8 points, 6.3 rebounds, and 2.1 blocks. The Raptors had the ninth pick in the 1997 NBA draft and selected an 18-year-old high-schooler named Tracy McGrady.

On November 20, 1997, after the Raptors started their third season with a 1–9 record, Thomas formally tendered his resignation to Allan Slaight and the ownership group. (He also sold his ownership stake.) Glen Grunwald was named the team's new general manager.

Thomas was right about selecting Stoudamire as the team's first-ever draft pick. He was also correct to try and trade up to acquire Kevin Garnett, who would go on to play 21 seasons in the NBA and be a 15-time All-Star, four-time All-NBA First Team selection, nine-time NBA All-Defensive First Team selection, and retire as one of the greatest power forwards to have ever played. Ed O'Bannon, who the fans wanted on draft night, ended up spending two NBA seasons with New Jersey and Dallas before finishing his professional career overseas.

Stoudamire made it clear after Thomas' resignation that he would not return to Toronto as a free agent at the end of the 1997–98 season. In his third year with the Raptors, the point guard started a public campaign to push for a trade. As the deadline neared, Stoudamire started criticizing the organization every day, in hopes of pressuring the team into moving him. "I just didn't feel like there was a direction," Stoudamire says. "The ownership group was changing. I was like, 'Fuck it. I'm out too.' I could have handled it better. I didn't go about it the right way. It tore the team up. But I was young and trying to see how much power I had."

On February 12, 1998, the Toronto Maple Leafs' ownership group announced the acquisition of the Raptors for $500 million. The group included Larry Tanenbaum, who had originally lost the ownership bid to John Bitove Jr. in 1993. The takeover would include the acquisition of the Air Canada Centre, the proposed arena at the Canada Post location.

The following day, Grunwald sent Stoudamire, Carlos Rogers, and Walt Williams to the Portland Trail Blazers in exchange for Alvin Williams, Kenny Anderson, Gary Trent, two first-round picks, and a second-rounder. On the same day, head coach Darrell Walker resigned. Butch Carter was named the interim head coach. "I don't mind coaching an expansion team," Walker said. "But I wanted to see some light at the end of the tunnel. I don't see any light."

The Raptors finished the 1997–98 season with a 16–66 record.

Žan Tabak was traded to the Boston Celtics in 1998. He spent a year playing in Turkey before signing with the Indiana Pacers. He left the NBA in 2001 and played four years overseas before retiring in 2005.

After he was traded to Portland with Stoudamire in 1998, Rogers spent four more seasons in the NBA before retiring in 2002.

Stoudamire spent seven-plus seasons in Portland and almost made the NBA Finals in 2000 until the Blazers blew a 15-point, fourth-quarter lead to the Los Angeles Lakers in Game 7 of the Western Conference Finals. Towards the end of his career, Stoudamire reached out to Malone and thanked him for being an important part of his career. The two had not spoken for years.

"I didn't go out of my way to tell him that because I felt guilty," Stoudamire says. "I did it because I meant it. Brendan was important to my development as a player. He helped jump-start my career. I was able to do my thing and exceed a lot of people's expectations."

Michael Malone says the conversation provided his dad with some closure. "It made my father feel good," he says. "Maybe Damon didn't realize it at the time. Maybe he was getting mixed messages from different people in the organization. But when he reflected on his career, I think he realized how Brendan always had his best interest at heart. Things didn't work out. My dad got fired. That's the profession. But knowing his impact on the players and the city gave him great joy."

Liz Washington worked for three more years after the Raptors drafted Stoudamire. "I wasn't about to quit and give up my pension," she explains. "I didn't even know if Damon would be in the NBA for two years."

When Stoudamire signed a seven-year, $81 million contract with the Blazers in 1999, Liz finally allowed herself to retire.

As her son's NBA career started to wind down, she was the worried mother figure again, wondering what was next. "When he was playing, I was always like, 'This boy's never had a real job in his life,'" Liz says. "I didn't know what he would do when his playing career was over." After retiring in 2008, Stoudamire decided to get into coaching. In 2016, he was named head coach of the University of the Pacific. The Boston Celtics hired him as an assistant coach in 2021. "He kept pursuing what he loved, and that is the game of basketball," Liz says. "I hear him talk about how he got his work ethic from me because I always worked to put food on the table. I'm more proud of Damon now than when he played in the NBA." In March 2023, Stoudamire was named the head coach of Georgia Tech's men's basketball team. His coaching journey continues today.

On June 24, 1998, inside General Motors Place in Vancouver, British Columbia, the Toronto Raptors selected North Carolina forward Antawn Jamison with the fourth overall pick. Grunwald had already agreed to a trade with the Golden State Warriors, who had the following selection at number five, and was going to swap first-rounders with them. Jamison was headed to Golden State in exchange for his North Carolina team-mate Vince Carter.

The person making the official trade call to the league was Robin Brudner, who had joined the franchise before the start of the 1995–96 season.

"It was the first time I was on a trade call alone," she recalls. "I remember phoning my father and letting him know I just made my first trade, and it was for some guy named Vince Carter." Brudner ended up spending 17 years with the organization, and took on a larger role in basketball operations after Grunwald was named general manager. "He's one of the smartest people I've ever known," Brudner says. "I would go into a meeting thinking he was not right about something, and I would go back to my office, and sure enough, he was always right. He was always there for me and gave me opportunities to work on the basketball side. I think the world of him both professionally and as a person."

Carter averaged 18.3 points and 5.7 rebounds in his first season and was named Rookie of the Year. In 1999, the Raptors officially moved into the Air Canada Centre. They started to garner national attention in the United States for the first time thanks to Carter's gravity-defying performance at the 2000 Slam Dunk Contest. The Raptors star drew comparisons to Michael Jordan for his high-flying ways and became one of the most popular players in the league.

On April 23, 2000, Carter and the Raptors played their first-ever post-season game on the road at Madison Square Garden against the New York Knicks after finishing with a franchise-best 45–37 record in the regular season. The Raptors would lose 92–88 and be swept by the Knicks in three games. In the summer, McGrady, who had formed a one-two tandem with Carter, became a free agent and signed a seven-year, $92.8 million contract with the Orlando Magic.

After American businessman Michael Heisley purchased the Vancouver Grizzlies in 2000, the fan base became skeptical of the new owner's intentions. Heisley publicly declared his intentions to keep the team in Canada, but the talk of relocation only intensified as the 2000–01 season began.

Massenburg was a member of that Grizzlies team. "All anyone would talk about the whole year was whether we were staying or going," he recalls.

Andy Dolich was the team's president of basketball operations and takes responsibility for the management team not doing a better job of selling the game of basketball in Vancouver. "We didn't sell enough season tickets," he says. "We didn't have enough local sponsors."

According to Dolich, the U.S.-Canadian foreign exchange rate made it impossible to continue running the team in Canada. The revenues were in Canadian dollars. The expenses, including player salaries, were paid in U.S. dollars. "It wasn't a sustainable business model," Dolich says.

Dave Doroghy, who joined the Grizzlies before the start of their first season as their director of sponsorship sales, says Toronto did not have to face the same uphill climb because of the financial stability of their ownership group, the more prominent corporate sponsorship pool compared to Vancouver, and a larger metropolitan area of fans to tap into.

Toward the end of the 2000–01 season, Heisley and the ownership group had narrowed their relocation options to four cities: Anaheim, Louisville, New Orleans, and Memphis. The Disney corporation asked the ownership group to purchase the NHL's Anaheim Mighty Ducks as part of their condition to allow the NBA team to relocate, which crossed them off the list. Louisville had a dedicated college basketball fan base and didn't seem thrilled at welcoming a pro team. New Orleans was not known as a basketball hotbed, which left Memphis as the number one candidate.

On March 26, 2001, Heisley officially applied for relocation to Memphis.

The Grizzlies played their final home game in Vancouver a few weeks later on April 14, 2001, as the Houston Rockets rallied from a 19-point second-half deficit for a 100–95 win. After Shareef Abdur-Rahim scored

24 points and grabbed eight rebounds in the loss, he showed his appreciation for the fan base.

"The hardest part of this for me is that I've always been made to feel so at home here," he told reporters. "I've been blessed to be able to play here. It's been an honor and pleasure for me to go out and play in front of them every night. I appreciate them, I love them for that, and I don't know if we'll find that anywhere else."

In six seasons in Vancouver, the Grizzlies never won more than 23 games in a season and finished with a 101–359 record. A fan at the final home game held a sign that read, "100 WINS, 6 YEARS, HAVE FUN MEMPHIS!"

The Raptors would be the only Canadian NBA team remaining at the start of the 2001–02 season.

Doug Christie was the only player from the 1995–96 season who remained on the roster when the Raptors finally made the playoffs. After getting swept by the Knicks, Christie was traded in the summer to Sacramento for forward Corliss Williamson. The trade put an end to the expansion era for the Raptors. The original ownership group had moved on. No one from the first-year roster remained. The team no longer called the SkyDome home and was now led by a new franchise player.

The Raptors won just one playoff series with Carter before he requested a trade and became a New Jersey Net during the 2004–05 season. The franchise would return to the postseason in 2007 with forward Chris Bosh, who the team had selected with the fourth overall pick in the 2003 NBA draft. The Raptors would lose to Carter and the Nets in six games in the first round. They made the playoffs again the following season and lost to the Orlando Magic in a first-round series. After the 2009–10 season, when they finished 40–42 and missed the playoffs, Bosh signed with the Miami Heat in free agency. The Raptors would linger in mediocrity until the 2013–14 season, when they returned to the playoffs, winning 48 games and the Atlantic Division. They would lose again to the Nets in the first round. The Raptors would make the playoffs for the next five seasons, culminating with the franchise's first NBA Finals appearance in 2019. On June 13, 2019, the Raptors clinched their first NBA championship, beating the Golden State Warriors 114–110 at Oracle Arena in Oakland, California, in Game 6 of the Finals.

John Bitove Jr. watched the championship-clinching win with his wife, Randi, and his family inside Wayne Gretzky's Restaurant, where he'd celebrated his 33rd birthday and the ownership bid in 1993. After the final buzzer sounded, John walked out of Gretzky's onto Blue Jays Way. He smiled at the thousands of Raptors fans already flooding the downtown core, waving their flags, hugging one another, and honking the horns in their cars. The celebration had started. Bitove took a moment to take it all in. He had grown up dreaming of bringing an NBA franchise to Toronto and watching them win a championship. The Raptors had come a long way in two-and-a-half decades.

Randi admits it was hard to cheer for the team after the shotgun clause forced her husband to give up ownership of the franchise, but it was John who encouraged her to enjoy the team again. "It's still his baby," she says. "He's not part of the ownership group anymore, but it'll always be a part of him."

In 2022, Bitove was inducted into the Canadian Basketball Hall of Fame. "When you get this kind of award," he says, "you just look back on all the people involved, and you smile with pride and feel very thankful." Bitove's ownership run with the Raptors was brief, but he's at peace with it today. "I was a kid back then, and it was the best thing because I hired a bunch of kids, and I kept throwing more responsibility at them. That was the beauty of it. It brought this new energy and new ideas. We were a startup. It wasn't a bunch of old White guys saying, 'We've got a basketball team.' It was, 'What can we do today that's different and crazy?' That's how we left a mark," he says. "I wouldn't trade it for anything. I would do it all over again. There's nothing I would change. It's part of the history of this country."

The email landed in my inbox in August 2021. Over the past two decades, Elaine Quan has organized in-person reunions for everyone involved in the 1995–96 season. Quan, who worked in the community relations department and runs a successful PR agency in Toronto today, had to scramble in 2020 when the global pandemic shut down her 25th anniversary reunion party. So instead, she asked Brian Sherriffe to produce a series of Zoom meet-ups. In my inbox are the private YouTube links to these conversations.

I click on the first one and see Stoudamire, Murray, Miller, Christie, Earl, Massenburg, Pinckney, and King cracking jokes with one another. They're trying to remember Earl's nicknames and are still laughing about Esposito and Rogers playing one-on-one after practice. The second video features the television broadcast team, including Leo Rautins, Rod Black, Paul Jones, and Lori Belanger, sharing their favorite John Saunders memories and still shaking their heads at that one time the lights went out in Cleveland on live television. The next video features the game operations and entertainment team. Jamie Nishino, Kenny Solway, Sharon Edwards, and others are trying to count all the times they got notes from the league office for breaking the rules.

The camaraderie between everyone strikes me as something that can only be shared by a group of people who helped start an NBA franchise. Everyone played a part in building a foundation for the organization, from the players on the court to the people working on the television broadcast to the in-game entertainment crew.

In the final video, Bitove is laughing with David Peterson and Thomas about when Peterson had no idea who Thomas was when they first met. Later, Samuel L. Jackson surprises the group by joining the Zoom. He still keeps in touch regularly with Quan. "She has the best cuisine habits of anybody I've ever met. She's a total foodie," Jackson says. "You always want to keep a foodie on speed dial."

An in-person reunion is being planned for the summer of 2023 as of this writing.

While most of the people involved with the first season have moved on, some remained with the organization long enough to be part of the franchise's first NBA championship in 2019. Rautins was part of the Raptors' broadcast inside Oracle Arena in Oakland when the Raptors won Game 6 of the Finals. The first person he thought of when the buzzer sounded was Saunders, who spent five years as the team's play-by-play man until Chuck Swirsky replaced him. "I think that's the biggest mistake the Raptors have ever made," Rautins says. "John was shocked when they didn't renew his contract. He was devastated. He wanted to retire as a Raptor broadcaster, just like what Chick Hearn did in Los Angeles." Saunders passed away at the age of 61 in 2016. He co-authored *Playing Hurt: My Journey From Despair To Hope* with John U. Bacon, released in 2017. The memoir detailed Saunders' childhood traumas and his lifelong battle with depression.

On the day of the championship-clinching game, Rautins went for breakfast with Black. The two remained involved with the team's television broadcast and spent the morning reminiscing about the journey of the Raptors franchise. "Can you fucking believe it?" Black said to Rautins. The two had sat courtside and called the first-ever Raptors game at the SkyDome. After 24 years, they would be in the building to witness the franchise's first NBA title. Jones also remained part of the team's radio broadcast and could not believe he had spent enough years with the Raptors to see them reach the mountaintop. "For years I told people I might never cover a championship team," he says. "To get to see it was the pinnacle of my career. I had gone through everything from start to finish. I was like, 'Wow. This was worth it.'" Walking into an NBA arena remains just as exciting today as it did back when Jones first got the job. "It fills me with energy," he says. "The pageantry. The music. The smell of the popcorn. The intensity, especially during the playoffs. It'll never get old."

In Doug Smith's 24th season of covering the Raptors, they finally won the championship. The day after Game 6, *The Toronto Star* reporter called up John Lashway and Isiah Thomas to reminisce about the franchise's start.

Herbie Kuhn remains the team's public address announcer today and still *shhhh*-ushes the crowd whenever the Raptors shoot free throws at home.

Ryan Bonne remains the man behind the mascot uniform.

Nav Bhatia became well-known as the team's superfan and was inducted into the Basketball Hall of Fame in 2021, becoming the first fan to receive the honor. He still attends every Raptor game today.

The championship brought back memories for those involved in the first season. Tamara Mose, the coordinator and choreographer of the Dance Pak, is a sociology professor at Brooklyn College today. She celebrated the championship in 2019. "Once a Raptor," Mose says, "always a Raptor."

Tyler Stewart, a member of the Barenaked Ladies, who performed the Canadian anthem at the team's first-ever regular-season game, was on stage in Austin, Texas, opening for Hootie and the Blowfish on the night the Raptors won.

"We went to the dressing room the minute we got off stage to watch the end of the game," Stewart recalls, "then we went back on stage to do an encore."

The championship was also a special moment for fans who rooted for the Raptors from the very beginning. Damian Daniels grew up in Dartmouth, Halifax, in what he describes as a household which loved basketball. He was an eight-year-old when his older brother got them tickets to attend the franchise's very first preseason game back in 1995 at the Metro Convention Centre in downtown Halifax. "It was front page news in our local paper," Daniels recalls. "I don't remember much, but I still have a souvenir hat and a game program from the game." From Day One, he became a Raptors fan. Growing up, Daniels would regularly visit friends and family who lived in Toronto and attend games in person. The championship season brought back two-decades plus of memories for Daniels and his family.

On Monday, June 17, 2019, over a million fans attended the championship parade in downtown Toronto to celebrate the first NBA title in Raptors franchise history. As the parade buses exited the Princes' Gates at Exhibition Place at 10:00 in the morning, making their way to an anxious crowd waiting at Nathan Phillips Square, fans crowded the streets to serenade their hometown heroes.

Standing at the front of one of the team's many parade buses, Kyle Lowry raised the Larry O'Brien trophy with both arms in front of a record-setting crowd as fans gathered on the sidewalk of every street to celebrate a special day in Canadian basketball history. The starting point guard, the team's leader and heart and soul, stood as an NBA champion wearing a game-worn throwback Damon Stoudamire jersey.

The Toronto Raptors were finally historic.

Acknowledgments

I want to start by thanking my parents and my sister for all the ways they have supported me throughout my life. Also, a shoutout to my nephews, Henry and Owen, to whom I dedicated this entire book in hopes that they will still want to be friends with me and hang out when they grow up.

I want to say a special thanks to the entire team at Triumph Books, including Jesse Jordan, Josh Williams, Clarissa Young, Michelle Bruton, and everyone else who has provided me with the guidance I've needed, from finalizing the manuscript to all the behind-the-scenes planning to bring a story idea to life and into this physical copy I'm holding today. This is our third book project together already. Damn. Time flies.

Thank you to Sloan Brown, a.k.a. DrakeCereal. I love seeing your illustration style continue to evolve and am so glad to have you provide the book cover design for *Prehistoric*.

A special thanks to Elaine Quan, who helped introduce me to so many members of the first-year Raptors, from the players to employees to even getting me a five-minute calendar invite with Samuel L. Jackson to chat about what it was like to watch Raptors games at the SkyDome. (He even gave me eight minutes in the end.) This project would not have been the same without your help, and I am forever grateful for your generosity.

Thank you to everyone who agreed to be interviewed and trusted me to tell what I came to learn was a very personal story for the folks involved with the beginning of the Toronto Raptors. Specifically, I want to thank Damon Stoudamire for agreeing to hop on a weekly Zoom with me throughout the summer of 2022 and providing the foreword for this project. Also, a special thanks to Tracy Murray. You've always been so generous with your time over the years whenever I've bothered you with one of my many ideas about the first year of the team.

Thanks to all my colleagues in the sports media industry who continue to inspire and motivate me. There are too many people to name, but those in my inner circle know who they are. I am not the best at saying thanks, so consider this my best attempt. Thanks to Holly MacKenzie for providing helpful feedback on the project, and I also want to shout out all the editors I've worked with over the years who have helped me shape and evolve my writing style over time.

Finally, I want to thank everyone who has supported my work over the years. From something as trivial as sharing my work on social media to a complimentary personal email that would help lift my spirits, especially on days when working in this industry can be very discouraging and exhausting, all of the kind words and feedback have accumulated over time and given me the confidence to continue pursuing creative projects like this, which provides me with a level of self-fulfillment that is more important than any royalty check. (I'm just kidding. Please buy 50 copies of this book for your friends. Money is very fulfilling too.)

Thanks everyone! Maybe I'll write another one of these before my early retirement at the age of 50.

Interviews and Sourcing

Over 140 original interviews were conducted for this project with a focus on members of the 1995-96 Toronto Raptors organization including the ownership group, front office, employees, coaches, and players. The majority of the interviews took place during a period from July 2021 to January 2023. (Twenty-one of the interviews were from long-form features about the Raptors which I have written over the past decade, and are referenced in the Chapter Source Notes section.) I've also included a chapter-by-chapter reference in the Chapter Source Notes section of where information from each interview is included in the book.

A total of 19 players appeared in at least one regular-season game with the Raptors during the 1995–96 season. Twelve of the players—Damon Stoudamire, Tracy Murray, Oliver Miller, Žan Tabak, Tony Massenburg, Ed Pinckney, Jimmy King, Acie Earl, Vincenzo Esposito, Sharone Wright, Doug Christie, and Dan O'Sullivan—responded to interview requests and agreed to participate in the project, in addition to B.J. Armstrong, who was selected in the expansion draft by the team but never played a game for the franchise.

A majority of research was conducted from *The Toronto Star* via the Toronto Public Library Archive, including key dates for the franchise, player profiles, and game recaps. The research was specifically focused on a period from January 1993 to November 1996, covering the start of the ownership bid to the beginning of the 1996–97 season. Any references from *The Toronto Star* outside of this time period has been specifically referenced in the Chapter Source Notes section.

Below is a list of books which were critical in the research process:

Thomas, Isiah. & Dobek, Matt. (1989). *Bad Boys! An Inside Look at the Detroit Pistons' 1988-89 Championship Season*. Masters Press.

Batten, Jack. (1996). *Hoopla: Inside The Toronto Raptors' First Season*. McClelland & Stewart Inc.

Smith, Doug. (1997). *Airborne: The Damon Stoudamire Story*. Viking.

Challen, Paul. (2004). *The Isiah Thomas Story: From the Back Court to the Front Office*. ECW Press.

Rosen, Charley. (2008). *The First Tip-Off: The Incredible Story of the Birth of the NBA*. McGraw-Hill.

Saunders, John. & Bacon, John U. (2017). *Playing Hurt: My Journey From Despair to Hope*. Da Capo Press.

Smith, Doug. (2020). *We the North: 25 Years of the Toronto Raptors*. Penguin Random House.

Chapter Source Notes

Introduction

Young, Chris. (1993, September 20). Canadian bidders pack lot of charms in attempt to woo expansion committee. *The Ottawa Citizen*. Retrieved from newspapers.com

Christie, James. (1993, September 20). Canadians take shot at NBA franchise. *The Globe and Mail*. Retrieved from newspapers.com

Daniels, Craig. (1993, September 18). Final exam time for NBA bidding groups. *National Post*. Retrieved from newspapers.com

Diebel, Linda. (2011, January 28). Former Ontario premier David Peterson is more powerful than ever. *The Toronto Star*.
https://www.thestar.com/news/canada/2011/01/28/former_ontario_premier_david_peterson_is_more_powerful_than_ever.html

CatchTheTaste. (2011, August 31). 1993 News - NBA Announces Toronto Expansion. YouTube. https://www.youtube.com/watch?v=d65SQq5zLQA

Hensley, Laura. (2015, July 31). Businessman John Bitove Sr. dies at age 87. *Toronto Sun*. https://torontosun.com/2015/07/31/businessman-john-bitove-sr-dies-at-age-87

Love, Myron. (2017, July 14). Phil Granovsky gave his all for his community. *The Canadian Jewish News*. https://thecjn.ca/perspectives/opinions/phil-granovsky-gave-community/

Magicana Staff. (2021, September 20). Allan Slaight (1931-2021). *Magicana*. https://www.magicana.com/news/blog/allan-slaight-1931-2021

Gay, Carlan. (2022). Origin Story. *SLAM Canada 1*.

Relevant interviews in this chapter: Russ Granik, John Bitove Jr., David Peterson, David Strickland, Gord Hendren, and Himal Mathew.

The Season Ticket Drive

Gretzky and Cherry to meet in food war. (1993, July 5). *The Canadian Press*. Retrieved from newspapers.com

Daniels, Craig. (1993, November 5). Toronto's in, betting's out: NBA. *National Post*. Retrieved from newspapers.com

Young, Chris. (1993, November 30). NBA-province meeting on wagering weeks away. *The Toronto Star*. Retrieved from newspapers.com

Blatchford, Christie. (1993, December 17). Gretzky earned new address; other changes were survival. *National Post*. Retrieved from newspapers.com

Daniels, Craig. (1993, December 23). NBA betting impasse deepens. *National Post*. Retrieved from newspapers.com

Gallagher, Danny. (1994, January 29). Toronto NBA franchise sitting on the sidelines. *The Nanaimo Times*. Retrieved from newspapers.com

Picknell, Gary. (1994, February 11). Hoops: Here It Comes! *National Post*. Retrieved from newspapers.com

Bitove starts putting NBA franchise together. (1994, February 12). *The Associated Press*. Retrieved from newspapers.com

Smith, Doug. (1994, December 22). Drug chain buys 4,250 seats to relieve Raptors' ticket ills. *The Canadian Press*. Retrieved from newspapers.com

Relevant interviews in this chapter: John Bitove Jr., Jim Bullock, Steve Weber, Elaine Quan, Tom Bitove, Andrea Smith, Justina Klein, Steve Griggs, Dave Hopkinson, Shawn Moscoe, Tom Pistore, Doreen Doyle, Jeff Deline, and Chris Kelly.

The Toronto Raptors

Stainkamp, Michael. (2010, August 29). A brief history of the Toronto Maple Leafs. *NHL*. https://www.nhl.com/news/a-brief-history-of-the-toronto-maple-leafs/c-536475

The Story Behind The Flo-Jo's. (2015, January 30). *NBA*. https://www.nba.com/pacers/news/story-behind-flo-jos

The five most off the hook MLB uniforms of the '90s. (2013, January 23). *MLB*. https://www.mlb.com/cut4/the-five-most-off-the-hook-mlb-uniforms-of-the-90s/c-41023648

Proteau, Adam. (2016, February 19). Deep ties between the Maple Leafs and Canadian Armed Forces. *NHL*. https://www.nhl.com/mapleleafs/news/deep-ties-between-the-maple-leafs-and-canadian-armed-forces/c-869660

Lowe, Zach. (2016, April 8). Once upon a time, the Nets seriously considered becoming the Swamp Dragons. *ESPN*. https://www.espn.com/nba/story/_/id/15155466/once-nets-seriously-considered-becoming-swamp-dragons

Kuffel, Hunter. (2017). All-Time Indiana Pacers jersey power rankings. *8 Points, 9 Seconds*. https://8points9seconds.com/2017/08/30/indiana-pacers-jerseys-rankings/5/

Schaefer, Sandy. (2020, August 20). Jurassic Park:
   All 6 Dinosaurs That Appear In The First Movie
   Explained. *Screen Rant.* https://screenrant.com/
   jurassic-park-movie-dinosaurs-species-appear-explained/
The Hockey Writers. (2022, November 11). 5 '90s NHL
   Jerseys Gone Too Soon. https://thehockeywriters.com/
   five-90s-nhl-jerseys-gone-too-soon/
Wong, Alex. (2018, October 25). The Making of the GOAT Jersey:
   An Oral History of the Raptors Throwback. *SLAM.* https://www.
   slamonline.com/nba/raptors-jersey-history/

Relevant interviews in this chapter: John Bitove Jr., Tom O'Grady,
Anne Occi, and Paul Lukas.

Isiah and Brendan

Mavs Cooling on Thomas. (1981, June 7). *The Wichita Eagle.*
   Retrieved from newspapers.com
Lief, Fred. (1981, June 7). Mavs Think Thomas Is No. 1. *St. Louis Post-*
   Dispatch. Retrieved from newspapers.com
Berkow, Ira. (1981, June 9). He Survived Ghetto Draft Day; Now
   He's Ready For NBA Draft. *New York Times.* Retrieved from
   newspapers.com
Hawkins, Jim. (1981, June 16). There's magnificent seven right in Isiah's
   backyard. *Detroit Free Press.* Retrieved from newspapers.com
Cotton, Anthony. (1981, November 16). Finding a Profit in Isiah.
   Sports Illustrated. https://vault.si.com/vault/1981/11/16/
   finding-a-profit-in-isiah-indiana-sensation-isiah-thomas-is-
   leading-the-pistons-to-respectability
Nack, William. (1987, January 19). 'I Have Got To Do Right.' *Sports*
   Illustrated. https://vault.si.com/vault/1987/01/19/i-have-got-to-do-
   right-up-from-mean-streets-piston-hero-isiah-thomas-ushers-in-
   a-new-era-for-his-family

Albom, Mitch. (1988, June 20). They play like winners, but now they
    must do it again. *Detroit Free Press.* Retrieved from newspapers.com

Lapointe, Joe. (1988, June 20). Great Lakers' waves drown Pistons.
    Detroit Free Press. Retrieved from newspapers.com

Vincent, Charlie. (1988, June 22). Pistons, Isiah never give up hope.
    Detroit Free Press. Retrieved from newspapers.com

Albom, Mitch. (1988, June 22). Gutsy Pistons lose to LA, 108-105.
    Detroit Free Press. Retrieved from newspapers.com

Albom, Mitch. (1989, July 14). Not Bad, Boys! *Detroit Free Press.*
    Retrieved from newspapers.com

McCallum, Jack. (1989, December 18). A Perfect Fit. *Sports
    Illustrated.* https://vault.si.com/vault/1989/12/18/a-perfect-fit-
    coach-chuck-daly-an-unrepentant-clotheshorse-and-a-closet-
    baritone-and-the-nba-champion-detroit-pistons-seem-to-be-
    -tailor-made-for-each-other

Albom, Mitch. (1990, June 15). Sweet Repeat! *Detroit Free Press.*
    Retrieved from newspapers.com

Ownership part of Thomas deal. (1994, January 6). *The Associated
    Press.* Retrieved from newspapers.com

Vincent, Charlie. (1994, January 8). Here's to Isiah and a not-so-new
    supporting cast. *Detroit Free Press.* Retrieved from newspapers.com

Farrell, Perry A. (1994, February 19). How Bad Can They Get? *Detroit
    Free Press.* Retrieved from newspapers.com

Thomas's Injury May End Career. (1994, April 20). *The
    Washington Post.* https://www.washingtonpost.com/
    archive/sports/1994/04/20/thomass-injury-may-end-career/
    b5c18ad5-05b8-430c-b43d-cad93e419ce1/

Meinecke, Corky. (1994, April 20). Isiah's torn tendon ends farewell
    game at Palace. *Detroit Free Press.* Retrieved from newspapers.com

Picknell, Gary. (1994, May 9). Raptors close to acquiring a GM.
    National Post. Retrieved from newspapers.com

Vincent, Charlie. (1994, May 11). Time To Dial Daly. *Detroit Free
    Press.* Retrieved from newspapers.com

Lyon, Bill. (1994, May 12). Isiah Thomas retires after 13-year career. *The Philadelphia Inquirer*. Retrieved from newspapers.com

Vincent, Charlie. (1994, May 24). Isiah to become part-owner, VP of Toronto team. *Detroit Free Press*. Retrieved from newspapers.com

Meinecke, Corky. (1994, May 25). Running the Raptors is a dream come true for ex-Piston Thomas. *Detroit Free Press*. Retrieved from newspapers.com

The Associated Press. (1994, May 25). Isiah Thomas takes on new career in NBA: executive. Retrieved from newspapers.com

Albom, Mitch. (1994, June 21). The Isiah Tapes. *Detroit Free Press*. Retrieved from newspapers.com

McCallum, Jack. (2009, May 9). Remembering Chuck Daly. *Sports Illustrated*. https://www.si.com/more-sports/2009/05/09/chuck-daly

Relevant interviews in this chapter: Paul Beeston, John Bitove Jr., Randi Bitove, Tom Mayenknecht, and Brendan Malone.

The Expansion Draft

Daniels, Craig. (1994, September 16). Thomas prepares for Toronto move. *National Post*. Retrieved from newspapers.com

Daniels, Craig. (1994, September 21). Raptors sign top scout. *National Post*. Retrieved from newspapers.com

Robson, Dan. (2019, June 4). Started from the bottom: How the Raptors' rise is rooted in the franchise's humble beginnings. *The Athletic*. https://theathletic.com/1009105/2019/06/04/started-from-the-bottom-how-the-raptors-rise-is-rooted-in-the-franchises-humble-beginnings/

Farber, Michael. (1994, November 7). A New Ball Game. *Sports Illustrated*. https://vault.si.com/vault/1994/11/07/a-new-ball-game-isiah-thomas-has-gone-directly-from-the-hardwood-to-the-hard-job-of-running-the-expansion-toronto-raptors

Well, Mike (1988, June 26). Draft offers solid players, few stars. *Scrantonian Tribune*. Retrieved from newspapers.com

Conley, Bruce. (1980, July 9). Kramer opts for Italy. *Argus Leader*. Retrieved from newspapers.com

Kingston, Gary. (1995, June 17). Grizzlies win coin flip, decide on college draft. *The Vancouver Sun*. Retrieved from newspapers.com

MacIntyre, Iain. (1995, August 12). Fur Will Fly. *The Vancouver Sun*. Retrieved from newspapers.com

Beamish, Mike. (1994, August 12). Thanks a lot for blowing the back-to-school budget, Arthur. *The Vancouver Sun*. Retrieved from newspapers.com

Chapman, Paul. (1994, April 29). Search On For A Name. *The Vancouver Sun*. Retrieved from newspapers.com

Vancouver granted new NBA franchise. (1994, April 28). *The Associated Press*. Retrieved from newspapers.com

Tsumura, Howard. (1994, April 28). League spot may change. *The Province*. Retrieved from newspapers.com

Vancouver nets NBA. (1994, April 28). *The Canadian Press*. Retrieved from newspapers.com

Tsumura, Howard. (1995, June 25). Grizzlies set to deal. *The Province*. Retrieved from newspapers.com

Tsumura, Howard. (1995, June 25). Decisions, decisions. *The Province*. Retrieved from newspapers.com

Tsumura, Howard. (1994, February 14). Mounties to shine in '99? *The Province*. Retrieved from newspapers.com

Sherwin, Bob. (1996, June 5). Dennis Rodman: Bad To The Bank — The NBA's 'Bad Boy' Has Parlayed His Unique Image Into Lucrative Off-Court Deals. *The Seattle Times*. https://archive.seattletimes.com/archive/?date=19960605&slug=2332901

Lawlor, Frank. (1995, June 18). Expansion teams need to be shrewd. *Wisconsin State-Journal*. Retrieved from newspapers.com

NBA's Dallas club picks 'mavericks' in expansion draft. (1980, May 29). *The Associated Press*. Retrieved from newspapers.com

Crothers, Tim. (1995, October 23). Which Way Is Up? Our Handy Eight-Step Guide Identifies The Surest Routes To Expansion Success For The Vancouver Grizzlies and The Toronto Raptors. *Sports Illustrated.* https://vault.si.com/vault/1995/10/23/ which-way-is-up-our-handy-eight-step-guide-identifies-the-surest-routes-to-expansion-success-for-the-vancouver-grizzlies-and-the-toronto-raptors

Wise, Mike. (1995, June 24). Newest teams pick from NBA's rubble. *New York Times.* Retrieved from newspapers.com

Rud, Jeff. (1995, June 4). Vancouver and Toronto rosters will take shape on June 24. *The Times-Colonist.* Retrieved from newspapers.com

Isaacson, Melissa. (1995, June 16). New direction for the Bulls? *Chicago Tribune.* Retrieved from newspapers.com

Smith, Sam. (1995, June 24). B.J. is the best of the bland. *Chicago Tribune.* Retrieved from newspapers.com

Smith, Sam. (1995, June 25). Toronto picks Armstrong; may not trade him. *Chicago Tribune.* Retrieved from newspapers.com

Christie, James. (1994, June 4). Raptors' First Coach Wouldn't Shun Rodman. *The Globe and Mail.* Retrieved from newspapers.com

Taylor, Phil. (1995, April 3). Go North, Young Man. *Sports Illustrated.* https://vault.si.com/vault/1995/04/03/go-north-young-man

Relevant interviews in this chapter: David Peterson, Kelly Gianopoulos, Sandra Hamilton, Matt Akler, Arthur Griffiths, John Bitove Jr., David Doroghy, Tom O'Grady, Glen Grunwald, Elaine Quan, and B.J. Armstrong.

The Rookie

Gilchrist, Kent. (1995, June 29). Big bear hunt began with lucky coin toss. *The Province.* Retrieved from newspapers.com

Tsumura, Howard. (1995, June 29). Beautiful B.C. *The Province.* Retrieved from newspapers.com

Araton, Harvey. (1995, May 16). High schooler wants to jump straight onto NBA court. *New York Times*. Retrieved from newspapers.com

McCallum, Jack. (1995, June 26). Hoop Dream. *Sports Illustrated*. https://vault.si.com/vault/1995/06/26/hoop-dream-kevin-garnett-a-sure-shot-lottery-pick-is-jumping-from-high-school-to-the-nba

Rivera, Steve. (1995, June 27). Best Point Guard Available. *Tucson Citizen*. Retrieved from newspapers.com

Smith, Sam. (1995, June 29). Draft long on surprises. *Chicago Tribune*. Retrieved from newspapers.com

Lawlor, Frank. (1995, June 18). Expansion teams need to be shrewd. *Wisconsin State Journal*. Retrieved from newspapers.com

Del Grande, Dave. (1995, May 22). Warriors claim No. 1 pick in NBA draft next month. *Oakland Tribune*. Retrieved from newspapers.com

Benevento, Don. (1995, May 21). Homework will determine Sixers' draft success. *Courier-Post*. Retrieved from newspapers.com

Adande, J.A. (1995, June 19). McDyess soars from background to fore. *Washington Post*. https://www.washingtonpost.com/archive/sports/1995/06/19/mcdyess-soars-from-background-to-fore/67e88db7-07e0-4ad7-920f-09d78784c985/

Beck, Howard. (2015, May 18). A Man in Full: An Oral History of Kevin Garnett, the Player Who Changed the NBA. *Bleacher Report*. https://bleacherreport.com/articles/2421236-a-man-in-full-the-many-sides-of-kevin-garnett-the-player-who-changed-the-nba

Loung, Steven. (2015, October 14). Isiah Thomas: Raptors were ahead of their time. *Sportsnet*. https://www.sportsnet.ca/basketball/nba/isiah-thomas-raptors-were-ahead-of-their-time/

Relevant interviews in this chapter: Damon Stoudamire, Walker D. Russell, Glen Grunwald, Brendan Malone, Liz Washington, and Willie Stoudamire.

Training Camp

Smith, Doug. (1995, October 22). Raptors trample Grizzlies in battle for Naismith Cup. *The Canadian Press*. Retrieved from newspapers.com

Smith, Doug. (1995, October 21). Raptors, Grizzlies meet in inaugural Naismith Cup. *The Canadian Press*. Retrieved from newspapers.com

Taylor, Phil. (1996, January 15). The Mouse That Soars. *Sports Illustrated*. https://vault.si.com/vault/1996/01/15/the-mouse-that-soars-confounding-skydome-skeptics-torontos-diminutive-point-guard-damon-stoudamire-leads-the-pack-of-nba-rookies

Raptors lose fifth game as Cavaliers break tie. (1995, October 30). *The Canadian Press*. Retrieved from newspapers.com

McCallum, Jack. (1986, April 21). The Spur Of The Moment. *Sports Illustrated*. https://vault.si.com/vault/1986/04/21/the-spur-of-the-moment

Smith, Doug. (1995, October 13). Coach Malone stays patient with team. *The Canadian Press*. Retrieved from newspapers.com

Daniels, Craig. (1995, February 2). Raptors may have their first player. *National Post*. Retrieved from newspapers.com

Smith, Doug. (1995, October 18). Roster cuts have some Raptors in danger of becoming extinct. *The Canadian Press*. Retrieved from newspapers.com

Riggs, Randy. (1988, June 29). 'It Was Easy Decision.' *Austin American-Statesman*. Retrieved from newspapers.com

Whitfield, Tom. (1988, June 29). Anderson Already at Home as a Spur. *The Atlanta Constitution*. Retrieved from newspapers.com

Relevant interviews in this chapter: Brendan Malone, Doug Smith, Matt Akler, Damon Stoudamire, Ed Pinckney, Tony Massenburg, Oliver Miller, Žan Tabak, Jimmy King, and Vincenzo Esposito.

The Sharpshooter

Moore, David. (1995, February 19). Tomjanovich knew Rockets had to make a move. *Dallas Morning News*. Retrieved from newspapers.com

White, Lonnie. (1989, March 19). Murray scores 64, but Glendora loses. *Los Angeles Times*. https://www.latimes.com/archives/la-xpm-1989-03-19-sp-381-story.html

Crowe, Jerry. (1991, February 6). Murray Home Burns While Sons at Games. *Los Angeles Times*. https://www.latimes.com/archives/la-xpm-1991-02-06-sp-588-story.html

Harris, Bill. (1995, October 18). Two let go on eve of debut. *National Post*. Retrieved from newspapers.com

Relevant interviews in this chapter: Tracy Murray, Damon Stoudamire, and Brendan Malone.

Ted Stepien and the Toronto Towers

Fink, David. (1980, December 24). Stepien intends to operate Cavs his way … or else! *Pittsburgh Post-Gazette*. Retrieved from newspapers.com

Bradburn, Jamie. (2019, May 29). Before Toronto had the Raptors, it had… the Buffalo Braves. *TVO*. https://www.tvo.org/article/before-toronto-had-the-raptors-it-had-the-buffalo-braves

Fitz-Gerald, Sean. (2019, June 4). 20 Questions with Leo Rautins: On Wale, a fake ID and how Canada gave his parents 'a life.' *The Athletic*. https://theathletic.com/1008480/2019/06/04/20-questions-with-leo-rautins-on-wale-a-fake-id-and-how-canada-gave-his-parents-a-life/

Gay, Carlan. (2021, February 16). Stewart Granger: The first Black Canadian drafted in the NBA. *Basketball Canada*. https://www.basketball.ca/news/stewart-granger-the-first-black-canadian-drafted-in-the-nba

Jackson, Derrick. (1980, November 9). Ted Stepien and the Race Factor. *Newsday*. Retrieved from newspapers.com

Waters, Mike. (2020, September 11). Leo Rautins' crazy basketball journey is 'based on something that should not have happened.' *Syracuse Basketball.* https://www.syracuse.com/orangebasketball/2020/09/leo-rautins-crazy-basketball-journey-is-based-on-something-that-should-not-have-happened.html

Cook, Dan. (1983, June 16). Stepien involved in new ventures. *Akron Beacon Journal.* Retrieved from newspapers.com

Ryan, Bob. (1980, December 26). The Cleveland Cavaliers: How A Franchise Fell Apart. *Boston Globe.* Retrieved from newspapers.com

Berkow, Ira. (1982, December 6). Everything Changes On The Cavaliers But The Face Of Failure. *New York Times.* Retrieved from newspapers.com

McKee, Kent. (1983, March 16). NBA here sounding less of a tale. *The Toronto Star.* Retrieved from Toronto Public Library Archive.

McKee, Kent. (1983, March 15). $7.3 million bottom line for city to court Cavs. *The Toronto Star.* Retrieved from Toronto Public Library Archive.

Proudfoot, Jim. (1983, March 15). Who needs Cavaliers? Not Toronto. *The Toronto Star.* Retrieved from Toronto Public Library Archive.

Woolsey, Garth. (1983, March 20). Cav fans wonder what comes next. *The Toronto Star.* Retrieved from Toronto Public Library Archive.

Lyon, Bill. (1983, July 28). Top pick hopes to fit in. *The Philadelphia Inquirer.* Retrieved from newspapers.com

Pantages, Larry. (1983, April 10). For Cavaliers' fans, the nightmare is over. *Akron Beacon Journal.* Retrieved from newspapers.com

Cobourn, Tom. (1983, June 29). Sixers grab 6-8 Rautins. *The News Journal.* Retrieved from newspapers.com

Parrish, Wayne. (1985, February 1). Owner is blamed for Tornado mess. *The Toronto Star.* Retrieved from Toronto Public Library Archive.

Woolsey, Garth. (1985, December 26). Media blamed as Tornados leave town. *The Toronto Star.* Retrieved from Toronto Public Library Archive.

Taylor, Phil. (1994, August 22). Yes, It Was a Joke. *Sports Illustrated.* https://vault.si.com/vault/1994/08/22/yes-it-was-a-joke-dream-team-ii-as-expected-won-the-world-championships-in-a-real-laugher

Jasner, Phil. (1992, June 30). Rautins has no regrets. *The Philadelphia Daily News.* Retrieved from newspapers.com

Wong, Alex. (2018). How the Cleveland Cavaliers nearly became the Toronto Towers. *theScore.* https://www.thescore.com/nba/news/1588411

Relevant interviews in this chapter: Leo Roth, Leo Rautins, Dan Shulman, John Bitove Jr., Kent Schneider, Rod Black, and David Magley.

The First Game

James, Michael. (1995, November 4). Oh, no, Canada! Nets humiliated. *The Daily News.* Retrieved from newspapers.com

Nets rookie on the hot seat. (1995, October 11). *The New York Times.* Retrieved from newspapers.com

Romano, John. (1995, November 2). NBA Preview. *The Tampa Bay Times.* Retrieved from newspapers.com

James, Michael. (1995, October 26). O'Bannon picky when it comes to Raptors' draft. *The Daily News.* Retrieved from newspapers.com

Brunt, Stephen. & Sellery, Bruce. (Hosts). (2019, December). Canadian Club Presents: John Bitove Jr. [Audio podcast episode]. *Canadian Club of Toronto.*

A A. (2017, December 24). Toronto Raptors vs. New Jersey Nets (First Raptors Game, November 3, 1995). YouTube. https://www.youtube.com/watch?v=IFTaRHpIW94

Wong, Alex. (2019, December 24). The Raptors have come a long way since their very first game. *Yahoo Sports Canada.* https://ca.sports.yahoo.com/news/the-raptors-have-come-a-long-way-since-their-very-first-game-160010034.html

Relevant interviews in this chapter: Sharon Edwards, John Bitove Jr., Randi Bitove, Kenny Solway, Tyler Stewart, Ryan Bonne, Jamie Nishino, Brian Cooper, Rick Kaplan, John Lashway, Robin Brudner, Brendan Malone, Tracy Murray, Damon Stoudamire, Liz Washington, Willie Stoudamire, and Leo Rautins.

Note: *Kenny Solway also provided the original game-day script to the November 3, 1995, game between the Toronto Raptors and New Jersey Nets for reference.*

Fab Five

Tappa, Steve. (1995, October 28). QC Thunder could get its Kings. *The Rock Island Argus*. Retrieved from newspapers.com

Price, Dwane. (1995, October 22). Not so fabulous anymore. *Fort Worth Star-Telegram*. Retrieved from newspapers.com

Todd, Jack. (1995, November 3). King survives Raptors' cuts. *The Gazette*. Retrieved from newspapers.com

Stouda, Greg. (1993, April 6). Carolina Finer. *Detroit Free Press*. Retrieved from newspapers.com

Sharp, Drew. (1993, April 6). Whispers will start: Fisher to blame? *Detroit Free Press*. Retrieved from newspapers.com

Farrell, Perry. (1995, June 28). Snow, King now on same road. *Detroit Free Press*. Retrieved from newspapers.com

Kornacki, Steve. (1994, November 22). More light, less heat: King, Jackson squeeze into U-M's leadership shoes. *Detroit Free Press*. Retrieved from newspapers.com

Myslenski, Skip. (1995, January 17). Not quite fabulous, but getting there. *Chicago Tribune*. Retrieved from newspapers.com

Relevant interviews in this chapter: Jimmy King, Eddrick Watson, Rance Adams, Eric Miller, and Khary Scott.

"Practices Were War"

Carson, Greg. (1994, July 20). Warriors' Rogers visit hoops camp. *The Times and Democrat.* Retrieved from newspapers.com

Wood, Tom. (1993, March 17). Rogers kept hangin' in. *The Tennessean.* Retrieved from newspapers.com

Boaz, Mike. (1994, March 18). After all he's seen, basketball is easy. *The Messenger.* Retrieved from newspapers.com

Shelton, Gary. (1994, March 20). A survivor, now a star. *Detroit Free Press.* Retrieved from newspapers.com

Nevius, C.W. (1994, December 7). Happy Warrior survived life on Detroit's mean streets. *The Albuquerque Tribune.* Retrieved from newspapers.com

Fennelly, Martin. (1994, March 17). Carlos Rogers tells the story of a survivor. *The Tampa Tribune.* Retrieved from newspapers.com

Relevant interviews in this chapter: Brendan Malone, Damon Stoudamire, Žan Tabak, Vincenzo Esposito, Rich Dalatri, Frank D'Urso, Jimmy King, and Tracy Murray.

The Big O

Chandler, Charles. (1990, March 31). Duke faces Arkansas challenge. *The Charlotte Observer.* Retrieved from newspapers.com

Monserud, Scott. (1992, June 21). From Big O to Big? *Fort Worth Star-Telegram.* Retrieved from newspapers.com

Casstevens, David. (1992, June 25). Suns make a whale of a pick. *Arizona Republic.* Retrieved from newspapers.com

Price, Dwane. (1992, August 23). Fat chance. *Fort Worth Star-Telegram.* Retrieved from newspapers.com

Brown, Rogers B. (1988, April 18). Miller says no to Oklahoma, signs Arkansas letter of intent. *Fort Worth Star-Telegram.* Retrieved from newspapers.com

Brown, Rogers B. (1992, June 24). No better quality since Class of '95. *Fort Worth Star-Telegram.* Retrieved from newspapers.com

Young, Bob. (1992, June 24). Miller wants to be a Sun. *Arizona Republic*. Retrieved from newspapers.com

It's Miller Time for the Pistons. (1994, September 23). *The Associated Press*. Retrieved from newspapers.com

Meinecke, Corky. (1995, March 25). Miller's inconsistent play weighs on Chaney. *Detroit Free Press*. Retrieved from newspapers.com

Goodykontz, Bill. (1993, June 25). Burning To Win. *Arizona Republic*. Retrieved from newspapers.com

Cooper, Barry. (1994, December 4). For Athletes Who Fail To Shed Their Troublesome Girth, Their Future In Professional Sports Is Given Little More Than A Fat Chance. *The Orlando Sentinel*. Retrieved from newspapers.com

Relevant interviews in this chapter: Oliver Miller, Brendan Malone, Tony Massenburg, Tracy Murray, Damon Stoudamire, and Ed Pinckney.

John Saunders

MacDonald, Gayle. (1994, November 24). Raptors buy time on City-TV. *National Post*. Retrieved from newspapers.com

Riches, Hester. (1995, April 8). Moses' 11th commandment: thou shalt worship TV. *The Vancouver Sun*. Retrieved from newspapers.com

Gordon, Charles. (1995, April 12). Modern Moses spouts a lot of bull about his experience with rushes. *The Ottawa Citizen*. Retrieved from newspapers.com

Patch, Nick. (2009, August 29). Remembering MuchMusic's birth days. *The Toronto Star*. Retrieved from newspapers.com

Earl, Dennis. (2014, August 16). The Forgotten Influence of MuchMusic. *The Writings of Dennis Earl*. https://dennisearl.wordpress.com/2014/08/26/the-forgotten-influence-of-muchmusic/

Hickey, Pat. (1994, August 5). Holding Court. *The Vancouver Sun*. Retrieved from newspapers.com

O'Neill, Jay. (1995, November 3). Canadian TV ready to tip-off with NBA. *Edmonton Journal*. Retrieved from newspapers.com

Hickey, Pat. (1995, November 11). Rautins Star of CTV's New NBA Package. *The Gazette*. Retrieved from newspapers.com

Rud, Jeff. (1995, November 6). Rautins remains an integral part of Canadian hoop vision. *The Times-Colonist*. Retrieved from newspapers.com

Wong, Alex. (2016, August 16). John Saunders, the Original Voice of the Raptors, Never Forgot Where He Came From. *VICE Sports*. https://www.vice.com/en/article/4xzadd/john-saunders-the-original-voice-of-the-raptors-never-forgot-where-he-came-from

Relevant interviews in this chapter: Leo Rautins, Paul Jones, Rod Black, Chris McCracken, Brian Sherriffe, John Bitove Jr., Lori Belanger, Moses Znaimer, Peter McKeown, and Michael Grange.

New Year's Party

Ullrich, Lowell. (1995, December 8). Decisions, decisions. *The Province*. Retrieved from newspapers.com

Ullrich, Lowell. (1995, November 6). Exhilarating end excites Winters. *The Province*. Retrieved from newspapers.com

Tsumura, Howard. (1995, November 6). Unheralded King. *The Province*. Retrieved from newspapers.com

Gilchrist, Kent. (1995, November 6). Speed thrills in Grizzlyland. *The Province*. Retrieved from newspapers.com

Farrell, Perry A. (1995, December 19). Raptors aren't typical expansion NBA team. *Detroit Free Press*. Retrieved from newspapers.com

Meinecke, Corky. (1996, January 27). John Salley Warming Bench for Toronto. *The Daily Oklahoman*. Retrieved from newspapers.com

Winderman, Ira. (1995, December 3). Salley crosses border, finally feels at home. *South Florida Sun Sentinel*. Retrieved from newspapers.com

Fleischman, Joan. (1995, January 16). Holiday party is no fun now for Heat star. *The Miami Herald*. Retrieved from newspapers.com

Relevant interviews in this chapter: Damon Stoudamire, Jimmy King, Tracy Murray, Žan Tabak, Vincenzo Esposito, Oliver Miller, Acie Earl, Doug Smith, John Lashway, Jeff Mather, Rick Kaplan, Leo Rautins, Elliotte Friedman, Arthur Griffiths, John Bitove Jr., Tony Massenburg, Ed Pinckney, Brendan Malone, Elaine Quan, Al Quance, Clement Chu, David Kuo, Steve Gazmin, Bruce Kidd, Perry King, Jackelyn Lau, Darrick Tam, Ev Spence, Matt Piemontese, Frank Grespan, and Sandra Hamilton.

The Trade Deadline

Rohrbach, Bob. (2019, July 23). My Vet: Isiah Thomas on a rookie season that shaped his legendary NBA career. *Yahoo Sports*. Retrieved from newspapers.com

Hofmann, Rich. (1994, July 1). There's Myles to go before Wright sleeps. *Philadelphia Daily News*. Retrieved from newspapers.com

Jasner, Phil. (1994, October 13). Wright keeps dad forever in thoughts. *Philadelphia Daily News*. Retrieved from newspapers.com

Relevant interviews in this chapter: Damon Stoudamire, Ed Pinckney, Tony Massenburg, Doug Christie, Sharone Wright, Brendan Malone, Paul Jones, Mike Inglis, and Tim Bourett.

The SkyDome

Epstein, Edward Jay. (2006, February 13). North Expenditure. *Slate*. https://slate.com/culture/2006/02/why-are-so-many-movies-shot-in-canada.html

Holmes, Adam. (2020, June 15). Samuel L. Jackson's Famous Jurassic Park Line Has A Crazy Story Behind It. *CinemaBlend*. https://www.cinemablend.com/news/2548257/samuel-l-jacksons-famous-jurassic-park-line-has-a-crazy-story-behind-it

Jones, Dylan. (2015, December 9). The Hollywood royal: Samuel L. Jackson. *GQ*. https://www.gq-magazine.co.uk/article/the-hollywood-royal-samuel-l-jackson-hateful-8-eight

Feinberg, Hugh. (2022, March 6). Jackie Brown 25 years later — A Cinema Scholars Oral History. *Cinema Scholars*. https://cinemascholars.com/jackie-brown-25-years-later-a-cinema-scholars-oral-history/

Seal, Mark. (2013, February 13). Cinema Tarantino: The Making of Pulp Fiction. *Vanity Fair*. https://www.vanityfair.com/hollywood/2013/03/making-of-pulp-fiction-oral-history

Nayman, Adam. (2019, July 25). 'Forrest Gump' Won The Battle, but 'Pulp Fiction' Won The War. *The Ringer*. https://www.theringer.com/movies/2019/7/25/20726783/pulp-fiction-forrest-gump-quentin-robert-zemeckis-oscars

Raftery, Brian. (2019, June 22). Tarantinoesque: The Making of the Last Great Celebrity Director. *The Ringer*. https://www.theringer.com/movies/2019/7/22/20699665/quentin-tarantino-director-celebrity-pulp-fiction-reservoir-dogs-snl-er-roger-ebert

Taylor, Ella. (1992, October 23). Mr. Blood Red. *LA Weekly*. https://www.laweekly.com/mr-blood-red-ella-taylors-1992-quentin-tarantino-profile/

Lewis, Andy. (2018, April 3). Samuel L. Jackson: How I Became an Usher at Martin Luther King Jr.'s Funeral. *The Hollywood Reporter*. https://www.hollywoodreporter.com/lifestyle/lifestyle-news/samuel-l-jackson-how-i-became-an-usher-at-martin-luther-king-jrs-funeral-guest-column-1099033/

Dye, Dave. (1989, June 4). The SkyDome's The Limit. *The Des Moines Register*. Retrieved from newspapers.com

Simon, Peter. (1989, June 4). It's time to play ball in Toronto's SkyDome. *The Buffalo News*. Retrieved from newspapers.com

Donaghy, Jim. (1989, June 4). Who needs baseball with new SkyDome. *The Associated Press*. Retrieved from newspapers.com

Gates, Bruce. (1988, April 18). Making roof work the big test for
SkyDome designers. *National Post*. Retrieved from newspapers.com

Kennedy, Mark. (1988, April 9). The SkyDome: It's like a fun place. *The
Expositor*. Retrieved from newspapers.com

Cacciola, Scott. (2014, April 20). Raptors Fan in Bad Times Tastes the
Good. *The New York Times*. https://www.nytimes.com/2014/04/21/
sports/basketball/a-die-hard-fan-is-loving-the-raptors-success.html

Bowerman, Glyn. (2019, June 3). "It works, Toronto!": An oral
history of the SkyDome. *TVO*. https://www.tvo.org/article/
it-works-toronto-an-oral-history-of-the-skydome

Grosman, Ryan. (2020, November 6). Here's what it was
like being a Raptors fan back in 1995. *Raptors HQ*.
https://www.raptorshq.com/2020/11/6/21551668/
toronto-raptors-25th-anniversary-inaugural-game-fandom

Harris, Bill. (1995, December 14). Raptors cool to chilly 'Dome.
National Post. Retrieved from newspapers.com

Wong, Alex. (2018, April 12). The Anxiety and Fear of the Toronto
Raptors Fan. *The New Yorker*. https://www.newyorker.com/sports/
sporting-scene/the-anxiety-and-fear-of-the-toronto-raptors-fan

Relevant interviews in this chapter: David Peterson, Damon
Stoudamire, Jimmy King, Tracy Murray, Tony Massenburg, Ed Pinckney,
Sharone Wright, Doug Christie, Oliver Miller, Acie Earl, Doug Smith,
Brian Cooper, Jamie Nishino, Ryan Bonne, Sharon Edwards, Kenny
Solway, Samuel L. Jackson, Tamara Mose, Madonna Gimotea, Chris
Medina, Vanessa Cobham, Alma de Jesus, Melanie Allison, Theresa
Runstedtler, Jordan Bitove, John Bitove Jr., Rob Pagetto, Adam Nayman,
Nav Bhatia, John Bitove Jr., Zach Derhodge, Hunter Somerville, Kathrina
Lalog, Douglas Landry, Wendy Landry, Rick Bercovici, Elise Bercovici,
and Ryan Grosman.

"They Should Have Been 73–9"

Asher, Mark. (1997, January 18). Rodman Suspended At Least 11 Games. *The Washington Post*. https://www.washingtonpost. com/archive/sports/1997/01/18/rodman-suspended-at-least-11-games/11e85dab-7207-4dd1-80bf-72528bb4afb5/

Armour, Terry. (1996, March 24). Salley earns his spot on roster. *Chicago Tribune*. Retrieved from newspapers.com

twohlrab3. (2017, January 17). NBA - Bulls @ Raptors 1996. YouTube. https://www.youtube.com/watch?v=7nr1HtRNZVI

Wong, Alex. (2017, October 15). The Oral History of the 1996 Chicago Bulls. *Complex*. https://www.complex.com/sports/oral-history-96-bulls

Relevant interviews in this chapter: Sharone Wright, Oliver Miller, Damon Stoudamire, Acie Earl, Doug Christie, Tracy Murray, Brendan Malone, John Bitove Jr., Eddie Williams, Žan Tabak, Ron Harper, Nathaniel Bellamy, Charles O'Bannon, Kris Johnson, Grant Hill, John Salley, Jim Cleamons, Ahmad Rashad, Charles Barkley, Cedric Ceballos, Joe Pytka, Nigel Miguel, Marques Johnson, Phil Taylor, and Bob Costas.

Isiah vs. Brendan

Relevant interviews in this chapter: John Bitove Jr., Doug Smith, Damon Stoudamire, Brendan Malone, Jimmy King, Vincenzo Esposito, Tracy Murray, Glen Grunwald, and Michael Malone.

Dan and Acie

May, Peter. (1995, June 14). Carr has them still playing waiting game. *The Boston Globe*. Retrieved from newspapers.com

MacMullan, Jackie. (1994, March 10). Ford trying to work on Earl. *The Boston Globe*. Retrieved from newspapers.com

May, Peter. (1995, June 25). Earl is taken off Celtics' hands. *The Boston Globe*. Retrieved from newspapers.com

Doxsie, Don. (1994, May 20). Moline's Earl endures first NBA season. *Quad-City Times*. Retrieved from newspapers.com

DeVrieze, Craig. (1990, October 11). '90-91 Iowa hoops: 'The Great Unknown'. *The Dispatch*. Retrieved from newspapers.com

MacMullan, Jackie. (1993, October 14). After the fall, Celtics' Earl believes he's in prime position. *The Boston Globe*. Retrieved from newspapers.com

Doxsie, Don. (1995, June 21). Vancouver, Toronto: The right places, the right time of year for Acie Earl. *Quad-City Times*. Retrieved from newspapers.com

MacMullan, Jackie. (1994, October 12). Jurassic Earl ready for sequel. *The Boston Globe*. Retrieved from newspapers.com

Relevant interviews in this chapter: Dan O'Sullivan, Acie Earl, Damon Stoudamire, Tracy Murray, Jimmy King, Žan Tabak, Doug Christie, Vincenzo Esposito, Ed Pinckney, Terel McIntosh, and James Moses.

Caribana

Relevant interviews in this chapter: John Bitove Jr., Damon Stoudamire, Brendan Malone, Oliver Miller, Tracy Murray, Vincenzo Esposito, and Dan O'Sullivan.

Historic

Raptors' Sharone Wright injured in car wreck. (1997, July 26). *The Associated Press*. https://apnews.com/article/b886cf0a6a53836c2d2adaee301ecd42

McCready, Eldredge. (1998, June 28). A year after a devastating wreck, Sharone Wright awaits return to NBA. *The Macon Telegraph*. Retrieved from newspapers.com

Stoudamire goes home to Portland. (1998, February 14). *The Associated Press*. Retrieved from newspapers.com

CBC Archives. (2019, November 21). The Parting of Isiah Thomas
and the Toronto Raptors. https://www.cbc.ca/archives/
the-parting-of-isiah-thomas-and-the-toronto-raptors-1.5350722

Isiah Thomas cuts ties with Raptors after buyout fails. (1997, November
21). *The Associated Press*. Retrieved from newspapers.com

Smith, Sam. (1998, February 14). Chaos in Toronto: Stoudamire
dealt to Blazers, coach quits. *Chicago Tribune*. https://www.
chicagotribune.com/news/ct-xpm-1998-02-14-9802140022-story.
html

Morris, Jim. (2001, March 27). Grizzlies stung by relocation news. *The
Canadian Press*. Retrieved from newspapers.com

Hoops in Vancouver Nears a Grizzly End. (2001, April 16). *The
Associated Press*. Retrieved from newspapers.com

Abdur-Rahim says years in Vancouver a blessing. (2001, April 16). *The
Canadian Press*. Retrieved from newspapers.com

Ziemer, Brad. (2001, April 16). Grizzlies Thank Fans. *The Vancouver
Sun*. Retrieved from newspapers.com

Willes, Ed. (2016, June 8). The complicated, ultimately happy saga of
Arthur Griffiths and his Vancouver sports legacy. *The Province*.
https://theprovince.com/sports/willes-the-complicated-ultimately-
happy-saga-of-arthur-griffiths-and-his-vancouver-sports-legacy

Azpiri, Jon. & McElroy, Justin. (2015, October 30). An oral history
of the Vancouver Grizzlies. *Global News*. https://globalnews.ca/
news/2298192/an-oral-history-of-the-vancouver-grizzlies/

Relevant interviews in this chapter: Brendan Malone, Michael Malone,
Tracy Murray, Oliver Miller, Jimmy King, Vincenzo Esposito, Dan
O'Sullivan, Tony Massenburg, Ed Pinckney, Acie Earl, Sharone Wright,
Damon Stoudamire, Doug Christie, Glen Grunwald, Robin Brudner, Žan
Tabak, Liz Washington, Andy Dolich, Arthur Griffiths, Dave Doroghy,
John Bitove Jr., Randi Bitove, Elaine Quan, Samuel L. Jackson, David
Peterson, Rod Black, Leo Rautins, Paul Jones, Damian Daniels, Doug
Smith, Ryan Bonne, Tyler Stewart, and Ken Derrett.